"A MASTER[...]"
—PopMat[...]

Winner of the Toronto Book Award

Winner of the OLA Evergreen Award

Finalist for the Shaughnessy Cohen Prize for Political Writing

Finalist for the Rakuten Kobo Emerging Writer Prize

NAMED A BEST BOOK OF THE YEAR BY

The Globe and Mail

CBC

NOW

Indigo Books

Quill & Quire

"Read this book."
—*This Magazine*

"A powerful call to action. A superb synthesizer, the unstoppable Cole addresses racisms of all kinds across the country."
—*NOW*

"This is a story of confrontation and resistance, but also of deep listening and bearing witness. Written with power and verve, Cole's sharp, urgent, and lyrical prose reveals an author with a capacious intellect, moral clarity, and unwavering commitment to justice."
— **Shaughnessy Cohen Prize jury citation**

More praise for

The Skin We're In

"The sheer strength of this book arises from its insistent linking of policing, prisons, public education, migrant labour, impoverished neighbourhoods, and the fates of refugees. *The Skin We're In* is about the interlocking forces besieging Black life in Canada; and it is also about organizing resistance and imagining futures in bravely intimate terms. Desmond Cole is an urgent and essential voice from a generation that will be heard." —David Chariandy, author of *Brother* and *I've Been Meaning to Tell You: A Letter to My Daughter*

"In *The Skin We're In*, Desmond Cole offers us not only analysis of one year of anti-Blackness in the lands we currently call Canada: he also recovers disappeared histories of Black resistance, gives richly deserved credit to Black LGBTQ+ activists, shows solidarity with disabled and Indigenous folks, and, most importantly, reminds us of the power of Black genius and Black joy. This smart, powerful, essential book is an act of radical generosity—one we should all be grateful to receive, hold, share and revisit." —Alicia Elliott, author of *A Mind Spread Out on the Ground*

"Desmond Cole systematically dismantles any lingering illusions of Canada as a beacon of racial benevolence by exposing the multiple forms of state violence facing Black peoples of all ages and genders. His text, further, compellingly highlights the ongoing refusal of Canada's Black diaspora to submit to conditions of subjugation, bringing to light both historical and contemporary legacies of rebellion. A powerful read." —Robyn Maynard, author of *Policing Black Lives: State Violence in Canada from Slavery to the Present*

"It is not an exaggeration to say that Desmond Cole's book should be taught in classrooms, roiling in the minds of the next generation, lauded in social justice movements. It's a striking, searing, perspective-shifting book that draws attention to the injustices faced by Black Canadians on a daily basis. . . . [Cole's] prose contains the grace, clarity, caution, and cadence of someone familiar with speaking up and standing tall. He seamlessly integrates historical and theoretical material with analyses of recent events, making the text informative and incisive without sacrificing emotional resonance. . . . A solid introduction to themes of white supremacy, imperialism and power, anti-Black racism, and Cole's own life and values . . . [and] as Cole powerfully illustrates, Black pain—and the fight against it—does not always have a tidy, smooth, palatable ending." —*Quill & Quire*, starred review

"A masterpiece of reporting on racism. . . . [Cole] is one of the most talented and insightful journalists working in Canada today, and his new book further cements this reputation. *The Skin We're In* is critically important reading for all Canadians. If it leaves white Canadians with a shaken sense of national pride, that can only be a good thing—and perhaps the first step toward confronting racism seriously and building a nation for which all Canadians truly can be proud." —PopMatters

"A skillful blend of history and reportage . . . Cole describes his progression from journalist to activist on behalf of Toronto's black residents fed up with mistreatment at the hands of the police, lip service from politicians and media, and indifference from the community at large. Accomplished, timely, and powerful, *The Skin We're In* is a potent and urgent reminder that there is no place for complacency in the battle against racism." —Toronto Book Awards jury citation

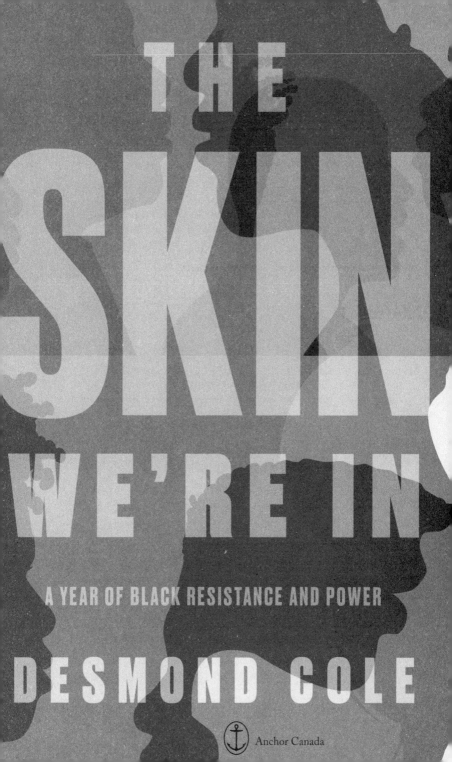

THE
SKIN
WE'RE IN

A YEAR OF BLACK RESISTANCE AND POWER

DESMOND COLE

Anchor Canada

Anchor Canada paperback published 2022
Doubleday Canada hardcover published 2020

LIBRARY AND ARCHIVES CANADA CATALOGUING IN PUBLICATION
Title: The skin we're in / Desmond Cole.
Other titles: Skin we are in
Names: Cole, Desmond, 1982- author.
Description: Previously published: Toronto : Doubleday Canada, 2020.
Identifiers: Canadiana 20190051132 | ISBN 9780385686365 (softcover)
Subjects: LCSH: Canada—Race relations. | LCSH: Discrimination in law enforcement—Canada. | LCSH: Discrimination in criminal justice administration—Canada. | LCSH: Police misconduct—Canada. | LCSH: Police brutality—Canada. | LCSH: Race discrimination—Canada. | LCSH: Minorities—Crimes against—Canada. | LCSH: Police-community relations—Canada. | CSH: Black Canadians—Social conditions.
Classification: LCC FC106.B6 C65 2021 | DDC 305.896/071—dc23

Cover and interior design by Terri Nimmo
Cover and title page images: smartboy10 / Getty Images
Interior photograph (page 82): Uranranebi Agbeyegbe

Printed in the United States of America

Published in Canada by Anchor Canada,
a division of Penguin Random House Canada Limited,
a Penguin Random House Company

www.penguinrandomhouse.ca

10 9 8 7 6 5 4 3 2 1

 Penguin
Random House
ANCHOR CANADA

For Adora

contents

preface to the paperback edition

In the spring of 2020, just after we first published this book, Black people ignited a global resurgence of resistance, organizing, education, and political mobilization. Black folks initiated this uprising in the name of George Floyd—who was lynched by Minneapolis police officer Derek Chauvin and his fellow officers—but also in recognition of the broader ongoing tyranny of policing and racial capitalism. We witnessed months of sustained demonstrations in the United States, and solidarity actions here in Canada.

Chauvin's act enraged Black people, and it also troubled the collective white settler conscience, as white people allowed themselves to feel sympathy for a Black man begging for his life while being slowly suffocated. White folks were, in general, less afraid to condemn this particular killing because they were allowed to watch Chauvin dominate Floyd, and were satisfied that the officer's violence was uniquely reckless and unnecessary.

In this moment of Black organizing and white guilt, our mainstream conversations about the police started to evolve. Author and scholar Robyn Maynard pointed out during a presentation that we were shifting from the rallying cry of "Black Lives Matter" to a specific demand to defund the police, and that this demand was extremely disruptive and effective. Local politicians in Canada began toying with the idea of transferring resources away from police and towards more caring and responsive services.

Maynard, who had advocated exactly this kind of transfer in her 2017 book *Policing Black Lives*, said in a public talk: "I never could have imagined that a few years later these questions would be asked widely across this country. The fact that this shift has happened is a victory in its own right." The work over years and decades by people like Maynard, and by the many people I cite in this book, has made it possible for these conversations to emerge in the Canadian mainstream.

Yet we're still so far from where we need to be. As I write this, Canadian media is marking the anniversary of Floyd's murder but has failed to give such primacy and sustained national coverage to Black and Indigenous people in Canada who have recently been killed by police or died in encounters with them, including Anthony Aust, D'Andre Campbell, Ejaz Choudry, Jason Collins, Moses Erhirhie, Jamal Francique, Braden Herman, Eishia Hudson, Julian Jones, Regis Korchinski-Paquet, Rodney Levi, Jared Lowndes, Sheffield Matthews, Chantel Moore, Caleb Tubila Njoko, Jean-Réne Junior Olivier, and Coco Ritchie.

And while the perpetrators and defenders of police violence are recognizing the change in attitudes, they've responded with symbolic gestures that keep police and other racist institutions intact. Prime Minister Justin Trudeau takes a knee while expanding Canada's racist federal prison system; Canadian university and college campuses issue solidarity statements while refusing to remove police from their campuses; corporations donate a few bucks to make us forget that their entire operations depend on the exploitation of Black people on stolen Indigenous lands around the world.

When I say the year of Black resistance and power I documented in this book could have been any year, I really mean it. Recent events are not evidence of a so-called "tipping point," but rather the cumulative and ongoing struggle of people forcing our elites to reckon with their crimes against people and the planet. Calls to abolish the police, prisons, and all systems of harm are not new, and will not simply take hold because of a new mainstream recognition. We have to fight like hell against the elitist desire to drag us backwards.

The COVID-19 pandemic and our responses to it show how desperate many of us are to return to a "normal" that has denied Black people our due. As scholar, author, and poet Dionne Brand wrote in 2020: "this normal, this usual, this ease was predicated on dis-ease. The dis-ease was always presented as something to be solved in the future, but for certain exigences of budget, but for planning, but for the faults of 'those' people, their lack of responsibility, but for all that, there were plans to remedy it, in some future time. We were to hold onto that hope and the suspension of disbelief it required to maintain 'normal.'"

We're not going back to a normal that never served us. We may not know exactly what the future we want looks like, and that's okay—our collective work will lead us there. We need to believe that a different future for Black people is possible before we can build it. Every day that we move closer to that belief, and every day that we act in service of something new, is a good day to be fighting.

negro frolicks
(january)

I remember wanting to escape the year 2016 like a kid in a haunted house, dashing from whatever real or imagined demon was chasing me. Running into empty space, terrified to look back—that was 2016. I imagine some Canadians remember it as the year a lot of beloved American artists and cultural figures died—Prince, Muhammad Ali, Carrie Fisher, Gene Wilder, Malik "Phife Dawg" Taylor—or the year that disgraceful celebrity was elected president of the United States. We're usually better at American culture and history than our own.

I marked the year 2016 through setbacks and losses closer to home. I mourned the deaths of Black people, many of whom I had never met or previously heard of, and more often I witnessed the ever-present impediments to Black life: policing, public education, prisons, the apprehension of our children, the discrimination against our parents at work, the disrespect of our elders on public transit.

I kept track of the violence done to Black people in my city, Toronto, and my country, Canada, as if it was being done to me, because it was, because it is, because that's what Black people are facing in Canada and around the world, and I'd never been more aware of it.

In 2016 I documented Black Lives Matter–Toronto's Tent City demonstration, a sixteen-day protest in front of Toronto Police headquarters during an unseasonably cold spring. The demonstrators were responding to a series of public injustices against local Black people, especially the decision not to criminally charge Andrew Doyle, a Toronto police officer who shot and killed a Black man named Andrew Loku in 2015.

At the time of the protest Doyle had not yet been publicly identified as the killer, despite months of campaigning by Black people. I hadn't seen this kind of demonstration of Black resistance in my adult life. I felt so connected to it that I not only reported from Tent City as a journalist, but I slept in it, helped clean it, kept watch over it at night. The demonstrators who maintained the camp day and night had opened a critical space for us to speak, to connect, to grieve, to hold each other.

During my reporting I met a recently arrived Black Tanzanian teenager named Michelle Erin Hopkins, who had been living in and helping to maintain the camp for a week. The police had attacked, beaten, and gassed protesters during their first full day of peaceful demonstration, and I was surprised that after so little time in Canada, this fifteen-year-old was so committed to engaging in such dangerous resistance of anti-Black racism.

"You can't ask people who have been oppressed their whole lives . . . to forget that and to ignore the fact that it might be happening again," Hopkins told me. The truth she spoke is a Black birthright, an inherited knowledge we need in order to survive no matter where we find ourselves in the world.

"People who refuse to acknowledge the fact that Canada has its race problems compare us a lot to America," Hopkins went on. "They say, 'Canada's not like America. Why are you bringing American problems into Canada? Why are you crossing borders?' But that's the thing—Black lives have no borders. We exist everywhere regardless of the fact they may not want us to."

The year was full of painful reminders that Black people are not wanted in Canada, that this is a land stolen from Indigenous peoples and ultimately colonized—just like my parents' native land of Sierra Leone—by white British settlers.

I danced away the final hour of 2016 in my own apartment with a couple of close friends—we drank champagne and sang and lit dollar-store sparklers. I needed the celebration. I grew up in Oshawa, a city about half an hour's drive east of Toronto. I can remember a New Year's party my parents hosted in the partly finished basement of our suburban home. I remember my relatives singing after the stroke of midnight. We didn't sing "Auld Lang Syne," the New Year's song that no one here seems to know the words to. My relatives sang in Krio, our native language, "Happy new year, me no die oh! Tell God tenki"—thank you—"for long life!"

In my head I sing that song every New Year's. I think about my relatives teaching me, in direct and subtle ways, that although Black people deserve far more than survival, survival alone is worth celebrating.

I woke up on the first morning of 2017 and made my friends pancakes with fruit and maple syrup. After they left I stared out my window, enjoying the tranquility of New Year's Day, the feeling that for at least a few hours nothing was going to happen. But the year's first local, well-publicized crisis of Black existence had already happened. As I sat on my couch scanning my Twitter feed, I saw posts about a young Black artist named John Samuels who had been attacked by the police in his art gallery on New Year's Eve. According to John, police had disrupted the gathering he was hosting, then repeatedly jolted him with a taser while his stunned guests admonished the police and filmed the attack on their cellphones.

My stomach somersaulted in my belly. In these moments of shock I sometimes ask "Why?" but it's more of a lament than a question. I already know why police choose, over and over and over again, to intimidate and attack and harm and kill Black people in my city, in Canada. It has nothing to do with any single incident, any presumed provocation or threat or misunderstanding. The police are just doing their job: a central responsibility of policing has always been to discipline Black people on behalf of the ruling class.

John's art gallery was within walking distance of my apartment. I wanted to jog over right away until I remembered it was a holiday and that John had likely spent his New Year's Eve in jail and probably wouldn't be there. The recognition of what I'd just read came in waves. I started to plan, to anticipate what John and his friends might need and how I might be able to help. This is how 2017 began—meet the new year, same as the old year.

The tweet from Vanny Lorde, a local Black photographer, was in all caps: "MY BLOOD IS BOILING BRO." It contained screen captures of a Facebook post by John describing the violence he'd experienced at the hands of police the night before. This is so often how news spreads, through the outraged cries of Black fam on social media, people I may never have met but with whom I am always swimming in the struggle.

Sometimes it's a phone call from a friend or acquaintance, sometimes it's "Did you hear about . . . ?" in live conversation, but these days social media is usually first, usually fastest, in spreading news of police brutality against Black people. I wasn't searching for such a story on New Year's Day, but Twitter is my Black bulletin board—a place where Black people can share experiences, thoughts, jokes, and struggles. The photographer's previous tweet read, "POLICE BRUTALITY IS FUCKING REAL IN TORONTO AND DON'T YOU EVER TELL ME IT'S 'AN AMERICAN THING.'"

I met John and several of his friends at the gallery the next day. They had already boarded up the storefront window that police had smashed during their assault. Those gathered all looked young, in their early twenties. As John described the attack in detail to me, with friends who had been there filling in some gaps, I got a better sense of how long the cops had been hassling him, and the long-term impact of their intervention.

The gallery had been operating for only about ten months. The site was scheduled to be demolished in favour of condos, but John had been able to secure a short-term lease to launch his dream, a gallery space for himself and other young artists. Plainclothes police officers started coming around almost immediately, usually unannounced, usually asking questions about drugs and searching the space. They never found anything, and John, a young man with no criminal history, said he was never shown a warrant or given any justification for the regular police intrusions.

When John applied for liquor licences for gallery events, the police found further excuses to harass him. Interestingly, John said white gallery owners who heard his story were surprised he even bothered to apply for liquor permits; they admitted that they never did. John took that chance on New Year's Eve, but liquor licensing officials appeared at the gallery and told him he had violated their rules by serving his guests champagne without a permit. John handed over his alcohol. Minutes after those officials left, several police cars showed up at the gallery.

Without giving a reason, police told everyone in the place they had to go home. John said one officer seized the cashbox at the front of the room. When John reached out and asked, "What are you doing?" several officers jumped him, pinned him to the ground, and repeatedly electrified him with a taser.

Despite the use of force against John, he was charged with assaulting the police. One of his friends who had stood up for him was also charged with assault. So now two young men were facing serious criminal convictions that could follow them forever. Damage to the gallery caused by the police cost John thousands of dollars; they also kept several hundred dollars from the cashbox. John said that as police were fingerprinting him after his arrest, one of them said, "You lost a lot of money today."

The police attack on John was calculated and it fits the pattern of disproportionate uses of force against Black people in general. In Canada, police are more likely to scrutinize Black people as they did John: to suspect us of selling drugs without presenting any evidence; to subject us to surveillance and physical searches without a warrant; to target our homes and businesses with multiple police units in response to non-criminal issues; to arrest us using overwhelming physical violence; to charge us with violence after using violence against us; to steal our personal property, particularly our money, as if we have no claim to it.

John lost his gallery space shortly after he was arrested—his guarantor on the lease got nervous and backed out of their agreement. Now John had to cancel several art shows he'd already booked, and he lost significant income.

John believes the police's initial scrutiny of his gallery was prompted by complaints from neighbours. He recalls that long before the raid, police would linger across the street during gallery events. "They tried to make me live in fear," he said. "I've learned so much about how things like noise complaints are continuously used to eradicate culture . . . which then eradicates our stories, which then eradicates our survival."

To appreciate how long local bylaws have been used on these lands to control Black people, we can go all the way back to 1785, to Shelburne, in what is now Nova Scotia. White settlers resented the recent arrival of Black Loyalists, over a thousand enslaved Black people who had fought with the British during the American Revolution. The British had promised the Loyalists freedom and land in their conquered territories, but didn't keep their word. Many Black people became the property of new white masters in Shelburne, while others worked for lower wages than their white counterparts, or were forced into a form of indentured servitude that closely resembled slavery.

In order to control the "freed" Black loyalists, Shelburne officials created a bylaw "forbidding Negro Dances and Negro Frolicks in this town." In this context, "frolicks" could mean anything from drinking to gambling to mere socializing. Obviously, white residents faced no such restrictions. John, a Black gallery owner who often hosted events by and for Black people, was subject to the same fear of Negro Frolicks as the Black folks in Shelburne who just wanted to gather and dance and be free.

White supremacy, which informs and fuels anti-Black racism, is an insatiable force. White supremacy is never personal, never individual, never isolated. The historic problems I explore in this book are not a matter of some police being too rough, or some government programs being too poorly funded. They have nothing to do with the political leaning of a particular government or the intentions of powerful people. We're talking about a system of power that seeks to benefit white people above all others.

The Canadian government and its institutions are the products of a white supremacist ideology that claims this land as the property of a white European colonial government. To maintain its stolen land, the government is engaged in an ongoing, centuries-long genocide of Indigenous peoples. Our government is designed to assimilate or eradicate Indigenous peoples, and unfortunately it works exactly as it was designed to.

White supremacy is a hierarchy, with whiteness at the top. Indigenous peoples of the Americas, whose lands have been colonized by white settlers, occupy a low place on this hierarchy—white supremacy is trying to replace them. But Black people, whom British and French colonizers brought to this land in chains four centuries ago, are at the bottom of the ladder. We are the scapegoats. Whiteness is constantly defined and reproduced through anti-Blackness.

In particular, white supremacy designates Black people as less than full human beings, as disposable labour, as chattel placed on earth for the benefit of white people. This is just as true for today's incarcerated Black people, whose criminalized existence feeds the state's courts, jails, and prisons, as it was for Black people forced to labour in fields centuries ago. White supremacy is a global phenomenon, and has been used to justify European imperialist conquest and exploitation in Africa, the Americas, Asia, and Oceania.

White power works in concert with other forms of power—including capitalism (the dominance of private profit over public benefit); ableism (the dominance of people deemed able-bodied); cisnormativity (the dominance of people who feel that their gender identity matches their body/ sex); patriarchy (the dominance of men); and heteronormativity (the dominance of people who, based on the gender binary, only accept heterosexuality as normal)—to create what feminist scholar and author bell hooks describes as "dominator culture."

In the schoolyard we had a rhyme whenever someone insulted us: "I am rubber, you are glue, it bounces off me and sticks to you!" Think of the "it," the ball bouncing around, as immorality, depravity, sickness, weakness, vice—all the things people don't want to associate with themselves. Whiteness is an unimpeachable rubber that deflects collective human failing. Nothing sticks to whiteness. Blackness is the glue, and every negative thing that gets hurled at it sticks.

A more concise version of the rhyme was the always popular "I know you are but what am I?" The modern incarnation of whiteness resists exposure and definition—white supremacy thrives in large part by avoiding being named or identified. When confronted with its own violence, whiteness simply flips the script. I know you are but what am I? Whiteness can rhyme off the sins of blackness even as it resists any collective agency or responsibility for itself. So long as the spectre of blackness looms largest, whatever whiteness is doing cannot be so bad, or at least can't be worth mentioning.

Whiteness has been celebrated and defended more overtly at other times in history, but today whiteness is often about endless disavowal. Whiteness pretends to forget its own name when called, and refuses to acknowledge its desire for dominance. White supremacy keeps stepping on your toes while insisting it was an accident. As U.S.-based writer Yawo Brown puts it: "White America has been playing a centuries-long game of 'stop hitting yourself' while holding the arms of Black America."

Institutions in today's white supremacist settler colonial context always come in peace and goodwill. They always tell us they mean well, but they refuse to own their endless violence against Black people. This is why in the city of Toronto, the self-styled multicultural mecca of the modern world, the police spent untold resources to surveil, document, interrogate, and ultimately raid and smash up a business owned by a young Black man with no criminal history. This is why they sent multiple cars and officers. This is why John was arrested and charged for receiving a beating from the police. And this is why Black people, whose ancestors have been engaged in the same continuous struggle, were lighting up the internet on New Year's Day when we heard about the raid.

John was born and raised in Scarborough, once its own borough east of Toronto and now a part of the amalgamated city. His parents, both immigrants from Jamaica, struggled to raise him and his brothers on modest incomes. John told me in a 2019 interview that from a young age the arts were his refuge. He loved visual arts, hip hop, and dance and ultimately formed a dance crew that gained local praise and earned spots in music videos and commercials. As John gained confidence in his craft, he and his friends started dreaming of their own space to meet, rehearse, host, and create.

"We were having meetings in Starbucks," he said, laughing. "We were just like, 'Yo, guys, we're gonna get our own spot.'" After interning with a local gallery owner, John felt ready to operate his own space and found a small storefront on Bloor Street West. "The vision was always about space, because in Scarborough I didn't have space," John said. "Autonomy was the word I kept playing with at that time in my life. I felt the way to get that was to create your own business."

The police raid changed everything. John was charged with obstruction of justice, assaulting a police officer, assault with the intent to resist arrest, and two non-criminal liquor violations. He told me, "That time was so hard . . . I don't know how I would have been able to do it without the support of my community." John spent the majority of 2017 fighting to get the criminal charges withdrawn, and even after he succeeded he had to start paying the heavy fines for the liquor violations.

In the weeks after the raid, John invited me over to view some of the videos his friends captured of his assault and the accompanying chaos. I broke down at one point as I witnessed the same acts of violence from yet another camera angle, my body anticipating the pitch of John's screams, the breaking glass, the confusion of his guests.

Luckily for John, the same community that had animated his space was ready to support him. Friends, patrons, and local art institutions came forward with donations, showed up at court dates, offered their own spaces in kind. "That was the first time I actually met [organizers with] Black Lives Matter, which was so cool," John said. "I kinda felt like they were superheroes who came out of nowhere and were like, 'Yo, what's up. We're here to support you.'"

Black people and others who understand our struggle showed up from the first moments we heard about what had happened to John. Limited as our resources, networks, and access may be, we came together in community with what we had and got to work in the courtroom, in galleries across the city, in our peer groups, on social media.

Most Black people aren't surprised by incidents like John's—our safety depends on us anticipating racial violence. We don't need surveys or academic studies to verify what we have collectively experienced for centuries. We can't wait for those who uphold white supremacy—knowingly or through ignorance—to value us. To paraphrase the courageous Black revolutionary Assata Shakur, it is our duty not only to fight for our freedom but to attain freedom, to live free of the physical and metaphorical chains white supremacy has fashioned for us.

———

My year started with news of a police attack against a Black person in Toronto, and such attacks were common in Canadian news throughout 2017. The year was bisected in July by Canada's 150th birthday, a celebration of colonialism and white supremacy that unwittingly highlighted the ongoing state violence against the Indigenous peoples of the lands we now call North America. It has taken me most of my life to even grasp the connection between my struggle as a Black Canadian and the struggle of Indigenous peoples on these stolen territories. Distinct and complex as they may be, our respective ancestral struggles have placed us here together, and we need to cultivate listening, partnership, and solidarity to carve out a better collective future.

I was born on the flat lands of Red Deer, in southern Alberta, in the early hours of a cold April morning in 1982. The Red Deer River forms the northern border of Treaty 7 territory, the land covered by one of eleven treaties between the government of Canada and Indigenous peoples living in what is now northern Ontario, the majority of the prairie provinces, and parts of British Columbia, Yukon, and the Northwest Territories. According to the modern-day government of Manitoba, the purpose of the treaties was to "extend Canada's nation sea to sea; to claim and use natural resources in northern Canada (oil, gold)." Treaty 7 specifically covered the traditional territories of the Bearspaw First Nation, Blood Tribe, Chiniki First Nation, Piikani First Nation, Siksika Nation, Tsuut'ina Nation, and Wesley First Nation.

Of course, we are all indigenous to somewhere. Like most people who have settled in modern-day Alberta, my parents are not indigenous to that territory. Both my parents were born in Freetown, Sierra Leone, on the west coast of Africa. My family's heritage is Krio, a name that describes both our language and our lineage. The Krio people are mainly the descendants of enslaved Africans who gained their liberation in British colonies and returned from England, Nova Scotia, and Jamaica to the same West African shores from which Europeans kidnapped their ancestors. Hence the aspirational name of the city where my parents were born.

My ancestors and the Indigenous peoples who signed Treaty 7 have a critical common experience: both were oppressed by a group whose legacy is so unquestioned today that we usually don't even name it. But someone had to compel Indigenous peoples here to sign treaties to "share" their land and resources, and someone had to build a slave post on Bunce Island in Sierra Leone and force my ancestors onto slave ships. It was the British, of course, the most successful colonizers and enslavers in human history. British imperialism, which led to the colonization of both Canada and Sierra Leone, produced me, and informed the stories I'm about to share with you. So when I talk about Black and Indigenous solidarity as necessary for our future survival, I'm not speaking in metaphors. I'm asking us to honour the history and struggles of our ancestors as we grapple with the aftermath.

As a child in Red Deer, I had no conscious understanding of racism. I knew that, outside of the few friends we'd sometimes visit, almost no one in town looked like us or spoke Krio. I knew that the woman I called Grandma Carless, who took care of me when my parents went to work, was white. I knew that Mister Rogers, whom I watched on her TV every day, was also white. I knew all my neighbours were white. I didn't especially know what it meant to be Black, white, or anything else. If I had recognized any of the experiences my parents would speak about as I got older—the stares, unwanted comments, questions, inquisitions, indignities, slurs, and other reactions to our blackness—I couldn't begin to process them.

We moved from Alberta to Ontario when I was five years old and settled in Oshawa. The area is the ancestral territory of the Wendat Nation.

The name "Oshawa" originates from the Ojibwe language, and one common translation is "that point at the crossing of the stream where the canoe was exchanged for the trail." In other words, Oshawa's natural harbour on Lake Ontario is a portage, a crossing place. By the time we moved to Oshawa, each of my parents had been able to sponsor their mothers to come to Canada. My dad's mom, Mary, lived with us in our first house in Oshawa, and Adora, my mom's mom, lived in the neighbouring town of Whitby.

As a grade one student in Oshawa, I began to feel conscious of my blackness. I was colouring with a group of my classmates, almost all of whom were white. We shared the pencil crayons as we drew the things kids draw: dark brown for tree trunks, bright green for leaves and grass, yellow for the sun. Someone asked for the "skin colour" pencil. Everyone else seemed to understand that a particular cream colour was what she wanted. None of my peers seemed to realize this label excluded me, but I felt it in my bones and never forgot it. As the year went on I noticed how the cream-coloured pencil crayons were the most used, and were always worn down to the nub by classmates drawing themselves, their families, their friends. The tree-trunk brown was my preference for drawing myself and my family, but I never referred to this crayon as "skin colour" and neither did anyone else. (I learned later that Laurentien, the company that made the pencil crayons we used, had for many years named one of its pinkish colours Natural Flesh. The company also produced an Indian Red.)

As I got older I experienced many permutations of the crayon incident, and I associated being Black in my surroundings with the feeling of being simultaneously invisible and all too visible. My classmates would never mention race unless they were talking about me, and my race seemed immediately relevant when someone was angry with me. I thought Christopher was my friend until one day we got into an argument on the playground and he reflexively blurted out "Black boy!" I remember the look on his face after he said it—he seemed surprised by his own words, or maybe just embarrassed he'd said them out loud in front of everyone. We still played together after that, but I was always wary of him.

When I visited friends' houses we would watch television. There were few Black people on Canadian TV in the late 1980s and early '90s. Whenever a Black person would appear onscreen, one of my white friends, like clockwork, would turn to me with a stupid smile and say, "Hey, that looks like you!" I had no response to this unwanted attention and soon realized none was expected. It was just something to say to me, to laugh over before moving on. I began to associate my blackness with shame and isolation, and as early as primary school I started to wish I hadn't been born Black.

The older I got the more I noticed. At least once a month, a stranger at the Oshawa bus terminal would ask me if I had a brother. In time I realized white people just assumed all Black people in their city were related. Schoolmates would ask me if I was the brother of the other two Black girls in my class—even though our families were from three different countries. One day at the lunch table a white student who sometimes ate with us pointed at the homemade lunch of my Caribbean classmate and said, "I don't understand how you can eat that shit."

I was now old enough to feel safe in sharing these experiences with my parents and relatives, who reciprocated with stories of their own: when my uncle worked in retail, customers had made racist comments to him; my dad was interrogated when he crossed the border; some white women my mother worked with treated her like she was invisible. I started to understand my personal struggle with anti-Black racism as more of a family and collective experience.

When I was nineteen and a student at Queen's University in Kingston, Ontario, two white police officers stopped me one night while I was walking home alone and demanded I identify myself. I was sure I'd noticed cops following me in their cruisers as I drove around campus, but this was the first time they'd actually confronted me. We were in a laneway behind the local pizza shop, a shortcut I took almost every day. The cops left me waiting in the glare of their headlights as they presumably ran my name through their computer. I was so afraid. I thought about screaming for help if anything happened—and I feared no one would hear me. One of the officers finally returned with my ID, and when I asked him why he'd stopped me, he casually offered that there'd been some "suspicious activity in the area." Over the course of the next few years I would be stopped or followed dozens of times by police in Kingston and Toronto, where I relocated shortly after dropping out of university.

I came to resent my blackness as a child because it made me feel powerless and scared. It has taken me most of my adult years to embrace this skin, this ancestry, this struggle. During this time I've begun to seek out my communities, a diaspora of Africans who understand so much of my experience without explanation, who love and support me specifically because I am Black. The more I celebrate my identity, the more I encounter white people who are existentially threatened by Black pride and self-love. Since they can no longer shame me for being Black, white people now complain that I make everything about race, and accuse me of profiting from the phony racial distinction their ancestors created to marginalize us.

Black people just can't win in this white supremacist construct called Canada, which only exists through the ongoing genocide and subjugation of Indigenous peoples and the theft and destruction of their traditional territories. We could choose any year since the Confederation of Canada in 1867 to illustrate how white supremacy functions here. We could go even further back in time to the centuries of British and French enslavement of Black and Indigenous peoples that helped pave the way for project Canada.

But the struggle for Black life in modern-day Canada is a living struggle, as urgent today as it has ever been. This book shares snapshots of Black resistance and power from every month of 2017. I write the year here as I lived it, in the pursuit of Black freedom, in the spirit of seeing and honouring our fight, of connecting with others in Canada and beyond.

The final tweet I sent out in 2016 was a retweet of Christina Sharpe, then a professor of English at Tufts University and a Black woman whose writing on Black life has fed and strengthened my mind. Sharpe said, "2017 is going to be hard in ways we know and don't know. Strength and love." A couple of days later I was sitting in that smashed-up gallery with John, witnessing the aftermath of another interruption of our Black lives.

zero tolerance
(february)

The radio was constantly on in my childhood home, as integral to the kitchen as food and dishes. My parents got most of their news from public radio broadcasts, and stories about Black people would emerge from the steady waves of sound and pull me in. I started realizing that blackness was central to news stories about crime. As a child I used to fear it would again be one of us on the news, in custody or at large. I was afraid someone was keeping score and that it didn't look good for my skinfolk.

White supremacy is always keeping score. The math is simple, as is the assumption of cause and effect: Black people get caught by the police so often because we break the law so often. Dominator culture tells Black folks that we not only bring this pain upon ourselves, but that we're so irresponsible we blame our suffering on someone else, jealously landing on white people. When I listen to the news today, I have to resist this racist math and remind myself that white supremacy is selling the idea of Black violence to distract us from its own.

When the media first reported that a Black, six-year-old, forty-eight-pound girl had been shackled by two police officers inside a public school in Mississauga, there was no information about the race of the police officers, or their possible histories of violence against other children, or the neighbourhoods they lived in. These details only matter when a crime is being committed, and Canada's mainstream news media doesn't consider state violence to be criminal, especially when Black people are the targets. In my industry, violence to control Black people is not called violence. It's called policing.

Neither the Peel District School Board nor the Peel Regional Police notified the public that six-year-old Symone was handcuffed inside her school in September 2016. (I call this girl Symone, not her real name, to protect her identity and the identity of her mother, whom I call Brenda and who continues to fight the system that treated her daughter so violently.) Few Black people take the risk of publicly calling out state violence, and those who do must confront a potential lifetime of threats, reprisals, public shamings, and social stigmas from mainstream white culture. But in February 2017, Brenda decided to take that risk. She hired a lawyer and filed a complaint of racial discrimination with the Human Rights Tribunal of Ontario. And then she shared the story with CityNews, their camera focusing on her hands and on the back of her head so she would not be identified, so Symone would not be identified through her.

On that day in late September 2016, Peel Regional Police entered Symone's elementary school after receiving a call from staff. Police spokesperson Josh Colley said school officials had called his force about a "violent child." Colley said two officers arrived at the school "and found a young girl who was acting extremely violent—punching, hitting, biting, spitting." The police did not report that Symone had injured herself or anyone else as a result of this behaviour.

Colley said the officers used "any de-escalation techniques that they could" to calm Symone down. He did not describe any such techniques or say how many times police attempted them. "At the time of [the officers'] interaction with this young child, in their mind the safest way to de-escalate and begin that process was to restrain her," said Colley. He confirmed that officers first handcuffed Symone's ankles together, then used a second set of cuffs to bind the girl's wrists. The tribunal later determined that police kept Symone laying on her stomach in handcuffs for 28 minutes. Colley said Peel police have no rules that prevent them from handcuffing children.

The officers said they specifically chose this form of restraint because Symone "was banging her head and they feared for her safety." There was no mention of when the police had decided to remove the restraints or how they had determined Symone was no longer a danger to herself or those around her. All we know is that at some point, her mother arrived at the school and was beyond shocked to learn what the police had done.

A teacher who chose to restrain Symone as the police did would almost certainly face discipline from their regulatory body, the Ontario College of Teachers. The college's misconduct regulations prohibit teachers from engaging in any act of physical, sexual, emotional, psychological, or verbal abuse. A teacher who shackled a student would also be at serious risk of criminal charges. But police enjoy a legal monopoly on violence—we expect cops to control civilians by using any amount of force they see fit.

The decision by school staff to call the police essentially transferred responsibility for Symone's care from the school to law enforcement. As Brenda noted, "They had office staff, principals, like everybody was there for support. I don't understand the role the police were playing that day." Although the police shouldn't have been inside Symone's school, they were in charge once they arrived.

Brenda said Symone had been suspended at least four times since starting junior kindergarten at age four, and that the school had called the police on her on two previous occasions. Staff accused Symone of violent behaviours Brenda had never experienced from her child outside of school. She told CityNews, "The first teacher my daughter ever had said, 'Your daughter's exceptionally bright, but I do notice that tags on her clothes bother her—the sound bothers her,' so she made accommodations in the classroom, and they didn't need to call me to come pick her up. 'Cause that teacher actually cared. When she moved to [senior kindergarten], that's when things started going downhill. It seemed like every day, every other day, I'm getting phone calls. And that's when it was really, I don't know, hard for me."

There were hints in the CityNews reporting of the level of adversity Symone's family had been facing in the years leading up to the police attack. Symone's father died when she was only six months old. Brenda, who had since been raising her daughter alone, began having health problems when Symone was in junior kindergarten, around the same time that Symone's teacher noticed some of the challenges she was having at school. Brenda was eventually diagnosed with thyroid cancer.

There's no way of knowing exactly how Symone's family struggle was affecting her, but the school's repeated discipline against her could only have complicated her struggle. After repeated police interventions, Symone may reasonably have anticipated the cops were coming for her even before they arrived. It's hard to imagine what kind of stress she might have experienced then. As Brenda suggested, Symone knew at age six that the police posed a danger to her. "How's she gonna trust that police are there to protect us in a time of need? How's she gonna trust to call the police if anything happened?"

On February 24, 2017, three weeks after CityNews broke the story of the police attack on Symone and five months after the actual incident occurred, Peel Regional Police Chief Jennifer Evans announced that the force would conduct an internal review. Between the initial news report and the review announcement, Brenda had filed a complaint to the police. It appears this complaint, and media coverage of the attack, prompted the police to finally review the incident.

To chain a child by her wrists and ankles for *her own* safety . . . the idea exists outside of reality.

Such an act negates a child's need to feel safe, and defines her safety through the eyes of those who fear her. In his book *The Civil War in 50 Objects*, Harold Holzer reflects on the significance of shackles specifically designed for enslaved Black children in the United States. Holzer notes that while European enslavers frequently used iron shackles to control Africans during the long passage from West Africa to the Americas, they usually reserved such cruelties for men. Only on the rarest occasions were restraints forced on women or children. Quoting the writer Corey Malcom, Holzer observes "people of any age restrained by devices like these 'were barely considered human, and would never again be free.'"

The shackling of a six-year-old Black child in twenty-first-century Canada reminds us we are still not free. In the words of Toni Morrison, this kind of cowardice in service of white supremacy "translates violence against the defenseless as strength." Conservative media treated the police who shackled Symone as victims of a hopeless situation. Wilfully ignorant media commentaries repeated the question, "What were the police supposed to do?" as if a child throwing a tantrum was novel. Some openly blamed Brenda for what the police did to her child. Jay Michaels of Newstalk 1010 radio, where I hosted a weekly show for several years, suggested her priorities were out of order. On the day the news broke, Michaels said, "When there's been two incidents where police have been to the school for your child, do you really think the first thing you should do is start doing TV interviews and talk about police brutality? Or do you really think what you should probably do is maybe worry about the safety of your kid?" I guess Michaels didn't realize Brenda was sharing her daughter's story more than four months after it occured.

Michaels's co-host, Ryan Doyle, took issue with Brenda's race-based human rights complaint, specifically her assertion that Symone's race was a factor in the way police treated her. "You just lose all credibility when you start to talk about the race card when we're talking about a little girl who's obviously got some emotional issues that she's dealing with." Grown white people, many with their own children, were asking us to consider that sometimes it's necessary to shackle a child for her own good, and that race has nothing to do with it.

The use of force against Symone, while it sounds exceptional, is an extreme example on a spectrum of disciplinary violence that schools use against Black students. This violence is not always physical, but it is potent—Canadian education systems suspend, expel, devalue, and discourage Black kids with efficiency and intention. The exclusion of our kids is not an accident. It's part of a centuries-old mindset that fears and devalues the education of Black people, especially alongside white people.

The fact that Symone was suspended at least four times by the age of six is devastating, but is consistent with how the public education system treats its youngest Black children. In 2006–2007, the Toronto

District School Board, the largest school board in the country, suspended Black students from junior kindergarten to grade six over three times more often than white students in the same grades. In the same year, the TDSB suspended about 13 per cent of all Black students in grades seven through twelve—that's approximately one in every seven Black students between the ages of twelve and eighteen.

Interestingly, students who identified as "mixed," especially those between grades seven and twelve, were more likely than most other groups to be suspended in 2011–2012, and although the board does not define this term, it surely includes many students of African heritage. For that same school year, the TDSB suspended about 3 per cent of white students between grades seven and twelve. A 2017 TDSB study found that 48 per cent of students who had been expelled from school over the previous five years identified as Black, even though only 13 per cent of TDSB students identified as Black. By contrast, 10 per cent of students who were expelled during this time identified as white.

But disproportionate violence against Black people is not the problem: it is a symptom of the white supremacist thinking that guides all Canadian institutions. The goal is not to balance out these statistics, to shackle or suspend fewer Black children. The goal is to end the institutional practice of harshly punishing children, since the school's power to do so reinforces white supremacy.

In the early 2000s, much of this discipline was a result of the Safe Schools Act enacted by Ontario Conservative premier Mike Harris in 2000. (Dear reader: always pay extra attention to laws that contains the word "safe" and ask whose safety is being addressed.) Harris and his education minister, Janet Ecker, won re-election in 1999 partly on the promise of a "zero tolerance" approach to violence and misbehaviour in public schools. The act outlined extremely broad categories of student behaviour that could result in suspension, including "opposition to authority."

Teachers and administrators then used this legislation to target Black students and other oppressed populations. Most Ontario school boards didn't collect any standardized data about race and school suspensions before 2000. However, a 2003 report by the Ontario Human Rights Commission noted that, based on public perception and some independent research, "the Act and school board policies are having a disproportionate impact on racial minority students, particularly Black students, and students with disabilities." The same report said that students who were suspended rarely received schoolwork while they were excluded from class, and that the meagre support programs for suspended students all had waiting lists because they lacked adequate funding.

After the Liberals defeated the Conservatives in 2003, Premier Dalton McGuinty vowed to review the act and reduce suspensions in Ontario, but he made no specific acknowledgement of the disproportionate disciplining of Black students. By 2012, schools had dramatically reduced the overall number of suspensions for students of all races. And yet that same year, Black students across all age groups were still suspended about three times as often as white students. Data also showed that schools were disproportionately suspending students who identified as lesbian, gay, bisexual, transgender, or queer.

Somali youth make up a significant portion of the Black population within the TDSB: in 2011, self-identified Somali kids represented approximately 17 per cent of the thirty-two thousand Black students in the school district. Somali students experience unique challenges and discrimination based on racist perceptions about their language skills, immigration, and social status. In 2014 the TDSB struck its Task

Force on the Success of Students of Somali Descent. The group's report found that, in 2011, only 66 per cent of Somali students had graduated on schedule, compared with 79 per cent of all students—one-third of Somali students had failed to graduate on schedule. Perhaps the report's most shocking finding was that three out of four Somali students had been suspended, had been placed in special education programs, or had failed to meet the standard for grade six standardized testing in English, math, and reading. In interviews for the report, Somali parents said their children were often placed into English as a Second Language programs even when they had been born in Canada and spoke English fluently. Somali-speaking students were also the most likely of any language group to be suspended.

In Nova Scotia, where Black people have lived in large numbers for well over two centuries, the education system is equally efficient at disenfranchising Black students. In 1994, a group of Black educators and community members called the Black Learners Advisory Committee wrote an extensive report on African Nova Scotian students. The report's introduction states that "racial discrimination, overt or covert, systemic or otherwise, has played a major part in denying African Nova Scotians equal opportunity to education. This in turn has had disastrous consequences in employment and access to other services. As a result, most African Canadian children are from birth trapped in a vicious cycle of societal rejection and isolation, poverty, low expectations, and low educational achievement."

Those words, written a generation ago, still ring true in Nova Scotia. In 2016 the Halifax Regional School Board reported that 22.5 per cent of the students it suspended were Black, though they made up only 7.8 per cent of the school population. And while Halifax schools saw an overall decrease in suspensions between 2015 and 2016, the suspension rate among Black students continued to increase. Young people who identified as Aboriginal (which in Nova Scotia can mean many things but primarily refers to members of the Mi'kmaq Nation) were also overrepresented in suspensions. While the board's report notes that 60 per cent of its students identify as European, there is no mention of this group's suspension rate. Instead, statistics are given for three groups: African Descent, Aboriginal, and "other." The word "white" does not appear in the document, and neither do the words "race" and "racism."

I know you are but what am I?

For nearly fifty years, Black researchers in Canada have been documenting the ways schools have continuously failed Black students through low expectations, isolation, and harsh discipline. Much of this research is summarized in *Towards Race Equity in Education: The Schooling of Black Students in the Greater Toronto Area*, a 2017 York University study by Carl James and Tana Turner. Since the early 1980s, researchers have noted that Toronto schools stream Black students into "basic," or lower level, classes more often than any other racial group. The York study includes findings from the 1990s that "by the end of 1992, 44% of Black students in the Grade 9 cohort had graduated, compared to 59% of White students and 72% of Asian students." The same study summarizes findings from "The Roots of Youth Violence," a 2008 report commissioned by the Ontario government: "suspended and expelled students were more likely to drop out of school entirely and often got involved with criminal activity and, because they were not in school during the day, came under increased scrutiny of the police."

It's impossible to quantify the psychological toll of this disproportionately harsh treatment of Black students and their families. The words of one participant in the York study give us some insight into the daily struggles and fears of Black parents: "I have found that it has been very difficult for my son. Early on, he was identified as having a speech and language delay; and due to his young age, he would become frustrated with teachers and ECEs that were not trained to address his needs. When the teachers grew frustrated they would send him to the office; at which point I would receive a phone call from the principal. There was one incident that I will never forget. The principal advised me that if my son, 4 years old at the time and in JK, had been in Grade 6 or 7, he would have to call the police on him for his behaviour. As shocked as I was, he said it in a very cavalier manner."

I don't like to think about the number of times I was singled out for punishment in elementary school. One of my teachers felt I talked too much in class, so he put my desk at the front of the room, in between a cupboard and a lab desk, so I couldn't look at or speak to my classmates. I wonder if my teacher ever thought about the impact of this humiliation on one of the only Black students in the entire school. His isolation tactic mirrored so much of the racism I was already experiencing in the schoolyard and in my city. My country will argue that my teacher didn't realize I took it that way, that he never intended it that way. But as long as teachers in Canada are allowed to shame and isolate their students, their actions will reflect the anti-Black norms all around them.

I tried to hide from my parents any discipline I received at school. My grades mattered most to them, and since they saw me as a capable student, I was scared they would agree that I was just misbehaving and deserved to be singled out. But the constant humiliation made school more difficult for me, and I still can't even think about these punishments without involuntarily clenching my teeth.

In June of 2019, more than two years after Brenda went public with her daughter's story, the Human Rights Tribunal of Ontario began hearing the discrimination case. Lawyers for the Peel Regional Police Board argued that the officers had had "no alternative" but to handcuff Symone. Lawyer Paula Rusak said, "The optics are not great, but I think we all know that children sometimes can be difficult to handle, and in this particular case, the officers had no alternative but to restrain her as best they could. At that time—it's easy to Monday-morning quarterback—but at that time, that was the best thing to do."

—

On February 17, 2017, Nancy Elgie gave up her elected position as a trustee at the York Region District School Board, the third-largest board in Ontario, resigning eighty-seven days after she called a Black woman a nigger following a public meeting on equity issues. For three months, Elgie, who is white, gambled that the public would forgive or forget her racist slur. Most people did. But a small, tenacious group led by Charline Grant, the target of Elgie's insult, demanded she resign. Grant and her family were not merely fighting Elgie, but navigating a deluge of public sympathy for the trustee's racism.

The previous fall, Grant had sought support from board officials after learning that school staff had repeatedly discriminated against her teenage son, the only Black boy in his grade nine Woodbridge class. In a complaint to the Ontario Human Rights Tribunal filed earlier that year, Grant said her son's soccer coach had singled him out for leaving practice early to attend a religious feast—the family are Israelites, a small Judeo-Christian group. According to the complaint, the coach benched Grant's son the next day and remarked that the boy must be "full" from eating.

According to Grant, a coach once warned her son's white teammates to check their bags after her son had gone into the change room alone.

On November 22, 2016, Charline Grant attended a meeting of the school board to learn more about its responses to racism. Two weeks later, the *Toronto Star* reported that Nancy Elgie was under investigation for having "referred to a black parent as a 'n-----' in front of others" following the meeting. The *Star* didn't spell out the N-word, and although I can understand their decision not to print Elgie's harmful language, not printing it was more harmful. White supremacy loves to play dumb, and without context it was easier for Elgie and her supporters to claim the word had, like a sneeze or hiccup, spontaneously escaped her lips.

In resisting calls for Elgie's resignation, her supporters asked the public to imagine a situation in which a white public official who called a Black woman a nigger might still be the right person to make decisions for thousands of Black children. Many of Elgie's constituents, and even teachers within the school board, had no qualms about making this argument. The writer of a letter to Elgie's local newspaper explained that "while she admits to using a highly pejorative word, she explains clearly that she did so only to describe the words used by someone else. At no point did she call someone by this name. In our view, this very important distinction has been largely overlooked by the media."

The media had never reported that Elgie had repeated someone else's words, yet Elgie's defenders made this claim regularly. In the absence of accurate reporting on the context of Elgie's comment, her supporters were free to imagine their own. (And did you catch the letter writer's reference to the word "nigger" as a "name"?) White supremacy encourages the people it benefits to create their own parallel universe, their own set of facts and explanations about the existence and prevalence of racism. Even as white people insist that "no one really knows what happened," they can immediately share an explanation that eases their anxiety and shame. I call this "white supremacist improv." You don't have to be a white supremacist to play this game—you don't even have to be white. White supremacy has a mission for all of us, if we choose to accept it.

In their eagerness to explain away the incident, Elgie's boosters ignored the well-publicized racism within the York Region school board and, more importantly, the extraordinary efforts by its leadership to maintain the toxic conditions. In December 2015, board chair Anna DeBartolo cancelled a survey meant to record demographic data about students, including their race and ethnic origin. Schools that don't regularly collect and compare this data can't provide accurate reporting on the racial breakdown of suspensions, expulsions, special education programs, or streaming practices. On the same day, DeBartolo announced that the board was dissolving its own equity committee.

In September of 2016, the school board announced it was investigating Ghada Sadaka, a principal at one of its schools who had repeatedly written and shared Islamophobic messages on her Facebook page. The board conducted an investigation but refused to publicize its findings. Sadaka then announced she was taking a leave from her job and was quietly reassigned within the board.

Charline Grant was one of many parents who said the board was failing to address racism and discrimination. Many had sought support from community organizations, including the Vaughan African Canadian Association and the National Council of Canadian Muslims. Frustrated parents were even contemplating a class action lawsuit against the board.

Elgie's constituency included the municipality of Georgina, a town whose population at the time of the 2015 census was 92 per cent white. The same census indicated that Black residents made up only 1.5 per cent of the Georgina-area population. York Region's school board is the fastest growing in the province, and nearly 70 per cent of its students identify as something other than white. I couldn't find any news reports of organized condemnation, or even criticism, of Elgie's comments from within her constituency. And since it's nearly impossible to legally fire an elected official in Ontario, only Elgie's constituents could decide her political fate. Neither Elgie's fellow trustees nor her board had the power to remove her, but they used the board's investigation into her conduct as an excuse not to publicly condemn her, to wait and see.

When the *Toronto Star* asked Elgie why she had used such a hateful word, she first tried, unconvincingly, to dismiss it, saying, "There is no merit in the accusation." When reporters asked if she denied calling Grant a nigger, Elgie replied, "I'm not saying anything like that . . . I'm just saying there is no merit in the accusation." Elgie must have realized, once the story became public, that this non-denial denial was weak, so she came up with a new explanation: she and her family said she had recently suffered a head injury, which had since caused her to accidentally say "nigger." In both instances, Elgie's defence was that good people like her cannot mean any harm against Black people, even when they use the most destructive words our language has to denigrate blackness. Once Elgie claimed she didn't mean it the way we heard it—once she appealed to her own good intentions instead of the impact of her words—she absolved herself of the hurt she caused.

In early February, the *Toronto Star* undermined its own reporting of Elgie's racist remark by publishing an opinion piece by two of her children, originally titled "Facts to Consider when Judging Nancy Elgie," suggesting the public didn't have all the facts. (The online headline was subsequently changed to "Consider This When You Judge Nancy Elgie, Her Children Say.") The piece didn't contain any new facts about Elgie's racist language—her adult children weren't present to hear her anti-Black slur and didn't deny she'd said it. Instead, the family argued that Elgie had "misspoken" as a result of her recent head trauma. "Such words—even used accidentally—are painful and hard to forgive," her children wrote. "But since a person's reputation and life's work hangs in the balance, we ask you to consider a few facts, and then judge for yourself." The so-called facts were that Elgie was cooperating with the board investigation; that she was eighty-two years old and fragile; that she had enjoyed an exemplary career; and that her late husband, Bob, a former provincial govern-ment minister, had fought for human rights.

None of these "facts" explained why Elgie was still refusing to take responsibility for her hateful words towards Grant, or why she believed she still had the authority to make decisions about Black children, about anyone's children, as a public official. As a final insult, the *Star* allowed Elgie's children to add their professional credentials (both are university professors) to the end of the piece, as if they had some detached expertise to offer about the shameful conduct of their own mother.

"Anyone who knows my mother will tell you she doesn't have a racist bone in her body," Elgie's son Stewart told CBC News. "Her whole life, there was zero tolerance for any kind of racism in her household." Vicky Mochama, one of the few Black women journalists in Canada's main-stream media, clapped back via Twitter, "People without racist bones in their body sure say racist things! Maybe racism is a skin condition."

On February 13, I joined Charline Grant, her husband, Garth, and several local community members for the next school board meeting. Elgie was not present, but her family was. The board allowed her chil-dren, accompanied by her grandchildren, to read a letter to the board before the meeting started. Elgie's position had evolved again: now she was just as outraged as any of us about her own conduct and demanded that she be punished—as long as she could define her penalty: "I propose a voluntary sanction that I be prohibited from participating in all board meetings for a period of three to six months, if my fellow trustees accept it," her letter read.

The school board wasn't ready for the vocal community presence at the meeting. Despite the chair's attempts to silence us, Grant's allies halted the meeting and ultimately forced the trustees to adjourn. The trustees, unsure what to do but reluctant to walk out, remained in the room. We demanded that they explain why none of them had publicly called for Elgie's resignation and why most had refrained from even saying her name in public. After many excuses and hesitations, one by one, trustees began to tell the gathering that they too believed Elgie should go.

That was a Monday. On Tuesday, after weeks of government silence on Elgie's conduct, Mitzie Hunter, the provincial education minister and a Black woman herself, called on the trustee to resign. On Wednesday, Ontario premier Kathleen Wynne called Elgie's language "unacceptable" but didn't say what the consequence should be. "She's going to have to search her conscience and make a decision for herself," said the premier. On Thursday I wrote an opinion piece for the *Star*—at the time I was writing a regular column with the paper. Although I was a columnist and not a news reporter, I was the first Canadian journalist to contextualize in print Elgie's full comment about Grant. I used the word "nigger" in my piece because I was tired of the abstract conversation about its use.

Charline Grant had attended that November meeting to keep current on the school board's equity policies. Reporters approached her after the meeting, and while she was being interviewed, board staff overheard

Elgie ask out loud, "Is that the nigger parent speaking to the media again?" Grant herself did not hear the comment, but learned of it later from a school official. That official said Elgie had made the remark to DeBartolo, the trustee board chair, and to J. Philip Parappally, the board's top executive.

There's a saying in politics that you take out your trash on Friday—meaning you wait until the end of the business week to release bad news, so news outlets are less likely to pick it up. On the Friday after the disruption at the board meeting, Elgie resigned via a YouTube video.

In the days after Elgie finally quit, Steve Paikin, a veteran journalist with Ontario's public broadcaster, argued in a post on his blog that Elgie's brain had "short-circuited" and caused her to say nigger. Paikin said that allowing Elgie to keep her position might "ultimately lead to a place of more understanding, more harmony, and frankly, more love."

Elgie's many apologists saw her as a potential agent of redemption for her own racist action. At the same time, they described the community holding Elgie to account as harsh or even divisive. I think this argument dishonours the realities of anti-Black racism, and it's the reason I will never watch Elgie's resignation video. Her claim to goodness is not our problem. Her redemption does not help Black people.

The loving and determined community response for Charline Grant and her family was the story most media couldn't tell. The care and support Grant's family received from parents, students, teachers, and other community members was the good-news story, but many people missed it because of their investment in redeeming a particularly stubborn white woman.

In April of 2017 the York Region school board fired its director, Parappally, after a provincial report denounced his handling of racism within the school board. In November the *Star* reported that the investigation into Elgie's conduct had cost the school board $30,000. In October of 2018, Charline Grant ran for a seat on the York Region school board against Anna DeBartolo, the former board chair who had overseen the cancellation of race-based data collection and the scrapping of the equity committee. Grant placed second. Weeks later, DeBartolo resigned. Instead of appointing Grant to the post as the runner-up, the board chose to spend $177,000 on a by-election.

Once again, Grant came in second place.

American journalist and author Ta-Nehisi Coates has said "racism is not merely a simplistic hatred. It is, more often, broad sympathy toward some and broader skepticism toward others." This definition is particularly relevant in Canada, a country that measures itself favorably against the brash American brand of racism. Yet we broadly sympathize with our racist school systems, and we broadly scrutinize Black mothers like Charline Grant and Brenda who report abuses.

Charline Grant's struggle at the York school board continues, as does Brenda's fight at the Ontario Human Rights Tribunal.

justice for abdirahman

(march)

In Canadian mythology, police exist as a force for good in our communities. But when the media publicizes an act of police brutality, especially if the target is Black, the story changes slightly. We begin to speak more of the necessity of the cops. Police apologists remind us what a hard job policing is, and that despite its harms, an armed police force with the discretion to kill is still essential for "peace" and "order." It's tougher to be the police than to be policed, they insist. Sometimes it takes the cops themselves to remind us exactly who they are and what role they continue to play on these stolen and colonized territories.

In early March of 2017, seven months after an Ottawa police officer had fatally beaten a man at the front door of his home, a police oversight agency laid several criminal charges, including homicide, against him. In response, police officers across Canada decided to defend this officer, to tie their collective mission of policing to his potential prosecution.

Police seemed to fear that the conviction of one officer in criminal court was a threat to all police officers, to policing in general. And they would know.

—

The last days of July 2016 brought a heat wave across much of southern and central Ontario and sticky nights for those without air conditioning or a basement. The morning of Sunday the twenty-fourth, Ottawa was hot and humid. People were in the streets jogging, sitting, meeting, running errands. Sometime after nine that morning Abdirahman Abdi, who lived in the city's Hintonburg neighbourhood, visited a community centre where a staffer interacted with him and said he was speaking incomprehensibly. The staffer said that on his way out, Abdirahman collided with a pastor coming into the building for Sunday services. The pastor asked the staffer, "Is that man with it?" Witnesses say Abdirahman walked around the neighbourhood and assaulted several women: a woman sitting in her car, two women inside a coffee shop, a woman outside the coffee shop who had a child with her and was parking her bike.

At nine-thirty, police received several calls saying a man had assaulted a woman inside a coffee shop in the residential neighbourhood of Hintonburg. As police made their way to the café, a patron tried to restrain Abdirahman, who was a regular at the café located a few blocks from his apartment. Some customers knew him and remarked that they believed he suffered from mental illness.

A witness inside the café said Abdirahman left the shop after the police were called, and when he tried to re-enter the café moments later, he was restrained outside by at least one customer, who then tried to hold him down until the police arrived. Abdirahman got away from the patron, who went back inside the coffee shop, and the manager locked the door.

Outside the coffee shop, Darren Courtney said he saw Abdirahman assaulting a woman with a child while she parked her bicycle. Courtney testified that as he called 911 he approached Abdirahman, who turned away from the woman and child and began to engage with him. The 911 call captured Abdirahman introducing himself to Courtney. Courtney said Abdirahman told him there had been a struggle inside the coffee shop and that people were upset with him as a result. "At one point I thought he said he was hearing voices," said Courtney. (The recording of the call isn't clear enough to make out most of what Abdirahman is saying. Courtney is heard repeating back to Abdirahman what he thinks he's hearing.) Abdirahman repeated the phrase "keeping the peace" and told Courtney, "I can't go my home." At that point a police cruiser arrived on the scene.

An officer got out of his car and told Abdirahman to put his hands against the window of the coffee shop. According to Courtney, Abdirahman turned to run away. Courtney said the officer tried to restrain Abdirahman by holding his wrist. The officer kicked Abdirahman in the leg, and although Abdirahman fell, he got back to his feet and ran, with the officer in pursuit. Witnesses would later recount seeing the officer hit Abdirahman with his baton during the chase.

Ross McGhie was coming from a morning run with his partner when he noticed Abdirahman on a street corner, fending off an officer's baton blows with a rubber weight from a construction site. The officer would later testify that when Abdirahman tried to pick up a construction sign, he took the opportunity to pepper-spray Abdirahman directly in his eyes. "He didn't even blink," the officer said on the stand, adding that it was after Abdirahman was pepper-sprayed that he picked up the rubber weight. The officer said he was afraid Abdirahman would strike

him with the weight, but did not say Abdirahman swung at or confronted him. Instead, he hit Abdirahman in the legs with his baton,
claiming again that this had no effect.

As Abdirahman got closer to his apartment, he dropped the weight and
tried to run to his building's front door. McGhie said the officer kept hitting
Abdirahman in the legs, arms, and upper body with his baton. Many witnesses in and around the building said they heard Abdirahman screaming.

According to McGhie and several other witnesses, a second officer
drove up to the apartment building during this time. This officer "immediately jumped into the altercation and administered a number of very
heavy blows to the head and face and neck of Mr. Abdi," McGhie said.
One of the witnesses was Abdirahman's brother Abdirizaq. He told a
CBC reporter, "I heard the screaming, and then I come out and I see my
brother lying down, police hitting so badly. Like, I've never seen something like that in my life." Abdirizaq said he and his family feared
Abdirahman, who was on the ground with police on top of him, would die
from the severity of the beating.

Several witness used their cellphones to shoot videos of police
standing and crouching over Abdirahman on the ground after they
had handcuffed him. The videos show that Abdirahman's powder-blue
button-up shirt and his white undershirt were soaked with patches of
blood. There was also a pool of blood beneath him. In one video, a
woman can be heard shouting, "I think he's dead. Where's the ambu-
lance, he's going to bleed to death."

Even after police had handcuffed Abdirahman's hands behind his
back and he lay face down and motionless on the sidewalk, an officer
pinned him down with his knee. The police talked to one another as they
crouched above Abdirahman, and at one point they left him unattended
while he was lying handcuffed and bleeding on the ground. Although

police are trained in life-saving techniques, there is no evidence from eye-witnesses or publicly released video that they tried to help Abdirahman before the paramedics arrived more than ten minutes later. Meanwhile, Abdirahman's mother and other witnesses watched from the apartment lobby while police barred them from leaving the building.

At 9:52 a.m., police contacted paramedics, the first of whom arrived just before ten. According to testimony from paramedic Yannick Roussel as documented by the *Ottawa Citizen*, the paramedics thought they were responding to a police pepper-spray incident. Roussel said it was not until he got close to the motionless Abdirahman and saw his head trauma that he suspected his condition could be related to trauma rather than a medical issue.

Roussel immediately identified Abdirahman as "vital signs absent" and called for assistance. Paramedics, with the help of police, began to perform CPR. As Abdirahman was on his way to the hospital, Roussel contacted hospital staff to say he had no vital signs. "We don't know the cause of death right now," he said in a recording played at the trial. He added that Abdirahman's facial injuries made it difficult to tell what had caused his apparent death.

According to Roussel, Abdirahman was taken to the Ottawa Hospital's trauma centre, where he was listed as being in critical condition upon arrival. Doctors worked on him for forty minutes and, miraculously, revived him. "I was surprised, relieved and happy because that is very unusual for someone in cardiac arrest," Roussel testified. "But at hospital, last time I saw him his heart was beating, and he was alive."

A press release issued by the Special Investigations Unit, or SIU—the provincial agency that examines cases of death, serious injury, and allegations of sexual assault involving police officers—claimed that "at some point during the confrontation, the man suffered medical distress."

In the late afternoon of the following day, the public learned that Abdirahman Abdi, thirty-seven, was dead. Nimao Ali, a spokesperson for the family, addressed the media: "According to the doctor's assessment, he had been already dead 45 minutes before he arrived in the care of doctors." Ali added that hospital staff had done their best to revive him, but confirmed his death with the family that afternoon. Neither the Ottawa Hospital nor the SIU commented on the suspected cause of Abdirahman's death.

When the SIU investigates police officers, it has a policy not to name them. However, the media used the many photos and videos of the incident to identify the first two officers on the scene. The CBC reported that the first officer to engage Abdirahman on the street was Constable Dave Weir and that the second officer, who was witnessed dealing several blows to Abdirahman's head, was Constable Daniel Montsion. The report noted that Montsion "usually apprehends gang members as a member of the direct action response team . . . but was assisting on patrol that day." A police source told the CBC that Montsion was wearing a pair of reinforced assault gloves during the arrest.

Subsequent reporting revealed that Montsion had assaulted a Somali-Canadian man named Abdullah Adoyta during a 2014 arrest. Montsion testified that he'd struck Abdullah and taken him to the ground after fearing he had a gun. But in court the judge called Montsion's testimony "difficult to both understand and accept" and acquitted Adoyta, who had testified that he was unarmed and that Montsion had assaulted him after entering his neighbour's apartment.

As the Abdi family mourned, Ottawa mayor Jim Watson said nothing publicly about Abdirahman or the police. Many people on social media questioned Watson's silence, but neither he nor his office offered any comment. Two days after police attacked Abdirahman, CBC

Ottawa tweeted, "For those curious why #Ottawa's mayor has been quiet re: Abdirahman Abdi, he's on vacation." The tweet did not say whether the CBC had contacted Watson's office to ask for a comment on Abdirahman's death. It linked to a July 21 tweet from Watson that read, "Taking a few days of holidays so will do my best not to tweet!"

Watson had managed to tweet about several other things since his vacation notice. The day after police attacked Abdirahman, for instance, he tweeted a message inviting the public to a local baseball game. More than forty-eight hours after the incident, his office issued a very brief statement saying the mayor was "saddened" to hear of Abdirahman's death and offered condolences to the Abdi family. "I am confident that Ontario's Special Investigations Unit will conduct a fair and thorough investigation that will provide comprehensive insight into this tragic incident," the statement concluded. Months later, in an interview with the CBC, Watson was asked again about his silence following Abdirahman's death. Watson reminded the interviewer that he had been on holiday at the time and said he hadn't wanted to comment until he had made contact with the Abdi family. He did add, "I've remained relatively silent because there is a police investigation. We don't know what the cause of Mr. Abdi's death is. Many people, through Twitter, have said, you know, 'He was murdered!' or 'The police killed him!' We just don't know. Unless you were a witness, it's hard to speculate."

Meanwhile, Ontario premier Kathleen Wynne made no public statement about Abdirahman's death, and neither did Prime Minister Justin Trudeau, who lives in Ottawa. While reporters for CBC Ottawa diligently followed Abdirahman's story, the news outlet offered little national coverage, and neither did many other mainstream Canadian media companies. Writer and communications professional Jared Walker described the silence in the days following the attack: "The same Canadian media outlets that have had no qualms about repeatedly circulating video of the deaths of black Americans at the hands of police and which were responsible for a veritable deluge of self-righteous condemnation in their editorial pages have fallen silent when faced with the same issue at home. When confronted about this deafening silence, some Canadian journalists have even gone as far as to express exasperation, asking what they could possibly have done better."

Ottawa residents, especially members of the Somali community to which Abdirahman belonged, began to mobilize. Almost immediately, several Somali people gave witness accounts and video footage to local media. Two days after the attack, community members organized a vigil in a park only steps from Abdirahman's porch, and an estimated five hundred residents attended. Two days after that, about two hundred residents in Montreal held a vigil for Abdirahman, marched to a police station, and engaged in a moment of silence to honour victims of police homicide.

The Ottawa Muslim Association stepped forward to cover the costs of Abdirahman's funeral. At that gathering, attended by more than two thousand people, Ottawa imam Sikander Hashmi read a statement on behalf of the family, their first public comment since Abdirahman's death: "He was such a kind-hearted person. What occurred to him that Sunday wasn't fair at all and shouldn't be justified by any means. No human being, especially someone as innocent as him, deserved to pass away like that. No words can explain the depth of our love for him."

Residents created a group called the Justice for Abdirahman Coalition, or J4A, with the stated goal "to obtain greater transparency, challenge racial inequity, increase support for mental health needs and bring positive change to our law enforcement institutions in order to secure justice for the late Mr. Abdi and his family." In the days following

Abdirahman's funeral, J4A released a list of demands directed towards the Ottawa police, the SIU, the provincial government, and other stakeholders. The demands included the immediate suspensions of Weir and Montsion, changes to the laws that govern police use of force, and new rules to allow residents to vote for their local police chief. The coalition also criticized Mayor Watson for his initial silence. "It's clear the mayor's response is sending a message to Black individuals that live in Ottawa that our lives are not as valuable as others," said coalition member Yamikani Msosa of the Sexual Assault Support Centre of Ottawa.

While Watson and Ottawa Police Chief Charles Bordeleau avoided further comment, the Ottawa Police Association, a private lobby group representing officers, sought to discredit any criticism or condemnation of its members' conduct. Police associations don't speak for the local police force—that's the police chief's role. But our media regularly treat association leaders as if they are public officials. Association spokesperson Matt Skof repeatedly responded to questions about the officers' violence by placing the emphasis on Abdirahman's actions. "The call came in, there was violence involved, there was assaultive behaviour, the officers experienced that when they attended," Skof said. None of the dozens of witnesses who spoke to media suggested that Abdirahman had acted violently towards the officers; many stated that he did use a piece of rubber to defend himself from Weir's baton, and he did run from Weir to his front porch.

Tracey Clark, the president of the Bridgehead coffee shop chain, confirmed that Abdirahman was a regular and that staff were aware that he may have had mental health issues. "He would stand and stare at customers, or get a little bit too close, and we were beginning to hear from customers that it was making them feel uncomfortable," Clark said in an interview with CBC Radio. "And so we had started to have those conversations where, 'Are you aware of this behaviour, could we ask you not to do that?' So there were some interventions like that that had taken place."

Clark said Abdirahman had harassed more than one customer that day, and that her staff felt they had no other option but to call the police. She regretted that the police were being widely criticized for their behaviour while many viewed Abdirahman as a victim. "It's a terrible story. But very quickly it emerged that the police were the villains and it emerged that Mr. Abdi is the martyr. Well, what about the person that was groped or assaulted? What about those people, and where is their place in the story?"

CBC Radio host Robyn Bresnahan ended the segment by inviting Clark to read a poem she'd written, addressed directly to the deceased Abdirahman: "It was not the colour of your skin / I knew you had mental health issues too / But I did not have a choice." The poem went on to explain that Clark felt "guilty" about what happened, and included the line "Activists are blaming me. They silence me." A refrain repeated throughout the poem was "I am not safe if you are not safe."

Clark was not in the café when her staff called the police about Abdirahman. I remember listening to that poem, in which she positioned herself as an innocent party in Abdirahman's death. I reflected on Clark's description of herself as silenced and invisible within the story of a man who could no longer speak or express himself.

Even as he implored the public not to prejudge the police in the wake of Abdirahman's death, Matt Skof went on a media blitz. In response to questions about the officers' knowledge of Abdirahman's apparent mental health issues, Skof said it wasn't the job of the police to make such assessments: "It may be mental illness, it may be from an intoxicant, it could be from just a state . . . at that moment, where they're incredibly upset. So to dissect it at that point, or try to diagnose, is not something that's the officer's priority. You can't sit there and say, 'Well, I'm going to diagnose this person in this second and say they're mentally ill.'" In a separate interview, Skof replied to a similar question about mental health by saying, "It doesn't really in any way change the decision that you are going to have to make to ensure public safety."

Skof rejected claims that Abdirahman had been treated harshly because of his race. "It's only a fact in this case, just like age and gender or height," he said. "Race is not a factor in how the officers reacted to the call." Skof also told media he believed criticisms about race were being inappropriately transplanted from the United States. "That's unfortunate that we're seeing the bleeding of that very difficult rhetoric into Canada now. And I'm very live to it, I can obviously be sensitive to it, I'm aware that it's occurring, but it's two separate conversations and not one that's applicable here."

The history of violence by the Ottawa police force is long. Since its creation in 1990, the SIU has only laid criminal charges against fifteen Ottawa police officers—although none have resulted in convictions. Another way of saying this is that approximately once every two years, the SIU has deemed an Ottawa officer's conduct worthy of criminal charges. Our criminal justice system presupposes that police are upstanding and law-abiding people, and this very low number of charges validates that notion, regardless of the experiences of Black people and the public in general.

In 1991, the SIU laid its first ever culpable homicide charge against an Ottawa police officer named John Monette, who shot forty-nine-year-old Vincent Gardner, a Black musician living in the city. Monette was one of seven officers conducting what police called a drug raid on a local residence. Monette, who entered the home, testified in court that he and his fellow officers believed there were weapons inside. He was climbing the stairs to the second floor, where Gardner and several other musicians were practising. Monette testified that Gardner approached him, that he yelled at Gardner to stop, then fired one shot, striking him in the abdomen. He said he believed Gardner was carrying a gun—it was his guitar.

Gardner died nearly two months later in hospital. Doctors said they had discovered cancer in his liver and were therefore unable to determine whether he had died from the gunshot wound or from the cancer. In 1993 an all-white jury acquitted Monette, who is also white, on charges of manslaughter, criminal negligence causing death and bodily harm, and aggravated assault. Monette remained a police officer with the Ottawa force for the next quarter century and retired in 2016, one week after Abdirahman Abdi died.

The CBC conducted a study of SIU investigations of Ottawa police officers from 2011 to 2015 and found that, of the seventy-two cases, only four resulted in criminal charges. Of those four cases, "all criminal charges were either acquitted, stayed, downgraded or withdrawn."

In a 2008 case that predated the CBC's investigation, Sergeant Steven Desjourdy arrested twenty-seven-year-old Stacy Bonds, a Black woman living in Ottawa, and charged her with the non-criminal offence of possessing open alcohol in a public place. Police took Bonds to a holding centre at police headquarters, and several officers pinned her down while Desjourdy used scissors to cut off her shirt and bra. Desjourdy and his colleagues then left Bonds half-naked in the cell for over three hours, and laid an additional charge of assaulting police. (In 2010, after viewing video of the police's treatment of Bonds, a judge threw out all charges against her.)

The SIU charged Desjourdy with sexual assault. He was acquitted five years later, in 2013. CBC reported that after the verdict, "as Desjourdy walked out of the courtroom, about 50 police officers who had gathered outside applauded." None of the officers who had pinned Bonds down—including Constable Melanie Morris, who allegedly kneed Bonds in the abdomen and pulled her hair—faced any criminal charges, and all were cleared in a subsequent provincial investigation into their conduct. In her first public comments about the incident, in 2010, Bonds remarked, "People do need to know that police do abuse their power, and people need to speak out. But there are a lot of great cops out there, too, and people need to know that."

In 2014, the *Ottawa Citizen* reported that only four days before Desjourdy cut Stacy Bonds's clothes from her body, he assaulted an unnamed woman who was in custody for public intoxication. Desjourdy acknowledged that he repeatedly kicked the woman and threatened her with a taser while another officer removed her pants and electrified her twice with his own taser. Desjourdy ultimately pleaded guilty to an internal police charge of unlawful exercise of duty, for which he was demoted from sergeant to constable for three months.

The SIU fails to inform the public of most of its active investigations, and much of the silence is intentional. Between 2007 and 2017, the SIU conducted 144 investigations of Ottawa police officers but issued press releases for only 45 of them, meaning that about 70 per cent of investigations into serious crimes involving the police were never made public. According to the CBC, "Three deaths involving Ottawa police in 2007, 2009 and 2013 were never publicized. Two other deaths in 2012 and 2013 were only publicized when the investigations ended after the officers were cleared of wrongdoing."

The SIU has a policy of not notifying the public of investigations that involve sexual assault allegations against officers. The SIU's reason for this deliberate omission, according to spokesperson Monica Hudon, is privacy. "To protect the identities and privacy of the complainant and the subject officer, the SIU does not release information in cases involving allegations of sexual assault, unless there is an appeal for witnesses or information, or the director causes a charge to be laid," Hudon said in a 2016 interview. Sunny Marriner, executive director of the Ottawa Rape Crisis Centre, questioned this logic, pointing out that the SIU can notify the public of ongoing sexual assault investigations without naming the complainant or the officer. Marriner asked, "If we're not even aware that sexual assault allegations are being investigated by the SIU how do we then ask the subsequent questions of what protections are in place for the vulnerable populations that they have access to?"

Province-wide, in 2016 and 2017, the SIU conducted 296 investigations and charged officers in 17 cases, meaning that about 94 per cent of officers under investigation did not face criminal charges. This is actually low for the SIU. Between 2001 and 2016, investigators cleared an average of 97 per cent of the officers it investigated.

Further, the SIU's historically high threshold for "serious injury" has meant that it did not investigate thousands of injuries police caused because they were not deemed serious enough. From its creation in 1990 until 2017, the SIU defined serious injuries as "those that are likely to interfere with the health or comfort of the victim and are more than merely transient or trifling in nature and will include serious injury resulting from sexual assault. 'Serious injury' shall initially be presumed when the victim is admitted to hospital, suffers a fracture to a limb, rib or vertebrae or to the skull, suffers burns to a major portion of the body or loses any portion of the body or suffers loss of vision or hearing, or alleges sexual assault."

Local and provincial governments in Canada fail to keep comprehensive statistics about police killings, so it's difficult to discuss the scope of such violence. In 2017, at least sixty-five people in Canada died during or after their involvement with police. The majority of these deaths were poorly reported by media and, in some cases, not reported at all. The available data suggested that Black and Indigenous people were disproportionately killed given their respective numbers in the general population. In Ontario, the SIU has laid charges of culpable homicide, including murder and manslaughter, only nineteen times in its thirty-year history. Only one of those charges has resulted in a conviction.

When police speak about their roles in taking civilians' lives, they tell us that their violence, although regrettable, is inevitable. In Toronto, Constable Andrew Doyle was never charged for shooting and killing Andrew Loku, forty-five, in his apartment building in July of 2015. At the coroner's inquest into Loku's death, Doyle described his own act of killing Loku as "an absolute tragedy for everyone involved." Peel Regional Police officer Ryan Reid was never charged for fatally shooting Jermaine Carby, thirty-three, during a traffic stop in September 2014. Reid told a coroner's inquest that if he could revisit his decision to shoot Carby, he wouldn't have done anything differently—he said this with Carby's mother and family members in the hearing room. Toronto constable Louie Cerqua was never charged for shooting and killing Michael Eligon, twenty-nine, on a residential street in February of 2012. Eligon had left his hospital room, where he was involuntarily admitted under the province's Mental Health Act, and wandered the streets in his hospital gown. Police officers surrounded Eligon, who was carrying a pair of scissors in each hand, and Cerqua shot him three times, killing him. Cerqua said at the inquest into Eligon's death, "With the high stress situation like that, you're going to resort to your firearm, it's the only real option you have."

———

On March 6, 2017, the SIU laid three charges against Constable Daniel Montsion in the killing of Abdirahman Abdi: manslaughter, aggravated assault, and assault with a weapon—this last charge related to Montsion's reinforced gloves. Montsion's criminal trial is ongoing as I write this.

The Abdi family had obtained surveillance video footage from the lobby of their apartment building. The family allowed Heather Badenoch, a communications worker with the non-profit housing corporation that operates the building, to view the footage and describe it to the media. Badenoch said Abdirahman did not resist the two police officers who struck him in front of his residence. "When Abdi is lying on the ground, face down and still, the constable who has been charged punches him in the head very violently, twice, and we never see Abdi move again." In response to a statement made by the Ottawa Police Association that the charges laid against Montsion had been influenced by politics, Badenoch told the CBC she believed the video footage justified the charges.

Daniel Montsion was suspended with pay following the charges. Matt Skof, the police association spokesperson, said Montsion was disappointed to have to leave his job. "As he's been working all the way throughout this, ever since the incident in the summer, it's incredibly difficult. He remained professional and would have continued to want to serve the community as best he could," he said. Skof had seemed prepared for possible charges against Montsion near the end of 2016 when he'd argued, "The SIU has a mandate to investigate, but I believe that they inappropriately criminalize our profession out of sheer public pressure, and the politicizing of their mandate."

By the end of March 2017, Ottawa police had started a wristband campaign in Montsion's honour. Officers wore blue-and-black stretch bracelets with the words "UNITED WE STAND" on the outside and

"DIVIDED WE FALL" on the inside, along with Montsion's badge number. Police said they were selling the wristbands for two dollars and that all proceeds would go to what the Ottawa police called a "police benevolent fund."

Skof dismissed the idea that the wristbands were disrespectful to Abdirahman and his family, or that they sent the wrong message to the broader community. He said, "This has nothing to do with the relations we have with the community. This has nothing to do with race. This is not a public campaign. It's a member-driven initiative, an internal initiative for expressing support for a fellow colleague, in a very difficult profession going through a very difficult time." The police association denied it had ordered and distributed the bracelets. By the time the CBC reported the story, Ottawa police said they'd sold over a thousand wristbands. Three days later, CBC reported that more wristbands had been ordered, as "police officers across the country are now buying the bands."

Police across Canada, and their supporters, felt comfortable paying for the privilege of wearing an accused killer's ID number on their wrists. These are the people who "serve and protect" in Canada every single day, with guns and tasers, with batons and handcuffs and pepper spray, with a licence to kill. Police understand that their ability to enact violence with impunity is the defining feature of their job. They know that if one officer's use of force can be criminalized, all officers' ability to use force indiscriminately is at risk, and they will stop at nothing to protect that power.

I continue to reflect on the Abdi family's statement that no one deserves to be treated the way police treated Abdirahman. Unfortunately, we as Canadians can't seem to agree on this appeal to human decency, especially as it applies to Black people we understand to be suffering from mental illness. For such Black people, our government and police regularly insist that violence is not only justified, but the only option.

The notion of mental illness features prominently in Abdirahman's public story, but also in the public stories of Eligon and Loku and Carby and also of Pierre Coriolan. In June of 2017 Montreal police shot and killed Coriolan, a fifty-eight-year-old man who had immigrated from Haiti. Neighbours described Coriolan as having a mental illness and said he was in crisis in his apartment when a neighbour called the police. He'd recently learned he would be evicted after having lived in the building for nine years. Multiple officers responded to the call, confronted Coriolan, and shot at him with rubber bullets and a stun gun. Then two of the officers shot at him with live ammunition and he collapsed. An officer shot Coriolan with additional rubber bullets after he'd been hit with gunfire.

In February 2018, Coriolan's family sued the City of Montreal over what they described as "brutal and excessive" actions of the police. In March, twenty-one months after police killed Coriolan, the provincial bureau that investigates police violence determined the use of force by all officers had been justified.

Winnipeg police shot and killed forty-three-year-old Machuar Madut on February 23, 2019. Madut's South Sudanese community said he'd recently been struggling with mental health issues. Police shot Madut around ten on a Saturday morning; according to provincial investigators, police received a call about a potential break-in at an apartment. A witness says Madut, who lived at the apartment, appeared to be in crisis as he used a hammer to break into someone else's unit. Madut's cousin would later explain that he'd recently been served with an eviction notice. Police arrived and fatally shot him. George Van Mackelberg of the Winnipeg Police Association said the police respond to the behaviour of people they encounter. "Unfortunately sometimes people, for whatever reason, they leave no other choice," said Van Mackelberg.

Sandy Deng, a South Sudanese community member, questioned the police's use of deadly force. "I was hoping that the police would give us a better picture of what really happened. But he was a human being; he was supposed to be supported. He was one day away from going to see a mental health specialist."

After the killings of Abdirahman, Andrew, Pierre, and Machuar, their communities—Somali, South Sudanese, Haitian—mobilized to support their families. In each case, local members of the broader African diaspora have joined in. We have decried the excessive force used against our Black family and pointed out the police's failure to de-escalate situations involving Black people whom the community knows to be living with mental health issues. We say that we care about these men whether we knew them or not, and that the violence they experienced can never be justified.

Matt Skof contends that the institution of policing has no time to account for the mental health of the Black men it encounters and deems to be threatening. He insists that the police don't see our race and don't care about it. But the reason people mobilized for Abdirahman and so many others is because their race, their mental health, and their safety matter deeply to us. We know the violence and stigma Black people with mental health issues experience across all institutions, across society in general.

A CBC News investigation that analyzed 461 fatal civilian encounters with police between 2000 and 2017 found that "70 per cent of the people who died struggled with mental health issues or substance abuse or both." The combination of this violence with the police targeting of

Black people makes Black people with mental health issues more likely to experience police violence. The CBC also found that, of the 461 deaths, "criminal charges were laid against 18 police officers . . . with only two ending in convictions."

In a 2017 report on police use of force in Ontario, Independent Police Review Director Gerry McNeilly stated, "We cannot ignore the fact that, in many of these cases, the deceased was Black or a person of colour. Unfortunately, it is unknown exactly how many civilians killed by the police in Ontario have been Black or of colour as no agency maintains race-based statistics on this issue. The absence of such information has been the focus of criticism for preventing the public from understanding and addressing the full scope of this issue. Regardless, there can be no doubt that overrepresentation of persons of colour who have been killed by the police has aggravated already existing tensions between racialized communities and the police."

When police argue that they don't care about a person's race or religion, they show how particularly unqualified they are to connect with Black people, to de-escalate encounters with us, to provide care to us. It's no coincidence that police disproportionately kill men with dark skin who are living with mental health issues, who are poor, who have immigrated from Africa or the Caribbean, whose native language may not be English, who may be separated or estranged from their families.

Vicky Durand, a receptionist at a community services centre in Abdirahman's neighbourhood, said that in the months before he was killed, Abdirahman would often drop in without an appointment and ask to speak with a counsellor. Durand described Abdirahman as a "teddy bear" and told the *Globe and Mail* that in their interactions, he "would clasp his hands in front of his chest in a gesture of prayer."

A woman who lived in Abdirahman's building was one of the many witnesses who shouted at police as they assaulted him. "I told the police he's a crazy man," she told local media. "They hit, they hit, they hit, they hit everywhere. Then he was unconscious." The neighbour's description of Abdirahman as "crazy" was a plea to police to treat him with care, a cry not to take advantage of a man with less power and social status.

In the days following Abdirahman's death, a collective of agencies that serve immigrants in Ottawa and across Ontario released a statement that read, in part: "Abdi's death and the manner of his passing has left our clients, communities as well as employees in a state of grief and shock. We are especially concerned about the impact on the Somali and other refugee and immigrant communities, and their sense of safety and security as they build a new life in this country. In that context, we cannot ignore the questions that have arisen about use of force and the socially significant intersections of refugee background, race and mental health."

Police take the lives of our community members, then tell us their specific identities and experiences are irrelevant. The violence of policing requires that we lose our individuality and become the nondescript Black spectres that police must immediately contain. Police often say they kill us because we engage, because we threaten, because we flash our teeth or our weapon and they get scared. But Abdirahman tried to run, and at that moment the police priority was to detain him, to control his body and make sure he couldn't escape, by any means necessary.

The possibility that Abdirahman might have mental health issues offered him no protection; ultimately, too many people wanted to be protected from him in that moment. The care and concern that family, friends, and neighbours had shown for him was nowhere in the police response. Police, and the state they defend, tell us that tenderness and care would have been misplaced in response to Abdirahman, that treating him too gently might have put him in further danger or imperilled those around him.

Abdirahman was engaged in conversation with a stranger when the police arrived. If we can't imagine a different outcome than the police's violence, that's on us. We have to imagine something less violent, less reactive and reckless. Daring to imagine kindness and fairness for Abdirahman is a truly revolutionary act in a country that offers no alternatives.

On January 31, 2019, a few days before Montsion's criminal trial began, Ottawa police shot and killed Greg Ritchie, a thirty-year-old man who belonged to the Saugeen First Nation near Owen Sound, Ontario. Ritchie's family said he'd struggled with mental health issues since his youth and was on his way to a pharmacy to buy his medication when police, responding to a call about a man with a knife at Elmvale Acres Mall, confronted and shot him.

Police killed Ritchie within sight of the family home he'd left minutes earlier. His sister-in-law Chantel Ritchie said that people in the community feared Greg and treated him with suspicion. "People just take one look and that's it. He's First Nations, he's been homeless before, and he is afraid. People just take all of that in one look and then make assumptions and then act on it. And it just really hurts that we weren't there to be able to calm him down because there's no way that any of this would have happened if we were there. There's no way."

In late 2017, Montsion's lawyer, Michael Edelson, made a predictable argument in a pre-trial hearing. "This is not a beating that caused the death of Mr. Abdi. Mr. Abdi died of a heart attack. That's what killed him," Edelson said. Just as we had been asked to believe that Vincent Gardner died from liver cancer and not from John Monette's bullet.

And what if it's true? If we could conclude, in courts of law or public opinion, that the bodies of Black people keep giving up at the precise moments when the police are closing in, who would sleep better at night?

direct action

(april)

"I say, the critic must keep out of the region of immediate practice."
—MATTHEW ARNOLD CARICATURE, *Vanity Fair* (1871)

When I was young I loved to write for myself. I wrote stories and poems and kept a journal. I always imagined that if I ever wrote anything for others to read, it would be fiction. I never dreamed of writing for a newspaper. And I never thought that after getting a job with one of the biggest in Canada, I'd ultimately walk away from it.

I wrote my last piece as a columnist with the *Toronto Star* on April 12, 2017. The circumstances made it easier to quit: I had started off with a weekly column, but by the time I quit, the column had been reduced to every two weeks; I had no contract, no membership in the union, no benefits, no apparent prospects for advancement in the company; the president of the board of directors had suggested I write less about race issues; and I'd just been advised that I had violated the paper's code of conduct by staging a sit-in at a meeting of Toronto's police oversight board.

My demonstration at the police board was in response to police carding, a racist surveillance practice the *Star* had devoted an impressive amount of time and resources to documenting over the last two decades. My editor at the newspaper said I had broken company rules by engaging in public protest and told me I needed to choose between my column and my activism; to restrict my Black struggle for the privilege of writing for the paper twice a month. Shit, I didn't even have a dental plan.

I knew what police carding was before I realized I knew. As a boy growing up in Oshawa, I used to watch plotlines about racial profiling and police harassment on television shows like *A Different World*, *In Living Color*, *The Fresh Prince of Bel-Air*. I overheard stories my relatives told about their interactions with the police, and as I got older they shared these stories more openly. Years before the term "carding" had become current in Toronto, I'd heard of "stop-and-frisk" in New York City. And I'd heard people here talk about getting "c-picked," a play on the Canadian Police Information Centre, which is exactly what it sounds like: a national database of civilians' "criminal histories and interactions with police."

The first time I heard the term "carding" was in 2012, at a meeting organized by York Youth Coalition, a group of mostly Black youth in the Weston–Mount Dennis neighbourhood of Toronto. Residents there called police stops "carding," referring both to the ID cards police might request during a stop and to the paper cards they filled out by the millions during the stops. The Toronto police refer to the practice as "street checks." Internally the police called the paper they filled out a Form 208, but with the public they used the term "community contact card." But I'll call the practice carding—that is, the police activity of stopping people who are not reasonably suspected of any crime and documenting their personal information before, during, or after the interaction. Even this definition has severe limitations, but I no longer sweat it. Call it what you will, Black people know what a violation of our personal space, privacy, and freedom looks like.

I could flood these pages with numbers on the practice of carding and its many harms, yet the numbers and the evidence don't matter to those who benefit from white supremacy. They didn't believe Black people before the numbers, and they don't believe us now. It isn't in their interest to do so.

Police treatment of Black people in Canada today is part of a centuries-long history. In *Policing Black Lives*, Robyn Maynard connects the country's legacy of slavery and its public documentation of runaway slaves to the modern reality of racist police surveillance:

> Public associations between Blackness and crime can be traced back to runaway slave advertisements dating back to the seventeenth century, in which self-liberated Blacks were portrayed as thieves and criminals. All free and enslaved people were subject to the surveillance of a larger white community and law enforcement officials, who together scrutinized the presence of Black bodies in space as possible criminal "runaways." After slavery's abolition, the associations between Blackness and crime serve important political, social, economic and cultural functions in maintaining the racial order, and the ongoing surveillance and policing of Blackness—and the corresponding wildly disproportionate arrest and incarceration rates—were quintessential in the late nineteenth and early twentieth centuries in Canada. These

associations with Blackness, today, while articulated through a slightly different language (thugs, gangsters or, in Québec, les "yos"), remain markedly unchanged.

In my experience, the average white Canadian doesn't know that British and French settlers enslaved Black and Indigenous peoples on these lands for two centuries, and simply shifted legislative tactics once they had abolished "legal" slavery. Those who do acknowledge slavery in Canada often add that it was "not as bad as in the States," a nod to the white Canadian proverb used as a checkmate end to a conversation. No need to consider anti-Blackness here.

This idea that Canada's racial injustices are not as bad as they *could* be—this notion of slavery lite, of racism lite, of what my friend calls the "toy version of racism"—is a very Canadian way of saying "remember what we could do to you if we wanted to." Passive-aggressive racism is central to Canada's national mythology and identity. White supremacy warns Black people against setting our own standards and pursuing dreams that stray too far from the global atmosphere of anti-Blackness.

The ongoing reality of police surveillance of Indigenous communities across Canada is also rooted in the country's colonial laws. In 1885, the federal government enacted pass laws to control the movement of Métis people in and around what is now Winnipeg who were engaging in armed resistance against white settlers. The practice soon expanded across the country and lasted for nearly sixty years without formal approval from Parliament. Hayter Reed, one of the government officials who lobbied for and implemented the pass laws, described his vision in a letter to a superior: "No rebel Indians should be allowed off the Reserves without a pass signed by an I. D. official. The dangers of complications with white men will thus be lessened, & by preserving

a knowledge of individual movements any inclination to petty depre-
dations may be checked by the facility of apprehending those who
commit such offences."

When police engage in what we now call carding, they are maintaining a tradition of surveilling Black and Indigenous people, suggesting
that our very presence as free people on the street is suspicious and in
need of investigation. At one time, the prospect of free Black people
informed the actions of slave catchers. In our time, white Canada continues to view Black people as an inherent threat to its safety and sense
of order. The fear informs the police practice of stopping and questioning us. Maynard is clear, though: police do not act in isolation. Rather,
they are carrying out the will of Canada's white majority, in the service
of maintaining a colonial settler state where whiteness is supreme.

The modern era of carding in Toronto began, as so many police interventions do, in the wake of a crisis. Toronto's media dubbed the summer
of 2005 the "summer of the gun," after the city witnessed twenty-five
gun-related homicides between June and September. In response, local
police vowed to step up their presence in areas where many of the shoot-
ings had occurred. The force created a new unit, called the Toronto Anti-
Violence Intervention Strategy, or TAVIS, to police so-called high-crime
areas. TAVIS and the modern carding regime quickly became the city-
wide norm, and the unit was responsible for a disproportionate share of
carding and, by extension, the disproportionate surveillance and profiling of Black people, particularly Black youth.

Carding data across Canada is collected sporadically and has historically been made public only after residents and the media demand
access to it. The data we do have is damning, and in conjunction with
the testimonies of people who experience police surveillance, it hints

at the overwhelming scope of police interference into the daily lives of the people they target: Black people, Indigenous people, sex workers, people in crisis, homeless people, poor people, queer and trans people, two-spirit and gender non-conforming people, and people living with physical disabilities, addictions, or mental health issues.

In 2012 the *Toronto Star* published "Known to Police," its most comprehensive investigation into carding. The paper reported that "between 2008 and 2012, police filled out 1.8 million contact cards, involving more than a million individuals, in stops that typically result in no arrest or charge. The data end up in a massive police database that currently has no purging requirements."

In every single police district in Toronto, police disproportionately stopped and documented Black people and other racialized groups without making arrests or laying criminal charges. During these years, Toronto police carded three times more Black people than the actual Black population of Toronto. The likelihood of police stopping Black people for nothing increased in predominantly white neighbourhoods, with police responding to calls from white residents about Black people on their streets.

In the areas of Toronto where higher concentrations of Black people live, the stats were equally devastating. According to the *Star*'s investigation, "from 2008 to 2012, the number of young black males, aged 15 to 24, who were documented at least once in the police patrol zone where they live exceeded the young black male population for all of Toronto." The report noted that, as police continued the practice of carding, it was likely that all young Black men in certain areas of the city would end up in the carding database. Subsequent reporting showed how carding records had destroyed education and job opportunities for the Black people police target. For example, in April 2014, Transport Canada revoked the security clearance of Ayaan Farah, a young Somali woman working for an airline at Pearson International Airport in Toronto. The RCMP used carding data to claim that Farah had contacts with criminals which jeopardized airline safety, but refused to name those people for privacy reasons. Farah could no longer work at the airport, and two years passed before the Federal Court ruled that stripping her of her security clearance because of unnamed contacts was unfair, incomprehensible, and unreasonable. But the judgment didn't include compensation for Farah's years of lost income and the assault on her reputation.

In 2014, two years after "Known to Police" had exposed the scope of carding, the *Star* documented that the total number of carding stops had decreased by 75 per cent from the previous year, yet the proportion of stops of Black residents had actually increased. The same report noted that Black residents, who made up roughly 8 percent of the city's population, were involved in 27 percent of carding stops. In one predominantly white area, Black people were 17 times more likely than white residents to be carded.

In one of its most striking revelations, the *Star* exposed that many police superiors had been using an informal quota system to encourage officers to surveil the public. One supervisor told her officers she expected them to perform at least three street checks per shift and that officers who failed to meet these standards might not qualify for a promotion.

"Known to Police" was part of a long effort by the paper's reporters to illuminate the practice of carding and its implications for racialized people. The *Star*'s 2002 series "Race and Crime" had revealed that police disproportionately took Black people to police stations for simple drug offences, kept us overnight more often than white residents, and ticketed us more often than white motorists after pulling us over for no apparent reason. In response to this reporting, the Toronto Police Association sued the *Star* for an astronomical $2.7 billion in damages for allegedly labelling every individual Toronto police officer as racist. Although the Supreme Court ultimately threw out the case, it was a clear instance of the police association leading the charge to discredit the *Star* and, by extension, Toronto's Black population.

"Known to Police" did re-energize media attention to racial profiling and surveillance and helped to elevate the ongoing resistance in local Black communities like Weston–Mount Dennis, where I had first heard the term "carding" at the York Youth Coalition meeting. They and other community groups, including the the African Canadian Legal Clinic, Jane Finch Action Against Poverty, No One Is Illegal–Toronto, Justice for Children and Youth, and later the Anti-Black Racism Network, and Black Lives Matter–Toronto, documented community experiences with the police and agitated for change. They were all continuing the 1980s and '90s work of the Black Action Defence Committee and community activists like Sherona Hall, Akua Benjamin, Dudley Laws, Charles Roach, and Lennox Farrell.

Despite the unwillingness of Toronto city council to challenge police authority on carding, community groups and individuals kept the pressure on. Mayor Rob Ford barely mentioned carding or racial profiling during his four-year term from 2010 to 2014, and the media scarcely asked him about it. Bill Blair, police chief from 2005 to 2015, took the communications lead on the subject. In the early days of 2015, when Blair could no longer defend the racist practice, he quietly released an internal memo ordering the police to temporarily suspend carding. Blair chose not to publicly announce the move, and only discussed it after news of his memo was leaked to the media.

Blair, who had overseen the creation of TAVIS and the subsequent explosion of carding, retired in the spring of 2015. His successor, Mark

Saunders, defended carding and promised to "keep the community safe but also minimize the collateral damage that [carding] is causing." Many were surprised that Saunders, the city's first Black police chief, would refer to the effects of carding as "collateral damage," but given his politics and the imperatives of the position, it was unreasonable to expect anything else from him.

Shortly after he was sworn in as chief, Saunders was interviewed by the CBC's Dwight Drummond, a well-known Black journalist who had spoken publicly about his experiences being racially profiled by Toronto Police. When Drummond asked Saunders if he'd ever been carded himself, the chief replied, "Yes, I have. I'm glad you've mentioned that because it taught me the value of proper training. There was a period of time where I was stopped multiple times, and I can tell you it was during that phase where Toronto really didn't recognize, or didn't admit, that we had street gang issues. The officers on the road kinda figured it out, but it wasn't translated to them, and so the officers were left to their own devices. And so I would be stopped multiple times, I mean, *multiple times*. Now, granted, I wore my baseball cap backwards but that's not a criminal offence. But it fit a persona, it fits what you see on TV as a bad guy, and I would get stopped." Saunders went on to explain that as he was stopped more regularly, even as a police officer, it became harder to listen to the excuses from police about why he was their target. He nevertheless said arbitrary stops were a thing of the past. "When we as a service started to train the officers on what street gangs were about and how they behave and what their characteristics are, and what to look for, it stopped."

Less than forty-eight hours after the appointment of Toronto's first Black chief was announced in April 2015, *Toronto Life* published my cover story "The Skin I'm In." The piece chronicled my own experiences with carding and police surveillance and gained immediate and

69

sustained attention. Many white people expressed surprise that my stories of harassment and detention could be true. Many Black people were just as surprised that a magazine catering to the tastes of Toronto's elite had printed the thing at all.

I had the privilege of being able to tell my personal story of police harassment, to have that story feature on the cover of a prominent magazine, to be interviewed by media across the country. I am a Canadian-born citizen, able to communicate in English and French; I attended university; I am an able-bodied, cisgender male journalist and I was allowed to be heard in a way that most people are not. I'd recently been to Ferguson, Missouri, where I covered protests around the decision not to indict police officer Darren Wilson for the fatal shooting of eighteen-year-old Michael Brown, a decision that fuelled a mass mobilization of Black Americans. As one of the few Canadian journalists who'd made that trip, I earned a lot of airtime with prominent national broadcasters.

I'd also done live coverage of Toronto's 2014 mayoral election for a major TV network. More people had come to recognize me, so the idea that I might directly experience police surveillance troubled a lot of white, liberal-minded folks. If I'd seemingly played by the rules and was still a target, what did that say about our presumably inclusive and multiracial city?

Despite the tireless emancipatory work of Black people and our comrades, it was under public pressure from members of his own social class—university presidents, retired judges, and former cabinet ministers—that Mayor John Tory changed his public stance on police carding. Tory, who replaced Ford in 2014 and had previously expressed his strong support for the practice, called a press conference and, with tears in his eyes and with reference to my now five-week-old article, announced that his administration would direct the police to end carding.

———

Three months after Tory professed he'd changed his mind on carding, the *Toronto Star*, whose data had supplemented the personal stories in my *Toronto Life* piece, recruited me to write a weekly column. They even announced my column's debut on the front page of the print edition. After being a struggling freelance journalist for over five years, I was sure I'd finally got my proverbial big break.

I took advantage of the opportunity my column afforded to explore a broader range of issues. I wrote about provincial and federal politics, cycling, taxation, public transit, food banks, cab drivers, government clawback of child support payments to mothers on social assistance, services for the homeless, and the indefinite detention of migrants in Canada. Carding remained newsworthy, and I wrote about it whenever there were updates or I had fresh observations.

Mayor Tory didn't end carding—it seems now he had never intended to. When he vowed to stop the practice, Tory had said, "Carding has eroded public trust to a level that is clearly unacceptable." He offered repeated reassurances of a "clean slate" for those targeted by police. Just eleven days later, at the next meeting of the Police Services Board, the mayor and his colleagues approved a policy that allowed carding to continue, though presumably under stricter rules. This wasn't what Tory had promised—he seemed to be betting that his announcement would drown out his actual policy decision. And the provincial government, which had since intervened, seemed prepared to maintain the practice as well.

Eight months into my tenure, my editor contacted me to say that John Honderich, the president of the TorStar board of directors and the acting publisher of the paper, wanted to meet with me. You know that feeling you get when a work superior you don't report to or work with suddenly wants to speak to you? I tried and failed to convince myself the boss might be calling to personally offer me a raise or, better, a full-time position.

Honderich was nearly seventy years old and was considered a legend in the industry. He had joined the *Star* in 1976 as a journalist and made his way up the ranks as an editor and then as publisher. In every picture I'd seen of him he wore a bow tie, and he appeared in typical fashion when we met for lunch in April of 2016.

He took me out to a fancy downtown spot—not his usual spot, he informed me, but unfortunately Biff's Bistro was closed for renovations. I had a nice plate of fish and some wine, and after a lot of awkward small talk, Honderich got to the point: he was concerned about the contents of my column. He said I was writing about issues of race too often, and that I needed to "switch things up" in order to keep my readers interested. I was confused by the suggestion: weren't my readers following me *because* of what I was already writing? Wasn't that exactly why the *Star* had recruited me?

I tried to hold my ground by offering an example. "Do you think it would have been weird for James Baldwin's publisher to approach him one day and say, 'Look, James, all this racial stuff is great, but don't you think your readers want you to switch it up?'" Honderich just smiled a smile I've often seen from powerful white men when a Black person is standing up to them. A wry look that says "nice try."

Honderich assured me he had offered this criticism to other columnists, and cited as his only example Haroon Siddiqui, one of the few prominent non-white journalists the *Star* has employed full-time in recent decades. He then paid the bill, and we chatted about the Toronto Raptors as I walked him back to the *Star*'s lakeside head office.

A couple of weeks later, my lead editor, Andrew Phillips, contacted me to say the newspaper was cutting my weekly column to a piece every other week. Times were tough, Phillips reminded me, as he assured me that the paper was also cutting the space of several other writers. I was upset, and worried about losing half the income from the most reliable gig I'd ever had, but there was nothing to do but keep producing my best work.

In late 2016, several months after the *Star* had reduced my column's frequency, one of my editors sent me the following message:

Hey Desmond,

One of the website editors was telling me today your column yesterday did really well online (desktop and mobile) and what was most notable was that the engagement time was high, meaning people were reading to the end. These are big numbers for us.

Two weeks ago you did even better!

Keep it up.

The message included the online readership for my last two pieces—each one had earned well over fifty thousand views. I received other messages like this one during my time at the *Star*, and with each one I offered up a silent "fuck you" to Honderich before getting on with my day.

On April 20, 2017, I attended a meeting of the Toronto Police Services Board, the civilian group tasked with directing the police. The meetings are held at Toronto Police headquarters, and this meeting's agenda included some procedural motions about carding. It was common practice for activists to speak in front of the board. You get five minutes, and the more critical or inflammatory your comments, the stricter the enforcement of your time limit. After covering the police board for several years as a journalist, I'd more recently stopped writing about meetings and had begun attending mainly to speak directly to issues.

As I took my seat at one end of the board table, I had a plan. I argued that by allowing carding to continue, the board had once again betrayed residents, especially the Black youth police so often target. I said the board's greatest betrayal was its decision to leave all historical carding data in police custody. Not only did this policy ignore the fact that police should never have collected this personal information in the first place, but by allowing the police continued access to the database, the policy enabled the use of the information by the police in the future. I told the board members and Chief Saunders, "I plan to stand here in protest until you commit today, here and now, to restricting the police from having our information." As I finished my comments I stood with one fist in the air in a Black Power salute.

I think the board members thought I was joking. One of them, Ken Jeffers, asked me some questions that had nothing to do with my remarks about the database. After our exchange, I kept my place at the table. Board chair Andy Pringle asked me to go back to the public gallery so the meeting could continue. I refused. Pringle then called a recess, and Saunders and the board members all left the room. I stood there alone, focusing on the doors, trying to ignore the media perched near me with cameras and microphones.

After twelve of the longest minutes of my life, the board members returned. They took their seats only to vote to adjourn the meeting. As they stood to leave, board member and city councillor Shelley Carroll gestured at me with an open palm, as if to say, "Now look what you've done." I was leaving with friends who'd been in the public gallery when, as if to prove exactly what I'd come to protest, four uniformed officers entered the room to see me out. The meeting was over, I was leaving, and if it's illegal to linger inside a meeting room to contemplate the coming apocalypse, I should have been arrested long ago. On this day, I left with my friends before the police could put their hands on me.

My disruption of the board meeting made the news. I experienced a racist backlash from colleagues and acquaintances, from online trolls, and through angry emails. I was also flooded with media requests and messages of support. Andrew Phillips, my editor, sent a note saying he needed to speak with me as soon as possible. The next day, he was waiting for me in his office with a highlighted set of papers in hand. It was like being called into the principal's office, only the principal looked as nervous as I was.

Phillips informed me that by participating in my protest, I had broken the *Star*'s code of conduct. He drew my attention specifically to the section on conflict of interest that read, "It is not proper for journalists to be both actors and critics. It is a journalistic obligation to ensure that our reputations as fair-minded fact-finders are not compromised by any open display of political or partisan views on public issues nor tainted by personal involvement or personal axe-grinding on issues the *Star* covers." My editor then directed me to another section of the code, which warned that "any breach of policy can lead to disciplinary action up to and including dismissal."

Not that I was being dismissed! Phillips took great care not to threaten me with that, nor to suggest there would be any punishment for my alleged breach of the code. "I just want to make sure you understand the rules," he said. I wondered why he hadn't ensured my understanding of the rules a year and a half earlier, when he welcomed me to the team.

No one at the *Star* had ever shown me this document before, let alone asked me to read or sign it. I was a freelancer; this agreement wasn't in my contract because I had never signed one.

Two days later I wrote a blog post sharing the news that I was leaving the *Toronto Star*. Nothing I wrote during my eighteen-month stint as a columnist there received half as much attention as my departure. Black people stopped me on transit and at the mall to tell me they were proud of me, that I should keep fighting, that they also knew what it was like to be bullied and singled out at work. In my resignation letter I recalled my year-old lunch with Honderich and the pressure I had been under since to alter the content of my columns. Honderich publicly denied having told me I was writing about race too often. Though he had been the publisher when the paper produced its groundbreaking series "Known to Police," he told a columnist at the *Star* he believed I was writing "about *carding* all the time." I wrote twenty-six columns before my 2016 meeting with Honderich—two of them were about carding.

The *Star*'s public editor, Kathy English, wrote a piece titled "Journalists Shouldn't Become the News," in which she explained why I'd been warned about my demonstration. English repeated the claim that by disrupting the police board meeting I'd crossed the line, "becoming the news." She ignored that I'd been hired precisely *because* I had become news, that while I wrote my column the paper continued to cover my activism in its news pages, that in that coverage the *Star* referred to me as "activist and freelance journalist Desmond Cole." The same newspaper that told me I could not be an actor and a critic had somehow managed, before my time, to give columns to internationally known activists such as Naomi Klein and Craig and Marc Kielburger. Had they been asked to halt their activism for the privilege of writing columns?

Just before I was hired, Catherine Porter, a columnist at the *Star*, had written about an environmental demonstration she attended. In her column she misstated some facts about her demonstration. The *Star* acknowledged the inconsistencies but defended Porter from claims that she should not be demonstrating while working for the newspaper. The same public editor who later admonished me for "becoming the news" wrote that "Porter is right in her understanding that she has explicit permission—and encouragement—to take a public stand and act in line with her views on social justice issues. Certainly the editors who asked her to write about the climate change rally understood that she was participating in the protest as a means of introducing her daughter to the power of protest."

The newspaper that had approved of Porter's lessons to her daughter now scolded me for fighting to end the racist police practice it had spent two decades documenting. In a column entitled "Quietism is activism for the status quo," legal academic and writer Azeezah Kanji responded to my plight by saying, "telling opinion writers of colour to refrain from activism is like telling someone being punched in the face that they can scream about the pain, but not raise a hand to stop the fist that is inflicting it." Another important response to the *Star*'s inconsistent application of the conflict-of-interest rule came from Michele Landsberg, in *NOW Magazine*, a few weeks after my departure from the *Star*. In the early 1970s Landsberg had begun a pioneering column for the *Star* and engaged in much activism during her years with the publication: "When I fought to prevent a child care centre closing, my editor printed petitions in the paper, and arranged for a photographer to record my delivery of the reader-signed documents to Premier Bill Davis. (He was a no-show.) They even made a TV commercial showing me knocking on the doors of welfare mothers to stir up trouble for bad landlords. I marched on picket lines; I protested at Queen's Park. I know I brought large numbers of readers to the paper. I know the paper valued and rewarded me. Is race less vital than poverty or sex discrimination? People of colour who are (or were) loyal to the *Star*, will not ignore the fact that one of their own has effectively been shown the door for his activism on their behalf."

But the *Star* wasn't concerned that I was breaking the rules. They objected to *how* I was breaking them. I was too loud, too brash, too effective in attracting the interest of other media outlets, and entirely too Blackety-Black for bow-tie man and his newspaper. The *Star* wanted my profile but not my voice, my "diversity" but not my blackness.

I wrote a popular and provocative column, but like most undervalued workers in the journalism industry, I had no salary, no contract, no job security, no prospect of advancement. I stood up for myself in part because of the many young Black journalism students I was meeting— most of them women—who would tell me they were encountering the same sort of pressures and prejudices from instructors at school. I wanted to make space for them by showing that we do not always have to accept our industry's low standards and misapplied rules. I wanted their future employers to know we are tired, and that we demand the ability to be ourselves at work and not the negroes they want us to be.

The false promise of objectivity in journalism reinforces white supremacy. My activism is my writing, and in the fight for Black life, I am by necessity an actor and critic at the same time. Plenty of people told me I'd given up my biggest platform for nothing, that I'd let the *Star* win. But Black folks who still hail me up in the street for my decision are the only people I can hear.

deep breath
(may)

Never have I been more grateful for flowers. The spring blossoms are finally here and I'm their paparazzo. No garden within two feet of the sidewalk escapes my glance, and I compulsively snap pictures on my phone. What are those called again? What tree is this? Have there always been this many bees? The news says they are disappearing, so when I see bees bobbing in front of crabapple blossoms or popping out of irises I quietly urge them on. Yaaas bees. It's animal encouragement season, it's bees and birds.

I post my flower photos online and start different conversations. A colleague I sometimes spar with on social media sends me a private message complimenting my shots, mentioning that his young son is fascinated by the growth of the tomato plants in their backyard. People start tweeting me flower pics of their own. Professor Christina Sharpe tweets spring colours too, and reminds us we need beauty in our lives every day.

I've been trying for the year and a half I've lived in my apartment to get a decent picture of one of the many neighbourhood cardinals. My cellphone is perfect for close-ups of flowers, but birds are elusive. One day I crawl into the bushes to get close to a cardinal. Not close enough, because I'm not quiet enough, not subtle enough. I come away with no photo but with seeds and twigs embedded in my velcro head of hair. Over time I believe I'm hearing and seeing this same cardinal everywhere, that I know its call, and I start running to the window every time I hear it.

There's a spot in High Park where moths and butterflies spread out. There are probably lots of spots like this, but this is the one I've found. Have there always been this many butterflies? One night my friends and I are walking near Dufferin Grove, and the scent of a thousand lilacs hidden in the darkness washes over us. I associate lilacs with my mom, who snips them and puts them in a jug of water on her table every spring. I realize my mom quietly taught me to appreciate beauty, to make a little time for it.

My friend and I go to the Royal Botanical Gardens in Burlington. We get off the city bus a bit too early and have to walk along the road to the welcome centre. My friend cradles a caterpillar up from the grass and bridges it along her fingers, hand over hand. I can't remember the last time I've seen a caterpillar, scooped one up, laughed as it pushes past the hairs above my knuckles. The gardens include spacious greenhouses with ferns and prickly plants, but we're also here to roam the outdoor trails. As we approach the first paths, we encounter a yellow sign fixed to a metal post: THIS AREA PATROLLED BY POLICE. The sign could travel three hundred years back in time and still be bang on.

Squirrels and chipmunks await us at the mouth of the trail, convinced we have food. The chipmunks are especially fearless. They are practically underfoot. We wind along the paths, across a boardwalk, along the main road, and into more gardens. The breeze is just cool enough to count, but sometimes the sun makes me forget it. We take the long way back to the welcome centre so we can cross a part of the path that's been flooded by a pond. We have to take our shoes and socks off to wade through, and I realize I haven't been barefoot outside all year.

No matter how many times I step in cold water I'm always afraid. Today the water is muddy and rocky and so refreshing. Never have I been so grateful for water, for the sun to dry my feet on the other side, for loving friendship, for life.

honoured group

(june)

A *Globe and Mail* headline from June 25, 2017, declared, "Black Lives Matter Toronto Makes Surprise Appearance at Pride Parade." Who was surprised? I wonder. The year before, BLM-TO had led the parade as the festival's "honoured group," and had used that spotlight to halt the parade for about thirty minutes to demand an end to anti-Black racism within Pride Toronto. A year later, journalists checked in with Pride organizers to see if BLM-TO had registered to march. People posted messages on social media claiming they wouldn't be back at Pride because of the activist group's disruption. CBC News ran an opinion piece by a Black gay man titled "Black Lives Matter doesn't speak for me."

People didn't get it—what did these radical Black people suddenly want with Pride? Why would the members of one marginalized group take over the space of another? Shouldn't Black people, more than anyone, understand the sanctity and importance of this celebration? The mainstream just couldn't fathom that Black people are also queer and trans people, that Black queer and trans people would unapologetically claim their historical and ongoing role in Toronto's queer liberation struggles.

BLM-TO didn't ask permission before stopping the 2016 parade, so the fact they appeared a year later without notice wasn't at all surprising. The Canadian public was still upset by a Black activist group's insistence on expressing dissent at Pride. But whiteness loves to act shocked by situations and people it would rather not reckon with.

BLM-TO co-founders and their supporters marched into the 2017 parade close to the intersection of Yonge Street and College Street where, a year earlier, they'd interrupted the festivities to call out Pride Toronto, the not-for-profit organization that runs the annual celebrations. This time the group's signs read, "May we never again need to remind you that we, too, are queer," and "May we never again need to remind you that WE built this" and that "we shut it down for ALL OF US." I remember this as righteous, bold, inspirational, and powerful—but not surprising.

More than two years since its creation in late 2014, BLM-TO had become a consistent and effective force in Toronto, a city where powerful white people endlessly boast about how good they are to the rest of us. The group's advocacy exposed the limitations and exclusions of Toronto's claims to multiculturalism and diversity. BLM-TO had forced governments and the public to consider blackness on its own, to account for the specific ways that anti-Blackness and white supremacy operate in Toronto and Canada, to connect anti-Black racism to the struggles of other oppressed peoples.

For every dubious claim that anti-Black racism stops at the U.S.-Canada border, BLM-TO had a new intervention to expose anti-Blackness here. The group was building on the strength of previous local movements for Black liberation. This new generation used language that changed public discourse, and it engaged in unapologetic direct actions that our respectable politicians couldn't handle. Most importantly, BLM-TO demonstrated that Black people on this territory are informing the global struggle for Black life; that we are leaders and influencers rather than consumers, spectators, or followers of Black struggles elsewhere.

On November 26, 2014, I wrote a news report from Ferguson, Missouri, a suburb of St. Louis, where protests continued after eighteen-year-old Michael Brown was killed by police officer Darren Wilson that August. Wilson had shot Brown six times, including once in the top of his head, after accosting him on a residential street. The day before I arrived in Ferguson to cover the story for *The Walrus* magazine, a grand jury had decided not to lay any criminal charges against Wilson. Local residents and their supporters, who had been holding sustained and disruptive public demonstrations throughout the three months since Brown's death, were outraged anew by this decision. They occupied the streets of the town, including the space in front of the police station, where police used several acts of local vandalism and looting as an excuse to detain or arrest any Black civilian.

Night and day, over two thousand soldiers with the National Guard patrolled the streets of the majority Black town. Soldiers with sniper rifles sat perched atop their armoured vehicles and took up positions on the roof of the police station, often pointing their rifles at demonstrators. I witnessed police arrest several peaceful demonstrators, none of whom appeared to be doing anything other than standing in the street, as they had been doing for months.

I flopped onto my hotel bed that evening and turned on cable news. I saw that demonstrations for Mike Brown were happening all over the world. In a protest rare for its size, thousands of people in downtown Toronto took to the streets not only in solidarity with the Brown family and the people of Ferguson, but also in acknowledgement of many instances of police violence at home. Demonstrators brought attention to the Peel Regional Police's fatal shooting of Jermaine Carby in Brampton two months earlier.

I was instantly homesick and sad I'd missed that gathering. I was travelling alone and had no one to speak with in person about what I was witnessing. I didn't realize it was the beginning of a powerful resurgence of Black liberation politics and activism in Toronto, a resurgence led by Black people of my generation, many of them younger than me. BLM-TO, the group born on the day of the Toronto solidarity event for Mike Brown, drew upon the collective pain we felt for Mike and grounded that pain in our daily experiences as Black people in our city and across Canada.

Canadian media reported extensively on police brutality in the United States after the Black Lives Matter movement in that country began shining its light. Our news networks echoed the widespread U.S. news coverage of police and vigilantes murdering Black people, among them Trayvon Martin, Sandra Bland, Rekia Boyd, Eric Garner, Tamir Rice, and Walter Scott. Our coverage would often include white commentators expressing relief that Canada was not home to a similar dynamic of racist violence. But then BLM-TO began using U.S. media as a mirror of our own country and culture, igniting uncomfortable conversations.

When Daniel Pantaleo, the New York police officer who fatally choked forty-three-year-old Eric Garner in the street, was not criminally charged in December 2014, BLM-TO held a die-in demonstration at Yonge-Dundas Square, in the heart of downtown Toronto. Once again organizers brought attention to Jermaine Carby's death, and to carding and surveillance by local police. And then, in the summer of 2015, a Toronto police officer shot and killed Andrew Loku, a father of five.

Andrew was having an argument with neighbours in his west Toronto apartment building in the early hours of July 5. A neighbour called the police, who fatally shot Andrew within seconds of encountering him. Robin Hicks, a neighbour and friend of Andrew's who lived on the floor where police killed him, said he was upset about noise coming from the apartment directly above his, and had been for months. Neighbours said Andrew, who had escaped war in Sudan and come to Canada as a refugee in 2005, would sometimes sleep in the laundry room to avoid the neighbours' noise.

Andrew was living with mental health issues, and his subsidized apartment unit was provided by the Canadian Mental Health Association to offer him stability and support. On this evening Hicks opened her door to find Andrew and the neighbours yelling at each other—Andrew had a hammer in one hand. Hicks intervened and took Andrew down the hall to her unit. Moments before police arrived, Andrew and Hicks were chatting in front of her door. Police entered the hallway, screamed at Andrew to drop the hammer, and then one officer shot him twice, killing him. Just as with Abdirahman Abdi in Ottawa, a civilian was engaging in conversation with Andrew, listening and de-escalating, immediately before the police acted violently.

With Andrew's killing, the Black community erupted with grief and rage, and Black Lives Matter–Toronto organized. The group interrupted the July meeting of the Toronto Police Services Board to demand the naming of the officers involved in Andrew's death (information that would not be released for nearly two years), compensation for Andrew's family, and the implementation of a series of recommendations to end police killings of people in emotional distress.

Five days later, on July 21, the SIU announced that it would not lay criminal charges against any Peel Regional officers in the killing of Jermaine Carby. Constable Ryan Reid shot Jermaine three times after a traffic stop in September 2014—Jermaine was a passenger in the car when Peel police questioned him. The SIU's report noted that although police had claimed Jermaine was armed with a knife, SIU investigators didn't find one on the scene. Instead, an officer from the same police force as Jermaine's killer approached SIU investigators several hours after the killing with a paper bag containing a knife, claiming that a fellow cop had removed it from the area. The SIU concluded that the knife had Jermaine's DNA on it. Although the SIU cleared all officers, SIU director Tony Loparco noted that the public might understandably doubt the police's story about the knife. "It is highly regrettable that one officer removed the knife from the scene," he wrote. "His ill-advised conduct has cast a pall over the integrity of the SIU's investigation."

BLM-TO organized a vigil in front of Andrew Loku's apartment on July 27. I was invited to speak, and it was my intention that day to honour Andrew rather than report on the event. Hundreds of us gathered, remembered our brother, then marched along Eglinton Avenue West, through a stretch of town often referred to as Little Jamaica for its historically high concentration of Jamaican residents and small businesses. By this time most of the media had collected its images and soundbites and left us. Reporters and cameras missed Black people coming out of their homes and shops to cheer the procession along Eglinton, hug and high-five each other, honk their horns as we passed. As we approached the Allen Expressway, someone whispered in my ear that organizers were about to lead us onto the highway. My heart tumbled into my gut—I was terrified to go. But as I looked around at all the Black people I'd been marching with, chanting with, crying and celebrating with, I knew I needed to be present for whatever was coming.

The majority of demonstrators occupied the on-ramp so no more cars could access the expressway, and a few brave souls made a human chain to block the off-ramp. Confused motorists honked and shouted, and a few got out of their cars to confront demonstrators, but from everything I witnessed, we managed to keep each other safe. I say "we" because I was beginning to recognize something: BLM-TO was in the streets fighting for me, and in moments such as this one, my presumed reputation as an "objective" journalist, who watches but doesn't get involved, was secondary to participating in my own liberation struggle. I could feel my priorities shifting in service with those willing to take risks for me and us. I was exactly where I wanted to be.

The media, it won't surprise you, came back once we'd shut down the highway—in Toronto, thou shalt not impede the flow of traffic. More than an hour after we'd blocked the ramps, I watched in disbelief as the cars in our distant view began reversing, turning around, and driving the wrong way up the expressway. I'd never experienced such a show of Black power in my own city.

Black Lives Matter–Toronto was different from most Black activism I'd seen. Its organizing crew seemed to consist almost exclusively of Black women and Black queer and trans people whose voices, the organizers regularly emphasized, have consistently been marginalized within Black decision-making and community organizing. The group's members all referred to themselves as co-founders. Many of the young organizers

I followed in those early months, including Alexandria Williams, Yusra Khogali, Sandy Hudson, Pascale Diverlus, and Rodney Diverlus, were students at local universities and were actively engaged in struggles on campus for free tuition, the creation or expansion of Black and African Studies, and better accessibility standards and services.

As I attended every BLM-TO event I could, I noticed the organizers often hired American Sign Language interpreters for deaf attendees. BLM-TO advocated for Black sex workers, for Black people who didn't speak English, for Black Muslim people. The media rarely explored the depth of experience and advocacy among these Black organizers—instead, mainstream media coverage focused on the unlikelihood of BLM-TO securing the approval of white people with its radical politics and unapologetic approach.

The 2016 Pride disruption made headlines around the world, but the media's response to a critical BLM-TO action only a couple of months earlier had been a relative shrug. At the end of March, the SIU had announced it would not charge the officer who had shot and killed Andrew Loku. (We now know that officer is Andrew Doyle, but the SIU's practice is to withhold the names of officers who are not charged with a crime. Doyle's identity became public during a 2017 coroner's inquest into Andrew Loku's death.) In response to this and other local denigrations of Black life, BLM-TO staged a demonstration, which started at Toronto City Hall and then moved to police headquarters. The group demonstrated continuously for fifteen nights and sixteen days, enduring attacks from the police while holding open a space for Black power and defiance it called Tent City.

The mainstream Canadian media was at Tent City when Toronto police attacked demonstrators and their allies on their first full day of protest, kicking and shoving them and using a chemical goop to permanently douse the fire they'd started inside a barrel to keep warm. And the media was there more than two weeks later, on the day the demo ended, as organizers confronted Premier Kathleen Wynne on the grounds of the legislature and organizer Yusra Khogali pressed her to utter the words "anti-Black racism" in relation to the struggle. Otherwise the media was absent, as if, other than our direct conflict with agents of the state, there was nothing newsworthy in the sustained gathering of Black people night and day against police brutality.

And then BLM-TO stopped the Pride parade.

▬

In February of 1981, approximately two hundred Toronto police officers engaged in one of the largest mass arrests in modern Canadian history: through an operation labelled Operation Soap, police raided four local gay bathhouses and arrested and charged nearly three hundred men. Nearly all of the charges were for being "found-ins"—persons found present, without lawful excuse, in a place the police believe is being used for sex work. Police also charged twenty men they claimed were operating the bathhouses, and accused two men of "buggery," the Criminal Code term for "unnatural" sex acts, which could include same-sex interactions as well as bestiality. Whatever the justification in law, police shamed and criminalized these men specifically for existing in the world as themselves.

Forrest Picher documented some of the testimonies of men arrested in those raids for a Canadian history website: "Men speaking out in the aftermath of the raids described severe misconduct on the part of the police. Some reported being photographed naked, others said police took down their employers' names and phone numbers and several men stated that police had referred to them as 'queers, faggots and fairies.'

Moreover, one man reported that several officers used sledgehammers and crowbars with abandon, smashing windows and breaking down doors."

The day after the police raids, thousands of demonstrators filled the streets in outrage. They chanted "Gay rights now!" and "No more raids!" while groups of counter-protesters along the march route linked arms and screamed homophobic slurs at them. Two weeks later, thousands more marched from Queen's Park, the provincial legislature, to Toronto Police's 52 Division. Gay activists engaged in hunger strikes, ran for political office, and organized in their communities. By May, after yet more bathhouse raids, activists formed Lesbians Against the Right. This group would soon join Gays and Lesbians Against the Right Everywhere (GLARE) and launch a committee to organize the 1981 Lesbian and Gay Pride march in Toronto.

The response to the 1981 raids was the beginning of a more militant queer movement, but that movement was overwhelmingly white. Queer people of colour had to carve out their own spaces and services. As activists dealt with the HIV/AIDS epidemic of the 1980s and '90s, ethnocultural groups formed outside the white mainstream to serve their own communities: Gays and Lesbians of the First Nations in Toronto; the Black Coalition for AIDS Prevention (Black CAP); the Gay Asians AIDS Project (GAAP); and the Alliance for South Asian AIDS Prevention (ASAP). The very existence of these groups shows not only the diversity within Toronto's queer communities but the persistent need for queer people of colour to do the work mainstream queer groups couldn't or wouldn't do.

Black queer activists, artists, and entrepreneurs struggled to create and maintain places for Black queer people to meet, socialize, and play in Toronto. Clubs like the Red Spot and Club Manhattan were havens for many queer people of colour in the '90s and early 2000s. DJs such as

Nik Red, Verlia, Vashti, Jo, Maria Elena, and Blackcat spun the music their diasporic audiences craved. Black drag queens such as Chris Edwards and Michelle Ross performed regularly in the Gay Village and earned large followings.

The work of Black and other racialized queer organizers informed the efforts of their white peers in the struggle. In September of 2000, Toronto police raided the Club Toronto bathhouse during a women-only all-night party called Pussy Palace. Police stopped the organizers from warning the approximately 350 women inside that they were about to search every room in the building. The cops charged two event organizers as keepers of a common bawdy house and documented the names of ten other women at the club.

Chanelle Gallant, one of the Toronto Women's Bathhouse Committee organizers, wrote in 2001, "To me, the raid on the Pussy Palace was clearly connected to the wide discretionary powers of the police to act against marginalized communities, evidenced in the historical harassment of gay men's sexual spaces (bathhouses, parks, porn bars) and 'community policing' of people of color in Toronto, and the domination of women through the incursion of a nonconsensual sexual gaze. It was with these broader social issues in mind that we began to design our responses."

Despite these very political evolutions within queer and trans communities, the annual Pride festival itself got bigger and more corporate, and political interests increasingly shaped the gathering. In 1995, Barbara Hall was the first Toronto mayor to march in the annual parade; that same year the city incorporated the Lesbian, Gay, Bisexual, Transexual and Transgendered Pride Committee, now known as Pride Toronto. In 1999, Pride organizers estimated their attendance had doubled from the previous year to 750,000 and credited "greater corporate involvement and investment in the parade." Pride Toronto became a not-for-profit entity in 1995. At some point the "Pride march" became the "Pride parade." By 2009, corporate sponsorship made up 41 per cent of Pride's revenues.

Black queer and trans people challenged the increasing corporatization of Pride while also resisting their marginalization and exclusion by white queer and trans communities. Beverly Bain, a professor in Women and Gender Studies at the University of Toronto, chronicles the story of a small group of Black queer activists, including organizers Dionne Falconer, Angela Robertson, Courtnay McFarlane, Douglas Stewart, Carol Allain, and Camille Orridge, who met in 1998 and began a conversation about the absence of a Black queer and queer of colour presence in the Toronto Pride festivities:

> This gathering was spearheaded by Jamea Zuberi, who felt that the Pride parade bore a resemblance to a Trinidad carnival but lacked the presence of bodies of colour. She suggested that the group approach the organizers of Pride with the intention of creating a section called Pelau, which would form part of the parade comprised primarily of black queers and queers of colour. Pelau is a Trinidad dish made with rice and peas and is often the signature dish at parties and carnivals. It also combines a mixture of ingredients and flavours that Jamea associates with the country's racial and ethnic diversity. . . .
>
> In 1999, the members of this group formed a coordinating committee named Blackness Yes. . . . They approached the Toronto Pride Committee with the offer to program a stage that would bring black queers together. It required some work on the part of Blackness Yes to convince Pride Toronto of the importance of a separate programming space for and by black diasporic queers.

In the summer of 1999 Blackness Yes! held its first Blockorama, in a parking lot on Wellesley Street, in the heart of the Gay Village. That first year, Zuberi recalls the space "overflowing with large crowds of Black queer people all celebrating, dancing, laughing and having fun. During the live steelpan segment, I looked up from my steelpan to see my father playing right beside me. In that moment, I knew that Blockorama had exceeded my expectations."

Although Blockorama grew in popularity over the years, attracting up to twenty-five thousand participants a day by 2007, its organizers refused corporate sponsorship and alcohol licences in an attempt to keep the celebration faithful to its original purpose. In 2007, Pride Toronto wanted Blockorama's usual spot for a stage and beer garden sponsored by TD Bank, and relocated the gathering to the parking lot of a nearby Beer Store. Blockorama organizer Syrus Marcus Ware (who later joined BLM-TO) described the move as another "displacement" for members of the Black queer and trans diaspora in Canada who have historically been forced from the places they called home. Of the immediate impact of putting Blockorama in a smaller venue, Ware said: "Of course we had our first ever medical emergencies at this space. And they were directly related to its size."

In 2010, Pride Toronto threatened to relocate Blockorama for the third time in four years. Dozens of Black queer and trans people and their allies packed a public meeting at the 519 Community Centre to once again assert their existence and their needs. Pride leader Tracey Sandilands negotiated with the group on the spot and agreed to let Blockorama stay in its current location for two more years.

Members of Blackness Yes! continued to fight for what they really wanted—a return to the original Wellesley stage. When Pride Toronto finally allowed Blockorama to return to its space in 2011, festival organizers said the stage had to remain licensed for alcohol, even though Blockorama organizers didn't want a licensed event. Licensing would mean that every person who entered Blockorama was subject to searches and ID checks, which forced partygoers to line up for hours just to get in. According to Bain, "The paradox of re-entering a space that was shaped and marked by black queer diasporic bodies wanting to celebrate our shared and multiple experiences, and having to submit to a racialized regulatory process of searches and proof of documentation resembling some form of prison lockdown aimed at regulating and confining black queer diasporic desires, was not lost on us."

In 2012 that fight was won, and Blockorama was held in its original space without a liquor licence.

In Pride Toronto's press release announcing that BLM-TO would be the honoured group at Pride in 2016, it noted that BLM-TO "continues to rally against sexual violence along with Take Back the Night, focusing particularly on the lives of Black women, Black Trans and queer people along the gender spectrum, Black people with disabilities and Black sex workers." Pride said its staff and volunteers "all openly welcome the opportunity to learn from the coalition, celebrate their successes and give support to the continued fight for Black lives."

Canadian governments and institutions have conducted very little research into violence against people who identify as intersex, two-spirit, queer, trans, bisexual, lesbian, or gay. According to a 2015 study on human rights and trans people in Ontario, "trans people are the targets of specifically directed violence; 20% had been physically or sexually assaulted for being trans, and another 34% had been verbally threatened or harassed but not assaulted. Many did not report these assaults to the police; in fact, 24% reported having been harassed by police." There is even less

THE SKIN WE'RE IN

data about the specific experiences of Black trans people. But a lack of data can't excuse a refusal to listen to Black queer and trans people, who keep sharing painful experiences of police violence.

BLM-TO was one of many organizations with a presence at the 2016 Pride Week festivities, with a booth and volunteers and pamphlets. But organizers said they were not treated like most others by the police who'd been hired to patrol the festival. BLM-TO member Janaya Khan described how cops continually asked the group for its festival permits, saying the harassment became so aggressive that group members alerted Pride Toronto organizers. Khan would later ask, "What does it mean if, in Pride, I am criminalized within it as a queer Black person, and I am criminalized when I leave it?"

Syrus Marcus Ware of BLM-TO, who is trans and has spent two decades organizing spaces at Pride for Black queer and trans people, has noted that Toronto's larger Pride community has historically ignored the specific dangers and circumstances of Black queer and trans people. "The idea that we could be black and queer, black and trans, is unfathomable to too many people in our community. We don't belong because they've never expected us there," Ware said in 2016. Even as BLM-TO accepted Pride's "honoured group" acknowledgement in early 2016, its members expressed mixed feelings about the festival's history with police involvement. "In Pride, there is often a delegation of police who are there, waving and shaking hands," Khan said at the time. "And that's not the relationship that black queer and trans people have, and racialized queer and trans people have with the police. It never has been."

We can trace this truth back half a century, to the 1969 New York Police Department raid on the Stonewall Inn and the subsequent uprising of queer people in that city that energized communities across the United States and beyond. Stormé DeLarverie, a Black queer entertainer, was reportedly one of the first people arrested during that raid of the Stonewall, a club where the city's queer community often gathered. But Stormé fought back, recounting years later, "The cop hit me, and I hit him back."

The courage of Stormé and others inspired hundreds of people to pour into the streets to support those being arrested. The next night, thousands more mobilized to protest the raid. A Black trans woman named Marsha P. Johnson, who also frequented the Stonewall, reportedly climbed a lamppost and dropped a brick through the windshield of a police car.

BLM-TO highlighted the ongoing mistrust of local police by advocating for Sumaya Dalmar, a 26-year-old Somali trans woman found dead in a Danforth Village home in February 2015. Police said they found nothing suspicious about Dalmar's death, but acknowledged they'd received calls suggesting she had been murdered. "Pride is about being able to live with dignity," said Leroi Newbold of BLM-TO in a 2016 interview. "And we can't live with dignity when our Black trans sisters can be disappeared and murdered within the vicinity that we live with impunity, and the police aren't held accountable with finding out what happened to them, such as what happened to Sumaya Dalmar."

We have to consider Pride Toronto's commitment to "the continued fight for Black lives" alongside the fact that the largest delegation at Toronto's 2016 Pride Parade was a group of hundreds of police from across southern Ontario, including Toronto, Hamilton, Waterloo, Durham, York, and Peel, and University of Toronto campus police. A video of the police delegation passing by a stationary camera is almost nine minutes long. Many officers were in full uniform and were carrying their weapons. There was even a Pride in Corrections delegation of prison staffers, which included a bus with tinted windows. The *Toronto Star* had reported on this vehicle at previous Pride parades, describing it as "what looked like a prisoner bus decked out in rainbow flags." Does *your* parade have a prison bus?

Institutions and corporations that disproportionately harm queer people have invested heavily in branding themselves as queer-friendly—activists often refer to this practice as pinkwashing. One of the many police squad cars at the 2016 parade had a paint job with pink highlights and the words "Stop Bullying" plastered on it. As a former federal prisoner said, in writing about the connection between the corrections Pride marchers and discrimination in Canada's prisons, "In terms of its treatment of people of colour and queers alike, correctional services should not be allowed to hide behind Pride's flag."

As BLM-TO's contingent led the 2016 parade and approached the intersection of Yonge and College Streets, the group and its supporters stopped marching and announced that they were taking time to address the decades of anti-Black racism within Pride. Alexandria Williams told the audience, who had begun booing and chanting for BLM-TO to move along, that the apparent progress and safety queer people enjoy in Toronto is not distributed equally. "We are fighting for our people, how dare you!" said Williams in response to the negative reception. She continued: "We fought for you. We threw bricks for you. We got locked up for you. We made Pride political. We made Pride *something*. You'd better respect that. Don't you ever forget your queer histories. Don't you ever forget who made this possible. It was people of colour, it was trans people of colour, it was Black trans people of colour. You can wear your rainbow flags, and you can have the time of your life, but every time my partner walks out that door I am afraid."

BLM-TO's purpose in stopping the parade was to make nine demands of Pride organizers. The group had written the demands in consultation with other Black queer organizations such as Blackness Yes! and Black Queer Youth. One of the demands was the removal of police floats and booths from all Pride marches, parades, and community spaces. In my experience, of the nine demands, this is the only one most people can remember. But eight other demands insisted on valuing the contributions, voices, and experiences of Black queer and trans people:

1. Commit to BQY's (Black Queer Youth) continued space (including stage/tents), funding, and logistical support.
2. Self-determination for all community spaces, allowing community full control over hiring, content, and structure of their stages.
3. Full and adequate funding for community stages, including logistical, technical, and personnel support.
4. Double funding for Blockorama (to $13,000 + ASL interpretation and headliner funding).
5. Reinstate and make a commitment to increase community stages/spaces (including the reinstatement of the South Asian stage).
6. A commitment to increase representation amongst Pride Toronto staffing/hiring, prioritizing Black trans women, Black queer people, Indigenous folk, and others from vulnerable communities.
7. A commitment to more Black deaf & hearing ASL interpreters for the Festival.
8. Removal of police floats in the Pride marches/parades.
9. A public townhall, organized in conjunction with groups from marginalized communities, including, but not limited to, Black Lives Matter–Toronto, Blackness Yes, and BQY to be held six months from today. Pride Toronto will present an update and action plan on the aforementioned demands.

These demands come from more than three decades of struggle among Black queer people for recognition and support at Pride. Many of those who stopped the parade with BLM-TO had been fighting long before Pride became the internationally known, corporately funded party it is now. It's also notable that BLM-TO and allies used their disruption to highlight the struggles of Indigenous peoples, South Asian people, and deaf people, and to demand better supports for them. Nearly all of this was lost in the media coverage and ensuing public reaction—all most people wanted to talk about was the presence of uniformed, armed police at Pride. BLM-TO did not seek to exclude individuals who serve as police from Pride. Their demand focused on official symbols of policing: the squad cars, the logos, and the hundreds of officers wearing their bulletproof vests and handguns to a community event. The media routinely failed to make this distinction.

Within half an hour of the start of BLM-TO's demonstration, Pride Toronto executive director Mathieu Chantelois and board co-chair Alica Hall had arrived to meet the organizers and review their demands, which were printed on large paper sheets. Chantelois took a novelty-sized feathered pen from BLM-TO co-founder Rodney Diverlus and signed the demands on the spot. He then hugged Diverlus and other demonstrators. The parade resumed, and the people who had staged the intervention celebrated. Moments later BLM-TO tweeted, "We shut it down. We won. #blackpride." Chantelois told media, "Their requests were completely reasonable" and "everything was making a lot of sense."

The very next day, Chantelois revoked his commitment to the demands he had signed. He told the *Toronto Star* that he and Hall didn't actually have the authority to honour the demands. Chantelois offered this explanation of his decision to sign: "What I did yesterday was made the parade move." In other words, Chantelois wasn't sincere when he signed, when he hugged the protesters, when he posed for the cameras. He just needed to get the negroes out of the way.

During a press conference a few days after the parade disruption, Janaya Khan focused on the conversations BLM-TO had ignited around the world. "That's one of the most successful things that have come out of this—there's been a huge cultural shift. We're asking questions about the role of police, we're asking questions about safety, we're looking at what Pride is going to be in the future, we're looking at how to make it more inclusive. Any time there's a cultural shift, we are winning," they said. "This is more than just policies, legislation and institutional shifts. This is a shift that has to happen on the public level, on the communal level."

Of course, media was eager to return to the old narratives that separate blackness from queerness. Regarding Chantelois's reversal on BLM-TO's demands, a reporter asked Khan, "Is it not then right for Mathieu to go back to his community, as it were, to his board, to then present that list to them? Because he is only one man, isn't the counter too that he should then go back to his community and put that list to them for more discussion?" Khan replied, "We are his community. When we're queer and trans, and when the vast majority of [BLM] members, not only in this chapter but overall are queer and trans, we are his community." BLM-TO members held this press conference as they were receiving death threats from across the country, including from people who identified as white and queer.

Despite the overwhelming success of the demonstration, or maybe *because* of it, the media and public backlash was immediate and vicious. *Globe and Mail* columnist Margaret Wente penned a piece titled "The Bullies of Black Lives Matter." Critics routinely said BLM-TO had "hijacked" the parade. The disapproving opinion pieces flowed for days, and many of them sought to completely rewrite the history of

Pride—a revolt against the hateful policing of queer people—as a non-descript celebration of "inclusion."

Many commentators said BLM-TO had harmed its own cause by stopping the parade. One columnist went further and suggested advocates were making deadly interactions with police more likely by demanding an end to police floats, uniforms, and weapons. "Lacking familiarity of 'the other'—gays, blacks or the mentally ill—and lacking proper training, can be a deadly combination," wrote columnist Martin Regg Cohn. "That's why police participation in the Pride parade, which increases familiarity and enhances understanding, is surely a good thing. Most of us understand, intuitively, that for all the systemic and institutional challenges facing Toronto's cops, demonizing them is a dead end. And can sometimes prove deadly." In other words, police lack "familiarity" with the people they kill in disproportionate number, and by resisting interactions with the police, Black queer people are partly to blame for future acts of police violence. This sort of helpful advice was everywhere.

But BLM-TO refused to back down from its demands. In the days after the demonstration, Pride organizer Jacqie Lucas resigned from her position in solidarity with BLM-TO. About six weeks after Chantelois had gone back on his word, he too abruptly resigned. Media obtained an email it attributed to Pride staff that said the executive director was facing allegations of sexual harassment and manipulative behaviour. In the months after Chantelois's departure, Pride Toronto seemed to work more closely with BLM-TO to honour its commitment.

In the fall of 2016, Pride Toronto issued a public apology, not only for its reactions to the BLM-TO demonstration, but for decades of racist behaviour: "Pride Toronto wants to begin by apologizing emphatically and unreservedly for its role in deepening the divisions in our community, for a history of anti-Blackness and repeated marginalization of the marginalized within our community that our organization has continued." Ravyn Wngz of BLM-TO replied that the group was still focused on its nine community demands. "All of the things that they apologized for are deeply appreciated but we still need action plans," said Wngz.

Only months after the parade, we were reminded of BLM-TO's insistence that there is no pride in policing. In November 2016, the group Queers Crash the Beat was formed in response to a Toronto police operation called Project Marie, which cops had named after Marie Curtis Park in Etobicoke. The group said the operation targeted men who had sex with men in that park and claimed that police used "elaborate and overreaching tactics, including going undercover and approaching men who were alone in the park, to target men who were seeking consensual sex." Toronto police charged at least seventy-seven men, mostly for trespassing or indecent exposure.

In early 2017, the Pride festival's membership voted to move ahead with all of BLM-TO's demands, including the removal of uniformed police and police floats. In response, some members of Toronto city council tried to deny city funding to Pride. A Toronto police group representing queer police officers wrote a letter urging the city to take its $260,000 grant away from Pride. It was a sobering moment: police violence had made Pride necessary, and now queer police were calling for Pride to be defunded. The majority of city councillors defeated the motion.

As Pride 2017 rolled around, the media speculated on BLM-TO's possible participation. Would the group march? Would it disrupt again? When BLM-TO didn't officially sign up, the media was perplexed. But BLM-TO ultimately showed up, as it had a year earlier, on its own terms. "Pride is actually ours," said co-founder Rodney Diverlus. "Queer and trans people of colour actually started this. We don't need to register for a deadline, we don't need to tell you we're coming, we don't need to pay money for a float. We're just going to take up space."

After Pride kept its city funding, the Toronto Police Association tried something else to save face: it announced that a hundred of its members would march in New York City's 2017 Pride parade, which was taking place on the same day as Toronto's fête. "We should not be down here," association president Mike McCormack told the media. "We should be in our own city, marching with our own community that we police each and every day." Some of the locals apparently agreed that Toronto's police shouldn't be marching in New York. Activists from several groups made a blockade in front of the New York and Toronto police delegations near the Stonewall Inn. Local cops moved in and arrested a dozen demonstrators.

The collective of New York demonstrators, which called itself NO JUSTICE NO PRIDE in NYC, released a statement that afternoon. The group expressed its solidarity with Indigenous demonstrators fighting against the Dakota Access Pipeline, and noted that the same banks financing the pipeline were "investing in mass incarceration, environmental destruction, and police militarization." The demonstrators had something to say to Toronto's visiting police, too: "Police officers do not see themselves as part of the community. The 'thin blue line' mantra proves that. The NYPD invited officers from Toronto who, after being given an ultimatum by Black Lives Matter to march without their uniforms as members of the community or not be allowed to come, decided to boycott Toronto Pride instead. NYPD has no right to invite these cops into a community that they are not even a part of. The police have the blood of the poor and black and brown people on their hands."

I cannot say whether or not these organizers were directly influenced by the Toronto protest a year earlier, but there's a bigger point to consider. After BLM-TO shut down the 2016 Pride parade, activists all over Canada and the United States began making similar demands of their local police forces. Activists in Vancouver, St. John's, Calgary, London, Halifax, Winnipeg, Ottawa, and Edmonton all initiated public conversations about uniformed police participation in Pride festivities, and in some cases they successfully advocated to remove those officers or pushed them to voluntarily withdraw.

The movement continued to spread: in 2017 alone, activists in Portland, Chicago, Seattle, Washington, D.C., and the twin cities of Minneapolis and St. Paul joined New York in demonstrating against police and corporate involvement in Pride festivities. Again, I can't and don't wish to attribute this directly to BLM-TO. For example, Black Lives Matter–Bay Area boycotted San Francisco's 2016 Pride celebration after organizers announced a plan to increase police presence in the wake of a 2016 mass shooting at Pulse nightclub in Orlando, Florida.

What matters is that Black queer activism across Canada and the U.S. is experiencing a resurgence, and activists in Toronto, far from being observers or followers, are continuing their long tradition of connecting to, and often informing, the broader struggle.

the unsettling

(july)

What do you give a country that has everything? Canada officially turned 150 on the first day of July in 2017, and the government invited us to celebrate this round number of colonial conquest. Of course, we didn't recognize the event in quite that way. Instead we talked about diversity, progress, and obedient corporate patriotism. Canadians are so polite, we hesitate to brag about how well we've stolen this land. Ours is a humble colonialism.

In fairness, it's hard to celebrate nationhood when the Inuit, Métis, and First Nations our government has tried to wipe out or assimilate are still here. Indigenous peoples have not only survived, but during my lifetime they have made piercing interventions into the mainstream white settler Canadian story. Canada has destroyed a great deal of Indigenous knowledge and culture, has literally and figuratively starved Indigenous communities, and continues its efforts to absorb those who remain into its white supremacist narrative, to use indigeneity as a spoke in Canada's diversity wheel. But with every state-sanctioned land acknowledgement or nod to Indigenous languages, Canada reminds us of the peoples and histories it has tried to erase, and undermines its veneer of moral legitimacy.

In his book *The Inconvenient Indian*, Thomas King explores the concept of "Dead Indians" and "Live Indians" in the imagination of white settlers. King says that after white settlers colonized North America and decimated Indigenous peoples through aggression and disease, settlers expected those who survived to submit to their authority, to eventually die or assimilate into a presumably superior white culture. "Problem was," King writes, "Live Indians didn't die out. They were supposed to, but they didn't. Since North America already had the Dead Indian, Live Indians were neither needed nor wanted. They were irrelevant, and as the nineteenth century rolled into the twentieth century, Live Indians were forgotten, safely stored away on reservations and reserves or scattered in the rural backwaters and cityscapes of Canada and the United States. Out of sight, out of mind. Out of mind, out of sight."

In *Indigenous Writes*, Chelsea Vowel identifies another one of Canada's anti-Indigenous myths: the false notion of collective progress. Vowel, a Métis writer and teacher from Lac Ste. Anne, Alberta, observes that while many Canadians refuse to acknowledge the ongoing genocide of Indigenous peoples, even those who see it are quick to excuse it:

Canadians who do recognize historical injustice seem to understand it in this way:

- Bad things happened.
- Bad things stopped happening and equality was achieved.

- The low social and political status held by Indigenous peoples is now wholly based on the *choice* to be corrupt, lazy, inefficient, and unsuited to the modern world.

I appreciate Vowel's use of the passive voice of power. "Bad things happened" is a sentence without an actor. Ditto "equality was achieved." It's convenient not to have to name who did what, especially if we really don't know or don't want to know. What's important is that everything is fine now, and that the ongoing suffering of Indigenous peoples is presumably their choice.

Canada says "look how far we've come" without defining who "we" is, how we've arrived where we are, and from where we came, and in what condition we've arrived. Canada is a phantom train that God sent chugging up an endless hill. We never say progress means settler colonialism, means racial capitalism—that's obvious and so gauche to mention out loud. And we have lots of language to describe difference: multiculturalism, diversity, our cultural mosaic. My favourite word is "inclusive," as in, "Canada is an inclusive country." Inclusion requires the power to exclude. If Canada gives up its right to exclude, to decide who belongs here and who doesn't, it ceases to exist. And Canada has found a way to exclude both the racialized immigrants seeking to come here since Confederation and the racialized Indigenous peoples who were here millennia before white European settlers.

It was Vowel who set the tone for the sesquicentennial year, tweeting on January 1: "Fuck #Canada150. Going to be resisting all the colonial white supremacist myth making this year." The resistance to colonialism in Canada was louder in 2017 than I can ever remember, louder in the news, on social media, and in the streets. Those who wanted to mark Canada 150 had all the money and resources but nothing to celebrate, not outwardly anyway. And many of those opposed to colonial celebration simply forced their way onto the proverbial stage and grabbed the mic.

When the brand of the party you're crashing is politeness, a bold and unapologetic strategy can really pay off. When someone who wasn't invited shows up, a polite host welcomes with a smile and accommodates those who, in other circumstances, are not allowed in their home.

In November of 2012, two years before the rise of Black Lives Matter–Toronto, three Indigenous women in Saskatoon—Sylvia McAdam of the nēhīyaw Nation, Jessica Gordon of Pasqua First Nation, and Nina Wilson of Kahkewistahaw First Nation—and Sheelah McLean, who is white, coordinated a series of teach-ins to respond to the federal government's plans to weaken environmental protection laws and further erode Indigenous treaty rights. As similar actions spread across Saskatchewan, Manitoba, and Alberta, the name "Idle No More"—Gordon had first used it to name a social media organizing group—caught on.

The movement gained international attention after Chief Theresa Spence of the Attawapiskat First Nation in northern Ontario began a six-week hunger strike in December 2012 to demand that the federal government review its treaty obligations with First Nations. As researcher and writer Febna Caven wrote of Spence, "Her peaceful resistance, emphasizing the importance of dialogue, catapulted the Idle No More movement to a new level of urgency. What began as a resistance against an impending bill in Saskatchewan spilled across the border to the United States, ultimately spreading as far as Ukraine and New Zealand as a movement empowering Indigenous communities to stand up for their lands, rights, cultures, and sovereignty."

Idle No More became a banner for many Indigenous decolonial

struggles. In the same way that "Black Lives Matter" is a rallying cry beyond any group or structure, Idle No More frames the insistence within modern Indigenous movements to deal with imminent challenges: the proposed construction of the Trans Mountain oil pipeline and LNG gas pipeline in British Columbia; the ninety-four calls to action from the Truth and Reconciliation Commission report on Canada's residential schools; the murders of Indigenous people by white settlers who faced no serious legal consequences, including the killers of Cindy Gladue, Colten Boushie, and Tina Fontaine.

In its call to action on July 1, 2017, Idle No More quoted the late beloved activist and author of *Unsettling Canada*, Arthur Manuel of the Secwepemc Nation: "I do not wish to celebrate Canada stealing our land. That is what Canadians will be celebrating on July 1, the theft of 99.8% of our land, leaving us on reserves that make up only 0.2% of the territories given us by the Creator."

Idle No More organizers said its "Unsettling 150" day of action would remind Canadians that the framework of government that we celebrate "illegally confiscated our lands, territories, and resources, spawned the post-confederation Indian Act and attempted to write Indigenous jurisdiction—and Indigenous Peoples—out of existence."

In the late hours of June 28, 2017, dozens of Anishinaabe land and water defenders, some from northern Ontario and Manitoba, and several of their supporters appeared on the edge of Parliament Hill. The Hill was meant to be the main stage for Canada's birthday celebrations, but these demonstrators had come to partake in a different ceremony—the erecting of a tipi.

Many of the demonstrators came carrying the long wooden poles for the tipi frame, which they intended to set up on the lawn of Parliament

Hill. At first, the demonstrators didn't make it inside the gates—they were met by Royal Canadian Mounted Police officers, who blocked their path.

Can we pause for a second and appreciate what it means that the Mounties were at Parliament Hill to stop Indigenous people and their allies from putting up a tipi? Damn. Before there was an RCMP in Canada, there was the North-West Mounted Police (NWMP). When I was a kid, one of the Heritage Minutes that used to play on public television featured the NWMP. In the short feature, a red-coated officer stares down a gun-toting American gold prospector who is trying to bring gambling gear and weapons into Canada. It was quality propaganda. No one ever bothered to teach me, on TV or in school, that the NWMP was one of Canada's first official means of controlling and surveilling Indigenous peoples.

The upstanding Mountie is one of Canada's favourite tropes about itself, one that conceals its oppression of Indigenous peoples. The demonstrators arrived with tipi poles at the gates of Parliament Hill. The RCMP arrested at least nine demonstrators and issued them notices of trespass. Under these orders, the police said the demonstrators could not return to the Hill for six months and would face arrest if they did.

But the police could not stop all the demonstrators, who held their ground in the rain, the tipi poles resting on tired arms, backs, and shoulders, until police finally gave way and the ceremony continued. The demonstrators set up their tipi just inside the eastern gate of Parliament Hill—that's as far as the police would let them go. They drummed and sang as they erected the tipi. They emphasized that their action was a ceremony and an opportunity to educate the public about their struggle. In the words of Elizabeth Cooke of the Bawaating Water Protectors, who had travelled about eight hundred kilometres from Sault Ste. Marie to Ottawa, "This is not a protest and we are here to pray for solutions, we are in a peaceful state and we are welcoming everybody to come and join us and learn from each other."

The water and land protectors negotiated with police to move the tipi away from the gates and closer to Centre Block. The control of their movements, and the gates between them and the lawn of Parliament, mirrored much larger issues—several distinct Algonquin nations have an unsettled land claim involving 8.9 million acres of the Ottawa watershed, including all of the land that Parliament Hill occupies. The government regularly begins its own proceedings by acknowledging its place on unceded Algonquin territory. It isn't abstract to say that the Algonquin and broader Anishnaabeg still cannot live and conduct ceremonies on their traditional territory without government intervention, arrests, and punishments.

Prime Minister Justin Trudeau visited the tipi the morning after the RCMP allowed demonstrators to relocate it. He entered wearing a denim jacket with the words "150 years young" on the back. The demonstrators hadn't invited Trudeau; he just showed up. According to accounts from both sides, the prime minister did not make any concrete commitments to demonstrators or address their demands for immediate recognition of Indigenous land claims and rights. But he did commend them for "being these strong voices, for being courageous."

The federal government had set aside nearly $500 million for the 150th commemoration. In a poll of a thousand Canadians, 70 per cent thought it was too expensive. The budget did not include the cost of policing and security for major events, such as the party at Parliament Hill. So Canadians paid extra for those RCMP officers who blocked the demonstrators' path.

The government ultimately spent $610 million on Canada 150 celebrations. The Liberal government emphasized that most of the money was actually for community infrastructure, culture, and recreation programs. That was the design of Trudeau's predecessor, Stephen Harper, and his Conservative government, although at the time the Liberals called the money a "slush fund" to buy election votes.

The Liberals' tune changed after Trudeau took power. "The Trudeau government's first budget doubled the program's size," wrote the *Globe and Mail*. "Recipients are required to post black-and-white signs that tout the federal contributions in their facilities until March 31, 2018." The article highlighted a critical contrast between the two parties in the state's branding of the 150 fête: "The Conservatives wanted celebrations to emphasize Canada as 'strong, proud and free,' while the Liberals redrew public servants' marching orders to focus on diversity, reconciliation with indigenous peoples, the environment and youth."

Activists inside the tipi documented the incessant police presence around them, and indeed the RCMP engaged in heavy surveillance and documentation of the land and water defenders under the guise that their ceremony near Parliament "may not remain peaceful." Freddy Stoneypoint, a student originally from Sagamok Anishnawbek First Nation in northwestern Ontario, was one of the nine demonstrators arrested at the Hill. Stoneypoint knew the RCMP was watching him after the "unsettling" action even though he was told the trespassing notices issued against him and the eight other protesters had been dropped. "Just about a month ago," he said, "I was at a vigil for Missing and Murdered Indigenous Women on Parliament Hill and I was immediately recognized and they told me the notices were still in effect for four more months. So I was asked to leave or I would be charged with trespassing."

Six weeks after the Parliament Hill action, the Québec Provincial Police arrested Stoneypoint at a blockade of a disputed Junex oil exploration site near Gaspé. Stoneypoint and other water protectors said Junex was trespassing on Mi'kmaq territory—police brought an armoured car to the blockade. They charged Stoneypoint with mischief, theft, and break and enter. Stoneypoint, who reportedly stayed alone for several days at the blockade after police threatened to arrest demonstrators, was the only person police arrested when they arrived. A fundraising poster for Stoneypoint's legal costs read in part, "This unprecedented targeting highlights the colonial foundations underpinning the injustice system in Canada."

In June of 2018, a judge dismissed all the charges against Stoneypoint. After the ruling, Freddy reflected on his decision to stay at the camp when police rolled in. "There was a helicopter, around 50 militarized [police] officers storming in from the sides of the mountain, and I heard that they even brought a tank to the base of the mountain. They pointed assault rifles in my face. One pressed their weapon on my face with so much force that it snapped my glasses in half. They were all white cops. I took a pretty hefty beating, but I'm happy that I survived to keep on fighting."

The morning after the demonstrators began the tipi ceremony, another group held a press conference a short walk away in downtown Ottawa. They were family members of, and advocates for, some of the thousands of Indigenous women, girls, and two-spirit people in Canada who have gone missing or were found murdered over more than four decades.

In its 2004 report *Stolen Sisters*, Amnesty International cited many causes for the epidemic of violence against Indigenous women, including "the social and economic marginalization of Indigenous women, along with a history of government policies that have torn apart Indigenous families and communities, have pushed a disproportionate number of Indigenous women into dangerous situations that include extreme poverty, homelessness and prostitution."

The same report said police forces were repeatedly failing to protect Indigenous women. A 2013 Human Rights Watch report focused specifically on the role of Canadian police forces in abusing Indigenous women or failing to protect them. A passage from that report, *Those Who Take Us Away*, summarizes some of its findings: "In ten towns across the north, Human Rights Watch documented RCMP violations of the rights of indigenous women and girls: young girls pepper-sprayed and Tasered; a 12-year-old girl attacked by a police dog; a 17-year-old punched repeatedly by an officer who had been called to help her; women strip-searched by male officers; and women injured due to excessive force used during arrest." The report also documented multiple allegations of RCMP officers sexually assaulting Indigenous people. The individual stories highlighted in these reports shine light on a colonial system that abuses Indigenous women, girls, and two-spirit people and systematically denies them respect and safety.

After being sworn in as prime minister in November 2015, one of Trudeau's first major announcements was the launch of an inquiry into murdered and missing Indigenous women and girls in Canada. It was a commitment the previous government under Conservative PM Stephen Harper had repeatedly refused.

A press conference in Ottawa during Unsettling 150 was an opportunity for family members and supporters to share their vital perspectives on the inquiry's progress. The first speaker was Jocelyn Wabano-Iahtail, an Ininew Eeyou Eskwayow elder and activist from the Cree communities of Attawapiskat First Nation and Chisasibi First Nation. Wabano-Iahtail has been an advocate against gendered violence for years, and has courageously spoken about an attack she survived but which took the life of her daughter, Nitayheh, in 2001.

As she opened the press conference, Wabano-Iahtail addressed the media directly: "One of the most important things that I want you to take away today as reporters is when I say 'Ininew,' it means a human being in my mother's language. When I say 'eeyou' in my father's language, it means a human being. And that's what I want you to put in your reports today, that is my request—that you recognize me as a human being—because that is the fundamental problem, a crisis situation that we're facing on turtle island, that the settlers don't view us as human beings."

Wabano-Iahtail then shared a concern that so many of the families affected by the inquiry had been repeating for months: "This national inquiry that my brother and I and so many others have fought for has been colonially co-opted. This is not what we fought for."

Other speakers came forward after Wabano-Iahtail. Sophie McKeown, a grandmother from Moose Cree First Nation, held an eagle feather in her hand as she spoke about her cousin, Jane Sutherland, who went missing in the fall of 1984 and was ultimately found murdered—the case remains unsolved. John Fox, of Wikwemikong First Nation, noted that the inquiry's terms of reference did not include police accountability. "They've excused the police in this country from any wrongdoing," Fox said. His twenty-two-year-old daughter, Cheyenne Fox, died mysteriously in 2013 after falling from the balcony of a twenty-fourth-floor condo in Toronto. The coroner's office first ruled her death a suicide, but later changed its finding to say the cause of death was undetermined. John and his family believe Cheyenne was murdered.

Candace Day Neveau, who had also participated in the tipi ceremony, condemned the government for choosing to celebrate colonialism while

Indigenous people continue to suffer under it. Neveau said, "the way Canada is investing so much in money into this celebration, it's absolutely disgraceful when there's children out there who have no clean drinking water."

For forty-five minutes, the speakers shared their pain and frustration, but also their hope that the Canadian government and people would listen, would learn from their teachings and interventions. Then they took questions from the media.

Julie Van Dusen, a CBC reporter, introduced a familiar narrative. "Most Canadians think that Justin Trudeau is making an effort—I gather you don't feel what he's doing is worthwhile," she said. It wasn't really a question.

Neveau responded with reference to the recent disappearances of Indigenous teenagers in Thunder Bay as further evidence of government inaction. Van Dusen shot back, "How can [Trudeau] be blamed for that? I mean, if you don't think that anything he's doing is helping the situation, is he an improvement over Stephen Harper?" Van Dusen didn't specify what Trudeau might be doing to help. She seemed to be advocating for the PM instead of asking the speakers about all they'd shared. Wabano-Iahtail wasn't having it.

"Excuse me, did I just hear you correctly? 'How can he be blamed for that?' Excuse me—don't speak to us that way." She and McKeown told Van Dusen that if she didn't wish to be respectful, she should leave the press conference. Van Dusen kept going, insisting that she had merely asked a "simple question." Wabano-Iahtail then addressed Van Dusen in Cree.

"You're a guest here, and you don't even know how to speak to us," Wabano-Iahtail continued in English. "You don't even recognize the tone in your voice and your delivery!"

But the press gallery would not be denied. CTV reporter Glen McGregor spoke next and repeated the exact question Van Dusen had just asked. Wabano-Iahtail was called on once again to speak truth.

"You know what, white people? You've had your voice here for 524 years—524 years you've been visible, white lady. . . . Look how fast your white man comes and steps up for you! Where is everybody else to come step up for us?" Wabano-Iahtail went on to say that as far as Trudeau was concerned, she and other Indigenous leaders were appealing to the United Nations to lay charges of genocide and other war crimes against the Canadian government.

"None of your governments have clean hands," she continued. "You haven't changed because you haven't started your healing journeys. The moment that we have our voice and our backbone, you want to shut us down. And you think you have your privilege to disrespect us the moment we tell you, because of your colonial mindset, and your colonial way of being, your white privilege, your white fragility, you can't take our truth. Look how many people came to bat for you, white lady," she said to Van Dusen, "and you're a guest here. Without us you'd be homeless! This is over," she declared, and walked out of the room with the other speakers.

I was watching a live feed of the press conference from my apartment, and I was shaking as Wabano-Iahtail clapped back at the press gallery, rocked by her strength and clarity.

Three months after that memorable stand, Edmonton police boarded a city bus and questioned Wabano-Iahtail and her family. They were on their way to the National Gathering of Elders in Edmonton, and as an elder, Wabano-Iahtail's pass to the event included free transportation. The police accused Wabano-Iahtail and her family of riding without paying the fare. The Edmonton transit authority later apologized to Wabano-Iahtail and her family.

———

In July 2017 I partnered with the advocacy group Progress Alberta to host events in three Alberta cities—Lethbridge, Calgary, and Edmonton—to engage residents in conversations about their experiences with police carding. Activists in the province had pushed local police forces to publish data about carding and race. As expected, the data showed that Black and Indigenous people were far more likely than others to be carded. The profiling of Indigenous people, especially women, was particularly high. In Edmonton, for example, police carded Indigenous women at ten times the rate of white women. Local police insisted the disproportions had nothing to do with race.

Indigenous women, girls, and two-spirit people in Edmonton and beyond continue to go missing, continue to be abused and murdered. At a community meeting in Edmonton, a woman shared her experience of vulnerability. "I grew up in a neighbourhood with sex workers on the street, many of whom were Indigenous women. I would crawl through glass today to thank those women because I would have never made it to school on multiple occasions if it wasn't for women chasing away those creeps and some of those women were obviously hurt, were taken, were murdered. I know this because they would disappear."

In some cases of violence, the perpetrators are police themselves, but our governments and courts routinely refuse to hold police criminally accountable. In 2015, several women from the town of Val-d'Or in Québec came forward to Radio-Canada with allegations of sexual violence against officers with the Sûreté du Québec, the provincial police force. After Radio-Canada published its report, more women shared similar stories. The police force in Montreal investigated, and submitted to Crown prosecutors thirty-seven cases of suspected abuse by six police officers.

The Crown decided not to lay a single charge against any officer. Many of the complainants were not able to identify their alleged abusers, which contributed to the decision not to lay charges. Once police were cleared, forty-one Sûreté du Québec officers responded by filing a $2.3-million defamation lawsuit against Radio-Canada for publishing the story. As I write, that lawsuit is ongoing.

In mid-2017, dozens of Indigenous chiefs, elders, and grassroots groups signed a letter to the Missing and Murdered commission that began, "Across the country, families, advocates, Indigenous leaders, experts and grassroots people are loudly raising alarms that the Inquiry is in serious trouble. We recognize that you and your fellow Commissioners have undertaken a difficult challenge, however, it is now clear that you must take immediate action to mitigate the damage and fundamentally shift your approach in order to move forward in a credible way."

The signatories highlighted several critical issues with the inquiry: inconsistency in following Indigenous ceremonial protocols to honour their loved ones; the absence of many Indigenous family leaders, advocates, and experts, whom the signatories say were never asked to participate; the re-traumatization of families and communities as a result of the inadequate process. They also cited fears that the inquiry was overly influenced by the Privy Council Office, which provides support to the prime minister and his cabinet; concerns about proper supports for the families participating in the inquiry; and criticisms about poor communication and secrecy regarding the inquiry's schedule.

The government had originally set a two-year timeline for the inquiry, and later turned down a call from the commissioners, made at the urging of community members, to extend the deadline by two more years. When the Liberals countered with a six-month extension, the commissioners said "the extremely limited extension does a disservice to the thousands of MMIWG, survivors and families, some of whom advocated for decades for a National Inquiry." During the inquiry's work, nearly thirty of its staffers, including commissioners, lawyers, and communications staff, resigned or were terminated. Many said the process was doomed to fail because of poor leadership within the inquiry and within government.

The commissioners noted that several police forces, particularly the RCMP, had refused to fully cooperate with the inquiry. "There were a lot of people who did not want this inquiry to happen," chief commissioner Marion Buller said. "We've had push back from police. We've had to use our powers under law to get police files for us to look at and not all police have co-operated in providing police files and policy manuals."

The inquiry released its final report in June 2019. It included testimony from nearly 2,400 family members, survivors of violence, and Indigenous knowledge keepers, and it described the decades of murders and disappearances of Indigenous women, girls, and two-spirit people as part of Canada's ongoing genocide of Indigenous peoples.

"Settler colonialist structures enabled this genocide, which takes into account both immediate policies and actions and 'the intergenerational effects of genocide, whereby the progeny of survivors also endure the sufferings caused by mass violence which they did not directly experience,'" the report states. "Genocide is the sum of the social practices, assumptions, and actions detailed within this report; as many witnesses expressed, this country is at war, and Indigenous women, girls, and 2SLGBTQQIA people are under siege."

The report contains 231 "Calls for Justice"—a comprehensive set of remedies and reforms in every aspect of Indigenous life, including education, health care, child welfare, criminal justice, self-determination, self-governance, cultural preservation, and, of course, land claims and treaties. The commission calls for a "decolonizing approach" to implementing the Calls for Justice. "A decolonizing approach aims to resist and undo the forces of colonialism and to re-establish Indigenous Nationhood. It is rooted in Indigenous values, philosophies, and knowledge systems. It is a way of doing things differently that challenges the colonial influence we live under by making space for marginalized Indigenous perspectives. The National Inquiry's decolonizing approach also acknowledges the rightful power and place of Indigenous women and girls."

Days after my return from Alberta in July 2017, Toronto police arrested me when I once again refused to leave the speaker's chair at a police board meeting. News had recently broken of a horrific act of violence against a Black teenager, whose suspected attackers were a Toronto police officer and his brother. City officials had said almost nothing on the subject, so I went to the meeting and called them out. I had been inspired by the actions of Indigenous demonstrators in Ottawa. I knew I would pay for my actions, but I was in good company.

here for dafonte

(august)

My year had begun with news of a police attack on a young Black gallery owner on New Year's Eve. I thought then about how attacks like this happen every day, that they are too common to all be documented and investigated. Only a couple of days before Toronto police attacked John, another one of its officers was involved in an assault of another Black youth, one that wouldn't be publicized until late July 2017. From the beginning I knew the assault of Dafonte Miller was awful—now I see it as one of the clearest publicly known illustrations of systemic racism and corruption in modern Canadian policing. Police have done to many others what they did to Dafonte; but in this country we rarely get such disclosure of the tactics they use to lie, manipulate, and cover for each other.

In telling Dafonte's story, I must contend with the cloud of doubt the police and politicians have cast over events to protect themselves.

Dafonte's lawyer, Julian Falconer, an accomplished human rights advocate, has publicized Dafonte's account of the assault against him. The charges against Dafonte's attackers are currently before the Ontario Superior Court as I write, and I will not pretend to adjudicate this case in the way a criminal court would. Long after courts deliver their rulings we still have to live with the truth. The following is Dafonte's story, as recorded by his lawyer, and reported by dozens of Canadian media outlets.

I believe Dafonte.

In the early hours of December 28, 2016, Dafonte Miller, nineteen years old, and two of his friends were walking in Whitby, a suburban city east of Toronto. They encountered two men sitting in a garage with the door open. The men were drinking beer and smoking cigarettes. One of them asked Dafonte and his friends where they lived. Dafonte answered that they lived in the area. The man then asked Dafonte and his friends why they were in the neighbourhood. When Dafonte asked the reason for the question, the man said he was an off-duty police officer and could ask whatever he wanted.

The off-duty officer was Constable Michael Theriault of the Toronto police, and with him was his brother Christian Theriault. Dafonte and his friends knew they had no obligation to answer questions and continued on their walk. According to Falconer, Dafonte's friends began running a moment later, and he turned around to see Christian and Michael Theriault running towards him. Dafonte's friends escaped but the Theriault brothers caught him.

When I share Dafonte's story, many people ask me if an off-duty police officer can legally behave in this way. There is probably a complicated technical answer out there somewhere involving the duties of a police officer under the Police Services Act, citizens' arrests, and so on. But my answer is, it does not matter. Where Black people and other oppressed groups are concerned, rules directing police behaviour become all but meaningless. When police take the law into their own hands, it is almost impossible to stop them. My parents taught me to obey police, not because of any law, but because police have the power and they will be believed, especially in their dealings with Black people. Dafonte says Theriault never ordered him to stop, and never said he was under arrest for any crime.

When the Theriault brothers caught Dafonte, they beat him with their fists, their feet, and a metal pipe, as detailed in an August 2016 complaint to the Office of the Independent Police Review Director—the OIPRD—which investigates public complaints against Ontario's police:

20. Christian Theriault caught up to Dafonte first and grabbed him by his sweater. Dafonte attempted to pull out of the grasp of Christian and asked why they were doing this. PC Theriault and Christian informed Dafonte that they saw some kids in their vehicle about 2 hours earlier. Dafonte repeatedly advised PC Theriault and Christian that they had the wrong guy and that he was never in their vehicle.

21. PC Theriault and Christian Theriault threw Dafonte to the ground and began kicking him in his head and his back. Dafonte tried to stand up, but he was placed in a headlock by Christian Theriault. While being held in the headlock, Dafonte was struck in his head and face by PC Theriault. PC Theriault struck Dafonte with his fists and with a metal pipe that he had with him when he left his garage.

22. At some point during the beating, Dafonte was able to escape from the headlock, but once he broke free he was struck in the face with the metal pipe by PC Theriault no fewer than ten (10) times.

Falconer says Dafonte struggled onto the property of a neighbour in the area and began banging on the door for help. At this point the Theriault brothers pulled him away from the door and continued to pummel him with the pipe and their fists. Dafonte collapsed onto the hood of a vehicle in the neighbour's driveway. Then, according to Falconer, Christian Theriault called the police and informed them that he and his brother, an off-duty police officer, had restrained someone who had committed a theft. Falconer says Michael Theriault can be heard in the background of the recording telling Dafonte, for the first time, that he is under arrest.

Dafonte never stopped fighting for his life. He managed to reach into his pocket for his cell phone and dialled 911. He claims Constable Theriault took the phone away before he could speak and that Theriault told the 911 dispatcher that he was a police officer and Dafonte was in his custody. The officer knelt down on Dafonte's head and neck in order to restrain him. When Dafonte repeatedly told Theriault he was having trouble breathing, he says the officer replied, "Shut the fuck up."

The calls to 911 prompted a response from the local police force. Officers from the Durham Regional Police Service arrived to evaluate the scene. According to Falconer, Dafonte was bleeding heavily, and pieces of his skin remained on the hood of the neighbour's car. His left eye was completely dislodged from its socket. This is the condition in which Durham police found Dafonte, and his complaint alleges that officers immediately treated him as the assailant instead of the victim of the attack:

33. DRPS Officers Jennifer Bowler and Barbara Zabdyr were the first DRPS officers to arrive on the scene. When they arrived Dafonte was face down on the ground. PC Bowler placed Dafonte in handcuffs and told him to stand up. Dafonte advised that he couldn't stand and

so PC Bowler dragged Dafonte up from the ground by the handcuffs and placed his upper torso over the hood of the vehicle parked in the driveway of [address redacted].

Durham police needed a reason to continue treating Dafonte like a criminal suspect, so they charged him with two counts of assault with a weapon, one count of possession of a dangerous weapon, one count of theft under $5,000, and possession of marijuana. The police handcuffed him and took him to hospital. According to the police complaint, a nurse had to ask police to remove Dafonte's handcuffs so she could treat him, because after everything else he'd endured, police had kept him hand-cuffed to take him for medical treatment.

Dafonte's injuries have been well documented: he suffered a broken left orbital bone, reduced vision in his right eye, a broken nose, a fractured wrist, and bruised ribs; his left eye was damaged beyond repair and he ultimately had surgery to remove it. According to the complaint, the arresting officers never asked Dafonte about the cause of his injuries, nor did they inform him of the charges against him or of his right to a lawyer.

As for the Theriault brothers, they were allowed to go home that eve-ning without being criminally charged or properly questioned. Dafonte's complaint says Constable Theriault and his brother both gave statements to the police saying Dafonte had attacked them with the pipe. "PC Theriault did not suffer any injuries as a result of the incident," the com-plaint states. "Christian Theriault suffered a scratch at the base of his thumb and was subsequently diagnosed with a concussion although all x-rays performed showed no signs of any injury." Durham police didn't test the brothers for alcohol or drugs.

According to Dafonte's complaint, Michael Theriault told Durham police "that he feared for his life and the life of his brother during the altercation." When police are on the job, their licence to kill is only valid if they claim to be afraid for their lives or for the lives of others. Even though Theriault had been off duty, in a police jurisdiction that was not his own, and even though he chased Dafonte, the cop claimed his life was in danger. When people say police need more training, I can't help but laugh—police are well trained to respond to Black people as an ever-present threat, to make the public choose between their lives and ours.

Theriault went back to work at Toronto's 42 Division, a Scarborough area that includes many neighbourhoods with high concentrations of Black residents. The public remained unaware of what had happened to Dafonte for almost seven months, and found out only because Dafonte and his family first fought to have the bogus charges against him with-drawn, and then found the courage and support to speak out.

—

Some time ago I was visiting my mom in Oshawa for the holidays. A storm had pelted Ontario and much of eastern Canada in the days before Christmas. Layers of ice draped the trees and paved the snow-covered ground. My childhood friend came over after dinner, and we sat chatting in the living room. After a while I got restless and sug-gested we go for a walk—it wasn't too cold and the icy scene was a rare treat. We put on our coats and boots and left.

My mother has lived in this neighbourhood since I was in high school. I know the area well and have walked the same streets my friend and I took that night hundreds of times. At one point we passed a park-ing lot and saw a truck spinning its wheels as it struggled up a hill. We jogged over to help but the truck started moving just as we got close and we waved the driver and passengers away.

It was late, maybe two or three in the morning, when we got home. My mom bounded downstairs in her housecoat, as if she'd been waiting. She was furious. Did we know what time it was? What were we doing out so late? *Walking?* You know that way your mom repeats what you've just said, so you can hear what you sound like.

I was embarrassed and angry—what was the point of owning a home in the suburbs if you were too afraid to take a stroll in your own neighbourhood? And anyway we were two grown men walking familiar streets together at night—what was going to happen to us? My mom just looked at me, her eyes squinting as they adjusted to the hallway light, then she turned and went back to bed. Even after I got back to Toronto I was annoyed.

Several years later I would read about what happened to Dafonte and realize that my high school was just a couple of kilometres from where the Theriault brothers attacked him, that I'd walked in that neighbourhood at night too, that the same police officers who charged Dafonte likely still patrol the streets where my family still lives. I would eventually talk with my mom about it. She didn't say, "This is why I'm scared when you walk at night." She didn't have to.

▬

In July 2017, the media began reporting on what had happened to Dafonte Miller and on the evidence suggesting a police officer and his brother were the attackers. Nearly every story featured two photos of young Dafonte—a cropped shot of him with a subtle smile, next to a gruesome image of his face after the attack. It was difficult to understand why we were hearing about such a violent incident so many months after the fact. But SIU investigators said they themselves didn't find out about it until April 27—four months after the attack—and that they had been notified not by Toronto or Durham police but by Dafonte's lawyer, Julian Falconer. Days later, on May 5, 2017, the Crown dropped all charges against Dafonte.

On July 18, 2017, the police oversight body laid three criminal charges against Michael Theriault: one count of aggravated assault, one count of assault with a weapon, and one count of public mischief. Three days later, in a highly unusual decision, the SIU laid identical charges against Christian Theriault—the first time it had ever laid charges against a civilian. In his decision, SIU director Tony Loparco said, "Cst Michael Theriault and Christian Theriault acted together and were parties to the same assault upon the 19-year-old man on December 28, 2016." Loparco added, "In view of the exceptional circumstances of this case, I am satisfied that the overall interests of justice are best served by trying both accused together in one trial." While Dafonte was initially charged with possession of a dangerous weapon (the metal pipe), the Theriault brothers face no such charge.

Dafonte's mother, Leisa Lewis, took the lead on speaking to the media when the attack on her son was first publicized. "I'm very disappointed in what happened and how it was handled," Lewis said. "And to know it was an off-duty police officer—someone who is trained how to handle themselves—that behaved like that, I'm very hurt by it. I'm very disappointed by the whole thing." When Lewis was asked if she believed race played a factor in her son's treatment, she replied, "I can't picture this happening to a group of white kids walking through a neighbourhood, so I do think race played some part in it."

The TV coverage of Michael Theriault's arrest often included video footage of him in uniform, approaching someone filming him and engaging in conversation. The video belonged to Joseph Briggs, a Black man who lived in the Scarborough area that Theriault patrolled before he was arrested. Briggs shot the video in 2015 after he saw Theriault confront a group of Black people sitting in their car at a local strip mall. He recognized Theriault and turned the video over to police.

In the video, Briggs accuses Theriault of racially profiling the people in the car, saying, "That's what you guys are paid for, man." An indignant Theriault replies, "To terrorize Black people—is that what you're saying? I don't think so, no." News agencies covering the attack ran the footage of this encounter nonstop, but almost always without the audio, and usually without explaining its origins or including Briggs' encounter with Theriault.

In 2011, Durham police pulled over Briggs, who is Black, after following him in his car. The police suggested Briggs was not allowed to drive the vehicle and forced him to leave the area on foot. When Briggs returned later, the officers followed him and arrested him. Briggs won a 2015 Human Rights Tribunal decision against the two Durham officers. His experiences with the same police force that ultimately charged Dafonte informed his decision to film Theriault in the parking lot.

Most of the media seemed uninterested in pursuing Briggs' evidence that Theriault had been harassing Black people on the job before he attacked Dafonte, or that he returned to work afterwards without consequence. The media didn't ask Black residents in Theriault's police division if they knew him or how he acted on the job. Yet Briggs had documented and shared Theriault's anti-Blackness long before the officer was charged.

According to the SIU, "all Ontario police services are under a legal obligation to immediately notify the SIU of incidents of serious injury, allegations of sexual assault, or death involving their officers." We know the Durham police didn't contact the SIU the night of the attack on

Dafonte or at any time afterwards. Instead of acknowledging this and pursuing disciplinary action against his officers, Durham Region police chief Paul Martin said it wasn't his officers' responsibility to call the SIU. "Under the legislation, it is the responsibility of the police service who employs the officer to make the determination about contacting the SIU," he said. Weeks after saying it wasn't his problem, Martin promised such inaction wouldn't happen again and he announced what the media called "new guidelines" for contacting the SIU. "There will be no exceptions," said Martin at a subsequent meeting of the local police board. "Whatever happens in Durham Region will be the responsibility of the Durham Regional Police Service. As the chief, I guarantee it."

There was no need for new guidelines—the SIU's rules and the public's expectation were clear. But Durham's police were not the only ones who knew about Michael Theriault's actions. Martin disclosed a critical fact about his officers' actions that night in December 2016: "During our investigation, when we became aware of the involvement of an off-duty Toronto Police officer, we contacted that service to share the information that we had at the time," Martin said in a statement. So the Toronto police were made aware of Theriault's involvement the night of the attack, and just like the Durham police, they failed to contact the SIU. When confronted with this fact, Toronto police made contradictory statements about what they knew and when they knew it.

First, on July 19, Toronto Police spokesperson Mark Pugash said that Professional Standards, the unit responsible for calling the SIU, was never involved in the case. One week later, Toronto Police Chief Mark Saunders contradicted Pugash, saying officers from Professional Standards "thoroughly" reviewed the incident and simply decided the SIU's mandate did not apply to Theriault's alleged attack. "I'm talking about officers that are well-versed in the law when it comes to SIU. In fact, you know, one of them is by far not only an instructor, but has been involved with SIU the longest in Canada."

Saunders went on to offer a bewildering explanation for why the unit's veteran staff chose not to contact the SIU. He argued that Constable Theriault never told Dafonte he was a police officer, thus invalidating the Toronto police's requirement to notify the SIU. "If nobody knows that that contact is police related, then it's not within [SIU's] mandate," said Saunders. "If two people are in an encounter, and nobody knows that person's a police officer, then it's not within the SIU."

There is nothing in the SIU mandate that requires civilians to know they are dealing with a police officer. The SIU's explanation of its mandate is clear: "The SIU's statutory jurisdiction does not differentiate between on-duty and off-duty police officers. Accordingly, the SIU's jurisdiction captures off-duty police conduct that results in serious injury (including allegations of sexual assault) or death, and police services are under a corresponding duty to report these incidents."

The SIU goes further in explaining exactly what it expects in cases of off-duty police officers: "As a matter of practice and given the limits of available resources, the SIU will not normally investigate conduct by off-duty police officers *unless* [my emphasis] police equipment or property is involved, or the off-duty officer's status as a police officer has been implicated in the course of the incident, such as may occur if an off-duty officer identifies herself or himself as a police officer." To accept Saunders's explanation, we have to believe his most experienced investigators did not know Theriault identified himself as a cop, which they would have learned through any serious inquiry. According to Dafonte's account submitted to the OIPRD, Theriault said he was an off-duty police officer, and both Constable Theriault and his brother Christian identified Michael as a police officer to 911 operators. In the 911 calls, Theriault clearly identifies himself and tells Dafonte he is under arrest. Durham officers proved they knew Theriault was a cop by notifying Toronto police on the night of the attack.

Durham police knew enough to contact Toronto police about Theriault, but simultaneously refrained from contacting the SIU about the incident. Whatever their explanation, they failed Dafonte. Toronto's police also failed him, and they may have had motivation beyond wanting to protect Constable Theriault. John Theriault, the father of the accused men, was a veteran Toronto police detective who worked in Professional Standards, the very same unit responsible for reporting its officers to the SIU.

Dafonte's OIPRD complaint contains a section titled "Interference in the DRPS investigation by Detective John Theriault." The document alleges that the elder Theriault "repeatedly contacted DRPS investigators to gain information relating to the status of the investigation and to provide additional false information about injuries suffered by his son Christian to aid in the concealment of the crimes committed by his sons, PC Theriault and Christian Theriault, against Dafonte Miller." John Theriault owned the Whitby home his sons were at when they engaged Dafonte and his friends.

For a week after it was first reported, news of Dafonte's struggle dominated local news coverage. Toronto-area media uncovered critical details about the story and asked police officials and Mayor John Tory many important questions. By coincidence, the Toronto Police Services Board was scheduled to meet the week after these new revelations of police corruption and cover-up. During a closed session before the regular meeting, Mayor Tory and the other members of the board discussed the Miller incident.

When the board members were seated for the public session of the meeting, police board chair Andy Pringle addressed the audience by saying, "Before I call the meeting to order, I want to read a statement concerning some of the media this morning around Dafonte Miller. This morning, consistent with established practices, the board discussed the matter concerning Mr. Dafonte Miller with Chief Saunders. This case is complicated, and there have been serious allegations made, which everyone is taking extremely seriously, especially members of the Toronto Police Services Board."

I came prepared. Despite Pringle's preamble, the Theriault brothers' attack was not on the board agenda, meaning no one from the public could formally address it. I signed up in advance to speak to a different issue. When I was called to speak, I began asking questions about Dafonte. Pringle told me I was out of order. I replied that the public had no opportunity to speak because the issue wasn't on the agenda. I brought up Chief Saunders's statement that his officers were right not to notify the SIU about Theriault. Pringle cut off my microphone, but I had the button to turn it back on at my fingertips.

I asked, "If this Toronto police force thinks that a man beating a teenager with a steel pipe is not in the interest of the SIU, what are you guys doing here? If you don't think that deserves a public conversation, what are you guys doing here? What are we paying you guys to be here for if not to discuss something of extreme public interest?" Pringle announced that the meeting would be adjourned, and just as had happened in April, Mayor Tory and the other board members walked out of the room, followed a moment later by Chief Saunders.

I didn't move from that chair. I just sat there trying to control my breathing. I exchanged a few glances with observers in the gallery, including friends who had come with me. After several minutes, two officers approached. One of them, Anthony Paoletta, said the police were asking me to leave the building. I thought again how convenient it is for the police that meetings about their accountability are held in their headquarters. I told Paoletta I didn't believe I was breaking any law and asked what would happen to me if I refused to leave the building. He didn't answer. I told him it terrified me that he considered it his duty as a police officer to confront me. Paoletta replied, "Mr. Cole, there's no reason to be terrified."

When I made it clear I wasn't moving, Paoletta and the other officer left me alone. Reporters who had turned out to cover the meeting, were perched near the meeting table. Some reporters asked me to comment during those tense moments. I tried to ignore them—board members had left water at the table, so I helped myself. A few minutes later, Paoletta and his companion returned with several other officers behind them. He explained that he had unsuccessfully asked me to leave and that if I didn't go now, the officers around him would be "escorting" me out of the building under the Trespass to Property Act.

I hate when people say "escort" when what they really mean is "throw out." I was immediately flanked by two officers wearing shorts and baseball hats. The one on my right explained that he was putting me under arrest. I told him I wouldn't fight, that he should do whatever he had to do. The police lifted me out of my chair and walked me through the back doors of the meeting rooms, which are inaccessible to the public.

Six officers accompanied me in the elevator. When we got to the first floor, the media was waiting with cameras and notepads. The police took me outside the building and explained that I had been arrested for trespassing. They gave me a $55 ticket and told me if I returned to the property, I could be arrested again for trespassing.

I returned to the police services board meeting the following month with more than a hundred demonstrators. We filled the meeting room and a hastily created overflow section in the hallway. Once again Dafonte's situation wasn't on the agenda. I spoke to it anyway, under the agenda item of armed police officers in Toronto schools. This time a distraught-looking Mayor Tory and his fellow board members managed to sit through my remarks. Someone in the gallery had made signs with a black marker and plain sheets of paper that read "Here for Dafonte."

When Mayor Tory rose to speak to the schools issue, we all got up and left the room.

In September of 2017, the Anti-Racist Network of Durham, in collaboration with Black Lives Matter–Toronto and with the consent of Dafonte's family, issued the following demands:

1. An independent investigation into Durham Regional Police Services and Toronto Police Services that will look as to which extent front line officers and administrative staff of both services colluded to cover up the assault on Dafonte Miller.

2. An apology from the Durham Regional Police Services and Toronto Police Services to Dafonte Miller.

3. The Firing of Michael Theriault from Toronto Police Services.

4. Monetary Compensation for Dafonte Miller and his Family.

5. The Firing of John Theriault from Toronto Police Services for his role in covering up the assault his sons committed.

6. Overhaul of the Special Investigation Unit that includes a commitment to releasing all names of police officers charged by the SIU, the annual collection and public distribution of race-based disaggregated data on SIU cases, the public release of all past and future reports of the special investigations unit and the immediate adoption of the 2017 Independent Police Oversight Review Recommendations.

As the weeks and months wore on, the media found little more to report about the case. At the request of both the Crown and the defence, the court put a publication ban on pre-trial court proceedings. On December 19, 2017, almost one year after the attack on Dafonte, we learned that John Theriault was under investigation by the OIPRD for his role in the investigation of his sons. Theriault had remained in his role at Professional Standards for almost a year before being removed pending the outcome of his investigation.

An OIPRD investigation is an employer–employee process: the elder Theriault can face criminal charges for his actions only if the Crown independently decides to go after him, as the Anti-Racism Network of Durham and BLM-TO have demanded. The same is true for the dozens of police officers in Durham and Toronto who knew what happened to Dafonte and covered it up.

As I write this, the Theriault brothers' criminal trial is scheduled to begin October 28, 2019, nearly three years after their attack.

uncontrolled movement
(september)

Some of us have decided that policing, as it exists today, will never contribute to our safety or freedom. Others can't imagine a world where police don't exist, and are terrified at the suggestion. For this second group, which I believe includes the majority of white Canadians, racist police violence is the cost of being "free." Violence is regrettable and no one wants it, but not all violence is equally threatening, and many prefer police violence to the chaos they fear might follow from being too soft on Black people. Keeping us under control is a top priority, restricting our movements a virtue. The constant denial of these anti-Black conditions means that Black people must take extraordinary risks just to expose the violence we experience. Many people don't appreciate it when we stop traffic or confront public officials, but it's usually the only way to get their attention.

When I was arrested at Toronto Police headquarters for speaking out of turn and led through the off-limits corridors, all I wanted was for the police to take me out the public doors. I remember being in the elevator with the six officers who were arresting me, and glancing up at a camera perched in one corner. That, I thought, is the camera that magically stops working if the police do something to me in here. I was tense until the doors opened and revealed the gaggle of media waiting to photograph us. I was grateful for the cameras that day, but all that exposure didn't stop police from arresting me for trespassing at a public meeting in a public building, and it certainly didn't compel the board to even utter the name of Michael Theriault, the cop who assaulted Dafonte Miller under their watch.

Back at police headquarters in September 2017, minutes before another scheduled board meeting, a Black woman in the building's cavernous lobby started screaming that she'd just been assaulted. At least one news reporter witnessed an officer grab the woman, D!ONNE Renée (pronounced "Dee-yon"), from behind and take her to the ground. When she started screaming, several reporters and camera operators were one floor up in the atrium and had a clear view of the spot where the officer forced D!ONNE down. That day there were no news stories about the officer's actions, no interviews with D!ONNE, no official comment from anyone within the Toronto police. The public likely wouldn't have heard the story if D!ONNE hadn't decided to tell us herself.

In the spring of 2017, Toronto police responded to several acts of resistance at police board meetings in their downtown headquarters by militarizing the public areas of the building. For May's meeting, police stationed four armed officers outside the boardroom's doors. At the June meeting, police tried to intimidate and physically block from entering the meeting room dozens of people who had come to speak against the presence of armed police in Toronto's high schools.

In July the police charged me with trespassing. In August, when I returned with over a hundred of Dafonte's supporters, police set up two tables just inside the entrance of their headquarters to screen visitors, search their bags, and inspect them with a metal-detecting wand. Police also erected a physical barrier in the meeting room between the public gallery and the board table, and stationed an armed cop on either side of the seat at the table that members of the public occupied when speaking.

These unprecedented measures set the tone for the September 21 meeting and the alleged assault of D!ONNE Renée by Constable Jamie Pardy, who was working at the reception desk at headquarters. D!ONNE is an advocate for police accountability and has been attending board meetings for years. Every reporter who's been a regular at police board meetings will have witnessed her call out police violence. D!ONNE has organized disability justice events and run for political office. She has a physical disability that makes it difficult for her to climb the stairs to the second-floor meeting room, and so always requests the use of the elevator just past the reception desk.

But this time when D!ONNE requested the elevator, Pardy refused to open the electronic gate that allowed her to access it. When D!ONNE asked again and was refused, she told Pardy to get a supervisor. Again the officer refused. At this time, another officer standing several feet behind D!ONNE informed her that she would have to return to the screening tables near the entrance, as she had not submitted to being searched. D!ONNE told the officer behind her she would not consent to being searched, and turned back to Pardy. D!ONNE says she saw Pardy searching around the reception area for something. When he located a pair of disposable gloves, he slipped one onto each hand.

D!ONNE says Pardy then came around the marble counter that separates the public reception area from the police workstation. According to D!ONNE, Pardy placed his hand on her buttocks and waist. She immediately shouted "Get your hands off of me!" She says she held on to the marble reception desk, whereupon Pardy put one arm around her throat, grabbed her breast with his other hand, and used his weight to pull her away from the reception desk. D!ONNE says Pardy threw her to the ground and ended up on top of her. At this point, other officers and witnesses in the lobby approached the scene, and Pardy got up and went back behind the reception desk as if nothing had happened while D!ONNE sat on the floor, her lip bloodied and swelling.

D!ONNE was not arrested or charged with any crime that afternoon. She had registered to speak at the meeting, and although an officer on the scene had recommended she go to the hospital, D!ONNE insisted on attending the meeting until other police officials allowed her to go upstairs to speak. She used the elevator Pardy had been denying her.

Then she went to the hospital, and a health care worker to whom she described the incident referred D!ONNE to services for victims of sexual assault.

The only mention of the incident with Pardy came that afternoon in a tweet from CityNews reporter Cynthia Mulligan: "Protestor calling out Police Service Board over this woman forced down after allegedly refusing to go thru security." Mulligan's tweet featured an image of Pardy lying on top of D!ONNE in the lobby. The media silence continued for two weeks, at which time D!ONNE held a press conference at Toronto City Hall to tell her story and demand accountability.

D!ONNE recounted her experience, often through tears. "I was shocked, I was traumatized, I was injured," she said. "It made no sense whatsoever." She said she had previously written to the police board citing her objection to being searched at the building's entrance. And she noted that when she'd attended the August meeting, she passed by the security desk without being searched, requested the elevator, and went upstairs to the meeting room without incident.

Cristina Tenaglia of the news network CP24 asked D!ONNE if she had done anything to Pardy before he had put his hands on her. I was among the dozen or so of D!ONNE's supporters hosting the press conference with her. Tenaglia seemed surprised when we immediately pointed out that her question put responsibility for an assault back on the woman reporting it. In a question a few minutes later, Tenaglia referred to CP24 video footage her news agency had that showed D!ONNE raising her voice at the police just after the incident.

We were stunned. None of us, including D!ONNE, were aware that CP24 had shot any video footage that afternoon. When we asked if we could see it, Tenaglia said she would have to check with her editor. After making a phone call, Tenaglia informed us that because CP24 had not yet confirmed everything that was on the tape, her editor did not want to show us the footage. We decided the press conference had run its course. After consulting with D!ONNE I tweeted: "we learned today that @cp24 has video related to the alleged @torontopolice assault of D!ONNE Renée—the public needs to see that footage" and "a reminder that this serious incident occurred almost 2 weeks ago, and a news agency that has footage has not aired it."

While D!ONNE and I were having lunch in the ground floor cafeteria of City Hall, I received a phone call, but when I answered, the caller hung up. I had received a call from the same number after the press conference, and the person had hung up then too. I found text exchanges I'd had with the person at this same number: Stephanie Smyth, a news anchor at CP24.

I called the number back. Smyth answered, and when I asked her if she'd been calling me and hanging up, she paused and then replied, "Well, yes, but it's only because I don't know what to say to you!" Smyth proceeded to berate me for my public criticism of CP24's coverage. "You're saying it like we did something wrong," she fumed. "You're questioning our journalistic integrity!" Which of course I was. But Smyth wasn't finished. "This is what you do, Desmond, you always twist things around." She suggested I had no proof that CP24 had any footage related to D!ONNE. When I responded that we'd learned of the footage directly from her own reporter, she ignored me and kept shouting.

I asked Smyth which part of my criticism was untrue. When she didn't answer, I encouraged her to respond to my public tweet instead of harassing me on my cellphone and hung up. No more than fifteen minutes later, as D!ONNE and I were still eating in the cafeteria, I glanced up at a television screen on the wall. It was playing CP24 without the sound. The station was airing a news story about D!ONNE and the press conference, which also included the two-week old video footage Smyth had just suggested did not exist—it showed D!ONNE in distress, sitting on the floor and surrounded by police officers.

That same afternoon, several media outlets broadcast footage from both CP24 and CityNews that showed D!ONNE pointing out her injuries to a police officer in the wake of the assault. Most news outlets said reporters did not see the confrontation and only began filming in response to D!ONNE's cries. But CityNews reporter Ginella Massa reported that her colleague Cynthia Mulligan, who had taken the photo of Pardy on top of D!ONNE, had heard "Renée yelling at a group of officers at the front desk, when one of them suddenly grabbed her from behind and put her to the ground."

To protect privacy, as a rule the SIU does not publicize its investigations into allegations of sexual assault, but because D!ONNE was willing to confirm the SIU had contacted her, the oversight agency acknowledged it was investigating her case and had started doing so a week after the incident. D!ONNE forced both the media and the SIU to acknowledge they had information about her claim, as both were silent about their documentation until she spoke out. Weeks after Pardy had put his hands on D!ONNE, activists photographed him still working at the reception desk. Although Pardy was under SIU investigation for sexual and physical assault, his superiors saw no issue keeping him at the desk.

During its investigation the SIU referred D!ONNE to Victim Services Toronto, an organization meant to provide support and consultation for presumed survivors of violence. D!ONNE never went to Victim Services: for one thing, she told me, she didn't feel comfortable going to an organization she believed to be affiliated with the police about an assault involving a police officer. What's more, the Toronto office for Victim Services is housed at police headquarters at 40 College Street, where Pardy had confronted her.

The SIU ultimately decided not to lay charges against Pardy. When informed of the decision, D!ONNE demanded and received a copy of the SIU's report. (Even after an investigation is complete, the SIU keeps its reports heavily redacted, often obscuring basic information about its investigations. I've been writing about police accountability in Toronto for nearly a decade, and D!ONNE's SIU report is the first unredacted report I've ever seen.) The report reveals that the SIU did not deem D!ONNE's physical injuries serious enough to invoke its mandate, and so only investigated the allegation of sexual assault. The twenty-two-page report confirms that Pardy did indeed grab D!ONNE, but SIU director Tony Loparco concluded that D!ONNE fell to the ground on her own: "I find that the fall was unintentional on the SO [subject officer]'s part, in that it was described as an uncontrolled movement and not a deliberate manoeuver on his part to take the Complainant to the floor. As indicated earlier, however, I accept on all of the reliable witness evidence that the Complainant intentionally and deliberately threw herself to the floor, dragging the SO along with her, in order to exploit the situation to her best advantage."

Thirteen of the sixteen witnesses the SIU interviewed were police officers or police employees who work at police HQ. Despite this fact, it took Toronto Police six days to notify the SIU of the incident. The report showed that D!ONNE's public accounting forced the police to follow its own rules. "On September 27th, 2017, the Toronto Police Service (TPS) informed the SIU that the Complainant had posted a picture of the Subject Officer (SO) on her twitter account and she stated that she had been assaulted and sexually assaulted by the SO."

Loparco determined that the officer who had the best view of the entire incident "did not witness or if he did witness chose not to say anything about this alleged inappropriate touching."

Police also claimed that a camera in the lobby that should have captured the incident had not been working.

Cynthia Mulligan confirmed with me that the SIU had not contacted her during its investigation, even though CityNews publicized her eye-witness account of the incident.

More than a year after the SIU investigated Pardy, activists noted he was still working at the police headquarters reception desk. Despite this, D!ONNE kept returning to police headquarters for meetings. People who knew what she'd been through went with her, sat next to her as she made deputations, and made sure she got in and out of the building safely.

D!ONNE told me in an interview, "the police will continue to do what they do: lie, deny, harm, and falsify. And as a community, we'll continue to do what we do. We continue."

Very early in the morning on September 19, 2017, I was one of several dozen demonstrators who filled the intersection of Yonge and Bloor Streets in downtown Toronto, stopping traffic to hold a press conference in the street. Yonge and Bloor is generally a miserable place, with endless construction, stunted trees, aggressive security guards, and inhospitable corners with almost nowhere to sit or linger. There are lots of places I'd rather be than Yonge and Bloor at 8 a.m. on a weekday, but this was an emergency.

We stood side by side at the four edges of the intersection with our arms outstretched to block traffic. Some of us were holding signs that read "Let Beverley Stay" and "Black Family Matters." Beverley Braham, who was thirty-eight at the time, was at risk of being deported and separated from her family for the second time in seven months, and we were once again fighting for her to get permanent resident status in Canada. Beverley was married to a Canadian citizen, and the government was in the middle of processing her husband's application to sponsor her. She had given birth to a son only four months earlier. Despite this, the government had plans to deport Beverley within forty-eight hours, to separate her from her family by force.

The Canada Border Services Agency, or CBSA, was after Beverley because she had overstayed the six-month visa she had used to enter the country from Jamaica in 2012. The government also suggested Beverley's relationship with her husband wasn't genuine. In Canada we spend small fortunes to monitor immigrants like Beverley, to subject them to deportation processes that can last months or years.

We often keep people without status in detention, and in some cases we house them in the same maximum-security prisons as people convicted in our courts, even when they haven't been accused of a criminal offence.

In January 2017, after the US administration announced its intention to ban immigrants from seven Muslim-majority countries, Prime Minister Justin Trudeau tweeted, "To those fleeing persecution, terror & war, Canadians will welcome you, regardless of your faith. Diversity is our strength #WelcomeToCanada." One year later, Trudeau's government increased targets for deportation by 25 to 35 per cent and boosted the budget of the CBSA in order to, as Public Safety Minister Ralph Goodale put it, "pick up the pace" of removals.

A 2016 University of Toronto report titled *"No Life for a Child": A Roadmap to End Immigration Detention of Children and Family Separation* outlined Canada's practice of detaining children. The report's summary states that "over the past several years, Canada has held hundreds of children in immigration detention. These include children from Syria and other war-torn regions, as well as children with Canadian citizenship who are not formally detained but live in detention facilities with their parent(s) as *de facto* detainees. Some children are held in solitary confinement. Children who live in detention for even brief periods experience significant psychological harm that often persists long after they are released."

As reported by the *National Post* in the summer of 2019, "The CBSA also says it is now prioritizing the removal of irregular asylum seekers whose claims have been denied, as it does people who are deemed threats to national security or who are involved in organized crime, crimes against humanity or other types of criminal activity." Unlike the United States, Canada has no limit on the amount of time people can be kept in immigration detention, and it keeps many of those whom it cannot deport in jails indefinitely, alongside people convicted of criminal offences. Since 2000, at least sixteen people have died while in immigration detention in Canada.

What does Canada get back for this investment in border agents, costly deportations, and immigration detention? I think we're buying into an anti-Black notion of national security, in which we understand that although immigration can be good, the unregulated entry of Black immigrants poses a specific and dire threat to Canada. For as long as Canada has been a country, it has gone to great lengths to keep Black people out, and to deport thousands who arrive. The point is never to keep all Black people out, but to control us through the constant reminder that we are here only because the state allows us to be here. Deportations, immigration detention, and draconian border police are a signal to Black immigrants that we are still not here as free people.

In Canada we stay ignorant or silent about the conditions of Black life many centuries ago, so we don't have to think about the legacy of white supremacy and anti-Blackness that has been passed down to us through our government, laws, traditions, and social norms. Rarely do we mention that for over two centuries on this land before Canada was a thing, beginning in the late 1620s, British and French settlers brought thousands of enslaved Africans here to work for them. Africans came to this land as commodities, as property who could be bought and sold by white colonizers, including white French settlers who came to New France. From *The Canadian Encyclopedia*: "The earliest written evidence of enslaved Africans in New France is the recorded sale of a boy from either Madagascar or Guinea believed to be at least six years old. In 1629, the child was brought to New France by the Kirke brothers, who were British traders. The boy was first sold to a French clerk named Le Baillif. When Le Baillif left the country, the little boy was given to Guillaume Couillart, who sent the boy to school. In 1633, the enslaved boy was baptized and given the name Olivier Le Jeune."

Nearly a century before the abduction and enslavement of an African boy, French colonizer Jacques Cartier was claiming that Haudenosaunee territory belonged to France, kidnapping people near what is now called Québec City and sailing them back to France.

We don't talk much about the practice of slavery in Canada. Technically, Canada didn't become a country until 1867, more than three decades after the official abolition of slavery in the British Commonwealth. But two centuries of slavery helped to sustain the colonial project that became Canada. We tell ourselves Black people arrived here by choice, arrived because we were invited, because we are safe here. We speak of the Underground Railroad. A common intro to blackness here is that during the nineteenth century, the British allowed a significant number of Black people fleeing enslavement in the United States to gain freedom in Canada. But as BLM-TO co-founder Sandy Hudson often says, our history books often fail to mention that the Underground Railroad flowed in both directions. Slavery was legal in British North America until 1834, and enslaved Black people also fled from here to the northern United States. "Free" Black people on this land sometimes lived in cities and towns where other Black people were simultaneously enslaved.

A complementary Black origin story teaches us about the Black Loyalists, the formerly enslaved Africans who fought with the British against the Americans in the Revolutionary War and were granted freedom and a new life in modern-day Nova Scotia. White settlers didn't welcome Black people to the territory they were stealing from the Mi'kmaq people, and their descendants have been mistreating African Nova Scotians ever since. Settlers in Shelburne, Nova Scotia, rioted against Black Loyalists in 1784, burned their homes, and drove them out of town. The Black Loyalists fled to nearby Birchtown, and the two towns lived in segregation for generations. Here's how the government of Nova Scotia's website describes those events:

> Founded in 1783, Birchtown was named in honour of Brigadier General Samuel Birch who was responsible for signing the majority of Certificates of Freedom held by Black Loyalists. At the time, Birchtown was the largest free settlement of Africans in North America and became a place of refuge for people of African descent escaping enslavement and difficult living conditions.
>
> In 1784, the first recorded race riot in North America took place in Shelburne when white soldiers returning to the area found it hard to find employment and took up arms, forcing many people of African ancestry to flee to Birchtown for safety.
>
> Due to adverse conditions, many Black Loyalists left Birchtown in 1792 to settle in Sierra Leone, Africa. Surnames of many who remained can be found in historical records, including Bailey, Bayard, Bruce, Crawford, Cromwell, Farmer, Hartley, Herbert and Hill.

"Due to adverse conditions." I would have loved to learn more about the circumstances that drove Black people from Nova Scotia to Sierra Leone. My extended family includes several surnames recorded in the *Book of Negroes*, the government registry of Black Loyalists, including Cole, Hamilton, and Johnson. As the child of Sierra Leonian immigrant parents, it would have been very powerful for me to know that my people may have been here centuries ago, that this may be our second time around, that some of us may have arrived here and never left. There's another lesson here: the colonial state has always sought out Black people as cheap labourers, and pitted us against resentful white settlers who believe they have more claim here than we do. It's tradition.

In the 1950s, Canada encouraged thousands of Black women to immigrate here as domestic workers in white households but under strict regulation and control. Government rules demanded that these women had to be single, between eighteen and thirty-five years old, with at least an eighth-grade education. A caveat in the agreement stated that "any women found unsuitable for work (i.e., pregnant) would be sent back to their home nation at the expense of the home government. Caribbean workers were subjected to gynaecological examinations to ensure their suitability, based on stereotypes of the promiscuity of black women."

This real-life Black origin story for thousands of Caribbean workers, who endured racism and indignities to serve as an underclass in Canada, doesn't fit with white Canadian mythology. But knowing these histories helps us understand the context of government insistence, in 2017, that it needed to forcibly separate a Jamaican woman who had just given birth.

In March 2017, BLM-TO mobilized people to call their federal member of Parliament and demand that Ralph Goodale, the minister of public safety, cancel Beverley Braham's deportation. At the time, Beverley was thirty-one weeks pregnant, and her doctor had deemed her pregnancy to be high-risk. Through social media, many of us sounded the alarm. Beverley's supporters picked up the phone and called the minister.

But I will never forget those who tried to waste our time by demanding we prove Beverley's worth. What had she done to get deported? they asked. Wasn't it true that a pregnant woman can safely travel for up to *thirty-six* weeks? Shouldn't she have thought about these things before she overstayed her visa? Wouldn't this set a precedent for other women to come here and get pregnant?

I was alone in my apartment on March 24 when Hudson of BLM-TO confirmed via social media that the government had suspended Beverley's deportation order for three months. I was elated at the small victory. The government should never have put Beverley and her pregnancy at risk, or made her fear they would force her to travel. Still, I knew we had done something very meaningful that day. Beverley's baby was born in July, and I didn't hear any more news about her until September, when BLM-TO announced that CBSA had apprehended Beverley and her infant and had held them in immigration detention. Beverley said that during a CBSA appointment, an official asked her husband to leave the room. She said the official then reported her to Children's Aid and took away her baby food. CBSA held Beverley and her son for nearly three days before releasing them and issuing her another deportation order.

That morning in September as we took over Yonge and Bloor for Beverley's press conference, I made my way to the south edge of the intersection. I was one of several people holding up a long, handmade banner that read "Which side are you on." The first vehicle stopped in line at the intersection was a blue Mack truck. When the driver realized we were blocking his path, he lurched the truck forward, stopping only a couple of feet from some of our volunteers. He continued to stare us down and blare his horn. (One month earlier, at an anti-racist rally in Charlottesville, Virginia, James Alex Fields Jr. was arrested and ultimately convicted of murder after he drove his car into a group of peaceful demonstrators, injuring nineteen of them and killing Heather Heyer, a thirty-two-year-old paralegal.)

We held the space for twenty minutes, long enough for the media to hear Beverley and her supporters. "All I'm asking is to stay with my family. That's all I want," Beverley said over the incessant blare of horns from angry motorists. "Canada is about family, so why do you want to separate us?"

This time, though, we were not able to stop Beverley's deportation order. In his decision, the Immigration and Refugee Board member stated the following about the prospect of separating Beverley from her husband and her infant son, both of whom are Canadian citizens (I have redacted her family members' names):

> I acknowledge that there would be a period of transition for both
> Ms. Braham and [baby's name] following Ms. Braham's removal to
> Jamaica and I can appreciate that Ms. Braham wishes to remain in
> Canada to continue providing care and support to her son. However,
> the information available is that [baby's name] will have the support
> of his father, [husband's name], during this time and I am confident
> that he will have the emotional and physical support necessary to
> adjust to his new circumstances. Moreover, I note that insufficient
> evidence has been provided to demonstrate that [husband's name]
> will be unable to travel to Jamaica to visit with Ms. Braham."

I wasn't able to reach Beverley after that, and heard no more news about her. I assumed she had been deported. But on February 28, 2019, BLM-TO announced that Beverley had received permanent residency. The collective action of people advocating across the country, and led by BLM-TO, had succeeded in keeping one Black family together. But when I think about how much work they must have done throughout 2017 with the one family, I see how unsustainable case-by-case activism is even when we succeed. As of 2019, the Liberal government is aiming to deport 10,000 people a year.

women of exceptional merit
(october)

In October of 2017, the RCMP detained 1,755 people who had entered Québec from New York State without permission from the Canadian government. In July, arrivals of this kind had increased from about 600 a month to nearly 3,000. In August the number nearly doubled again, to over 5,500 asylum claimants. Many of these travellers were Haitian asylum seekers who had been living in the United States but feared they would soon lose their status there. Overall in 2017, 8,286 Haitians applied for asylum in Canada; they represented 16 per cent of all applications made that year. At one point, the government deployed about one hundred soldiers to set up camps at the Québec–New York border and to assist the RCMP and border agents with security screening of the hundreds arriving each day. Marjorie Villefranche of Maison d'Haïti, a community service for Haitain immigrants, told media, "There is an enormous amount of fake information circulating saying that it is easy to come to Canada . . . They are hearing that Canada doesn't deport people."

The United States had been offering Haitians temporary status since 2010, when Haiti experienced a catastrophic earthquake that killed 250,000 and forced thousands to claim asylum in the States. In its first months in office in 2017, the new Republican administration had signalled its intention not to extend these protections.

The arrival in 2017 of these Haitian and other Black asylum seekers to Canada on foot, often with children, could become a Black origin story for the future. One day we might brag about how we welcomed so many Black folks fleeing the United States and the administration of its forty-fifth president. But in October 2017, the detention, processing, and eventual rejection, of so many Haitians showed that Canada didn't want Black asylum seekers, no matter what threats they might have faced south of the border. Seven years on from the earthquake, Haiti was still dealing with housing shortages and a cholera outbreak. Despite Canada's historic relationship with Haiti and our significant interventions into the country's governance, we tried to keep Haitians at arm's length in Canada, and to make their stay here temporary.

Canada's immigration system is a complicated set of ever-changing rules that are difficult to understand unless you spend your life studying them. But immigration isn't about an objective set of rules that have dropped from the sky for our collective benefit. Immigration laws did not apply to white settlers who colonized this land. Only after they claimed their place here did they decide they needed an entry system that strictly favoured their kinfolk. And while the rules continue to shift, the value of white immigrants over all others has not. In fact, when white people have needed to flee to Canada, rules have changed or simply not been applied.

The Canadian government can't tell us exactly how many U.S. residents came to Canada between 1965 and 1975 to escape being drafted into the U.S. military to serve in the Vietnam War—we just didn't count—but the government's estimates put the number as high as forty thousand. We had immigration laws back then, of course, but the government decided to make an exception for the mostly white people who wanted to resettle in Canada. A migration also happened in the opposite direction, as tens of thousands of Canadian citizens moved to the United States to enlist with the U.S. military and join the war. The Canadian Vietnam Veterans Association estimates that about twenty thousand Canadians enlisted in the U.S.; some historians put the number closer to forty thousand. This unregulated flow of mostly white men between Canada and the United States stands in sharp contrast with the strictly regulated flow of racialized people across the same border over the last half century.

In the years after the war, more than a million Vietnamese became refugees and spread out across the globe to find safety, and many came to Canada, often after surviving death-defying voyages to neighbouring Southeast Asian countries in small boats on the Pacific Ocean. For these immigrants, the normal rules applied, and even more were created to regulate their entry. Between 1975 and 1985, Canada admitted about 110,000 Vietnamese immigrants. Their passage was subject to newly created rules around sponsorship and distinct refugee status. Permanent resettlement of these immigrants was the government's goal, and in general Vietnamese refugees stayed in Canada.

In contrast to these influxes of refugees and asylum seekers, the mass arrival of Black people to Canada has historically been marked by the strictest regulation our government can design, and the welcome is often temporary. The general idea is that Black people are lucky to be here and should be grateful for whatever labour and living conditions we are offered. Black people seeking opportunity in Canada have often already been displaced by colonial forces—we can't escape colonialism just by leaving one plundered territory for another.

In 1955 Canada launched a program it called the West Indian Domestic Scheme to bring Black women from the Caribbean to provide cheap household labour for white settlers. At this time, the United Kingdom maintained its colonial rule over a significant number of Caribbean islands, including Trinidad and Tobago, Dominica, Grenada, St. Lucia, St. Kitts and Nevis, Barbados, Antigua and Barbuda, the Bahamas, Turks and Caicos, Bermuda, St. Vincent and the Grenadines, and Jamaica. Black people whose ancestors had been stolen by the British and forced into slavery in the Caribbean had so little opportunity on the islands that they had to consider labouring in Canada, yet another outpost of the so-called Commonwealth.

The thousands of Black Caribbean women who served as domestic workers in Canada after World War II paved the way for many, many other Black folks to land here. These Black women also made it possible for white women in postwar Canada to improve their skills and education, and in some cases to join the workforce. In the words of Bee Quammie, a journalist whose mother immigrated from Jamaica for work in the 1980s, "the disregarded work of women like Black Caribbean domestics enabled previous and current generations of white Canadian women to progress and be included."

The late Dr. Agnes Calliste, a professor of sociology and anthropology, observed that Canada's immigration policy for Caribbean Blacks from 1950 to 1962 was based upon "a demand for cheap labour, a desire to exclude blacks as permanent settlers, and a need to appease Caribbean people in order to further Canada's trade and investments in the British Caribbean." She cited a 1950 government regulation that limited immigration to British subjects who were born or naturalized in the United Kingdom, Australia, New Zealand, or South Africa; citizens of the Republic of Ireland; American citizens; French citizens who were born in France and were entering Canada from France; and non-immigrants who served in the Canadian Armed Forces. Other prospective immigrants, Calliste observed, including British and French subjects from the Caribbean and other "non-white" countries, "could only enter under special arrangement or if they satisfied the Immigration Minister that they were suitable immigrants."

White women who wanted to participate in Canada's growing economy—in factories, hospitals, offices, and schools—drove the demand for Black immigrant domestic workers. These white women needed someone to look after their children as they joined the workforce. Black women admitted as domestic workers confronted racist rules that kept them out of more lucrative professions like nursing. Many of these rules had been in existence before their arrival, as Joan Lesmond, a former president of the Registered Nurses Association of Ontario and herself an immigrant from St. Lucia, documents.

Take, for instance, Toronto-born Bernice Redmon, who wanted to become a nurse but was refused entry to nursing schools in Canada so instead headed down to the segregated South: "she went to St. Phillip Hospital Medical College in Virginia, and graduated with her nursing diploma in 1945. When she returned to Canada that same year, she became the first Black nurse allowed to practise in public health after getting a job at the Nova Scotia Department of Health." Lesmond names other trailblazing Black women—Ruth Bailey, Gwen Barton, and Marissa Scott—who also fought to get into segregated Canadian nursing schools with the help of Black churches and unionists.

Calliste wrote that in 1952 the government admitted a small number of Caribbean graduate nurses as "cases of exceptional merit." (Her paper on the subject is titled "Women of 'Exceptional Merit.'") She suggested the government did this to appease the concerns of Caribbean people who were essential to Canada's postwar economic success. One of the conditions for admitting Black nurses into the country was that the hospital administration that offered them work had to be "aware of their racial origin."

Calliste further noted that while the government evaluated white immigrant nurses on the basis of general admissibility to Canada, it additionally judged Black immigrant nurses on the basis of their nursing qualifications. Canada wanted Black women to prove they were exceptional in order to work as nurses, even while, in the immediate aftermath of the war, many places in Canada suffered from a shortage of qualified nurses.

These attitudes have shaped a country where today Black people are still near the bottom of what researchers Grace-Edward Galabuzi and Sheila Block have called "Canada's colour coded labour market." Their 2011 study showed that, on average, for every dollar a white man earned, a Black man earned 69 cents and a Black woman earned 56 cents; white women earned an average of 63 cents for every dollar a white man earned. Today, in addition to overqualified Black nurses who can't get a promotion, we have Black people with graduate degrees who clean hotels and drive taxis. A 2019 study on the health of immigrants, refugees, and racialized people found that "recent immigrants (arriving between 2011 and 2016) with a doctorate are 3.5 times more likely to be unemployed than non-immigrants with the same level of education."

Our labour is more welcome in dangerous settings like airports, garbage disposal, and construction. We have a Temporary Foreign Worker Program through which Black and Latinx workers from the Caribbean and Mexico toil in extremely unsafe conditions on Canadian farms.

These workers put in twelve- to fourteen-hour work days, operate heavy machinery, work from heights, handle pesticides, and often live in substandard housing. Immigrant farm workers enjoy few of the benefits Canadian workers do, and are routinely sent back to their countries of origin if they are injured on the job. We've done so much to facilitate white people's access to this country, but Black folks' desire to enter and to stay is ever under high scrutiny and regulation.

While Haitians were the largest single group of nationals crossing into Canada in 2017, many continental Africans were also risking everything to cross the border. Nigerians, for example, filed more claims than any group other than Haitians. On Christmas Eve 2016, two Ghanaians, Seidu Mohammed and Razak Iyal, crossed on foot into Manitoba from North Dakota. The two men wandered through frozen farmlands and became disoriented in the cold. A truck driver who saw Iyal and Mohammed on the highway stopped to help them and called 911. Mohammed, a twenty-four-year-old soccer star who left Ghana fearing for his life as a bisexual, lost all the fingers and thumbs on both of his hands. Iyal, thirty-five, who worked as a barber in Ghana, lost all his fingers and one of his toes. Canada eventually granted both men refugee status.

Many Canadians expressed sympathy for the men and offered to help, but Greg Janzen, a local reeve near the Manitoba border crossing, gave a different account. "They're criminals," he said. "If they're willing to jump the border at night and basically break the law, you don't know what they're capable of until they're fully processed. Are they good people?"

In March of 2017, a man from Ivory Coast named Mamadou crossed into Québec from the U.S. in the middle of the night. He collapsed in the woods in −15 degree cold after twice wading through freezing water along his journey, and was found by RCMP officers. Mamadou later said that as he lay in the forest he thought to himself, "That's okay, I want to die. Let me just die on my way. I don't want to go back." Only days earlier, Mamadou had walked up to the border crossing in Lacolle and tried to apply for asylum. When border agents turned him away, he decided to sneak through the woods at night.

Under a U.S.-Canada pact called the Safe Third Country Agreement, people cannot apply for asylum in Canada if they're coming from the United States, which is presumed to be safe. But this rule only applies if the person seeking asylum goes to an official border crossing. If they sneak in from a different point of entry, Canada is required by law to consider their claim. Even as the U.S. government was enforcing a ban on Muslims from African countries, even as its president was referring to African nations as "shithole countries," Canada continued to send Black asylum seekers back to the U.S., insisting that it remained a safe place for them. We don't usually argue that America is safe for Black people, but if the alternative is that Black people will try to come here, perhaps the U.S. is safe enough.

In February 2017, as Black asylum seekers continued to risk their lives dodging Canada's border agents and police, the Canadian Press tweeted a photo of an RCMP officer smiling as he held up a girl in a pink fleece jacket. The accompanying tweet read: "Here's Canadian Mounties greeting refugees from Somalia who walked across the border into Canada." Of course, that RCMP officer in the photo-op was detaining that child. The many photos of Black men in handcuffs at the same border crossing may not have worked so well with that caption.

In November we learned that of the 6,304 citizens of Haiti who had sought asylum in Canada between February and October 2017, only 298 had had their claims finalized, and of those, only 29—or 10 per cent—had been accepted. Immigration, Refugees, and Citizenship Minister Ahmed Hussen, himself a refugee from Somalia, reminded us that asylum claims were only for people whom the government deemed in genuine need of protection. "It's not for everyone," he said.

As our media focused on the U.S. threat to deny protection of Haitians within its borders, little was written about the already large population of Haitian immigrants in Canada, many of whom had sought refuge in response to decades of violent interventions in Haiti, including the ongoing armed presence of Canadian and other United Nations troops.

In 2003, under the pretense of regional stabilization, Canada had played a central part in the overthrow of the democratically elected Haitian government of Jean-Bertrand Aristide. As Pascale Diverlus, a co-founder of Black Lives Matter–Toronto and the child of Haitian immigrants, explains, "The federal Liberal government organized an assembly of Canadian, American and French leaders to discuss the state of Haiti—with no actual Haitian officials present. There, they decided to stage a coup-d'état." After ousting Aristide, thousands of troops were deployed in Haiti. The coup, as Diverlus observes, "would lead to thousands of deaths of Haitian civilians as collateral damage in the name of Canadian peacekeeping."

Although a number of countries participated in the removal of Aristide, Haitian officials pointed to Canada as one of the key players in the ongoing occupation. Haitian senator Moïse Jean-Charles said in 2013, "The real forces behind Haiti's military occupation—the powers which are putting everybody else up to it—are the U.S., France, and Canada, which colluded in the Feb. 29, 2004 coup d'état against President Aristide. It was then they began trampling Haitian sovereignty."

Diverlus and others argue that Canada's interventions in Haiti have created an obligation to help resettle Haitians here. After the 2004 coup, Canada did put a moratorium on deportations to Haiti, recognizing "a generalized risk to the population as the consequence of natural disasters, civil unrest or armed conflict." A pause on deportations may seem like a benefit to Haitians trying to remain in Canada, but people who testified before a government committee said the decision instead created instability and uncertainty for families.

"Having work permits of short duration (six months or one year) that must be renewed at a cost of $255 was identified as 'a hassle' that at best was an inconvenient loss of time and money and, at worst, cost people their jobs. Because it takes Immigration, Refugees and Citizenship Canada (IRCC) three to four months to process a work permit renewal request, they informed the Committee that people are often caught in a cycle of applying for and renewing work permits." On top of the constant fear of deportation, families also struggled to access education and health care because of an endless need to renew benefits and permits. The government could have alleviated so many of these hardships by simply making the Haitian immigrants permanent residents instead of long-term visitors under perpetual threat of deportation.

Canada reinstated deportations to Haiti in December 2014, when Haiti was in the middle of a cholera outbreak caused by UN peacekeepers. In August of 2016, the federal government stopped allowing Haitians who had arrived since 2004 the opportunity to apply for permanent residence or to stay in Canada under humanitarian grounds. So when the U.S. confirmed in late 2017 that Haitians would indeed lose their protected status there by 2019, it would have been fair to say the Americans were simply following Canada's lead. (Lawyers continue to fight the administration in court, and the deadline for Haitians to stay in America has been extended until January of 2020.)

In November 2017, Canada sent Black government officials to the United States to discourage Black migrants from Haiti and African nations from walking across the Canadian border to seek asylum. One of the envoys, Haitian-born member of Parliament Emmanuel Dubourg, described the effort by saying, "The main reason is to tell them we have a robust immigration law and that they should use the right channels to come to Canada instead of crossing in between the borders."

This isn't a new strategy. Early in the twentieth century, the Canadian government also sent officials to the United States to discourage Black migrants from coming to Canada: "Immigration officials sent two agents to Oklahoma, whose job was to dissuade Black Americans from immigrating. Both agents (one of whom was a doctor) went from town to town and employed many of the same tactics: they told Black Americans that crossing the border would be a difficult and even debasing experience; that once in Canada, they would encounter the same racial prejudice as in America; that Canadian lands were difficult to maintain; and, that the cold Canadian climate would adversely affect their health." In 2017, it was Black officials like Hussen and Dubourg who put a friendly Black face on an old message: Canada thinks it would be better for vulnerable Black people not to come, or at least not to come and expect to stay.

It has been more than a century since Canada denied entry to hundreds of Indians of Sikh, Muslim, and Hindu faiths, and also some Japanese immigrants, who landed in Vancouver in 1914 on a ship called the *Komagata Maru*. Canadian officials cited the "continuous journey regulation," a 1908 rule that said immigrants to Canada had to travel here without stopping anywhere. The rule was specifically designed to deter Indian immigrants, as there were no ships that sailed directly from India to Canada. Prime Minister Justin Trudeau apologized in May of 2016 for the 1914 detention and eventual expulsion of *Komagata Maru* passengers, saying in part, "Regrettably, the passage of time means that none are alive to hear our apology today, still, we offer it, fully and sincerely, for our indifference to your plight, for our failure to recognize all that you had to offer. For the laws that discriminated against you so senselessly, and for not apologizing sooner. For all these things, we are truly sorry." Trudeau didn't mention more recent history, including the government's lengthy detention of over five hundred Tamil asylum seekers fleeing war and persecution in Sri Lanka, who landed in Vancouver on two ships between October 2009 and August 2010 and were detained for months.

Meanwhile, Canada continues to discuss potential reforms to the Safe Third Country Agreement and is doing so as Black people are those most likely to cross over from the U.S. The *Globe and Mail* reported in 2018 on the progress of negotiations: "As the Liberals iron out their approach to STCA talks with the United States, they are touting their efforts to prevent more asylum seekers from crossing into Canada. For instance, Mr. Hussen said many of those crossing into Québec earlier this year were Nigerians carrying valid U.S. visitor visas. Canadian officials raised the issue with their U.S. counterparts, and the number of U.S. visas issued to Nigerians dropped."

Canada's politicians who restrict Black people's movements aren't simply bending to the will of their more powerful neighbours—the elites in both countries have the shared goal of white settler dominance, so it makes sense to work together.

The drive up North Preston Road during an October sunset, with Long Lake on to the left and rows of autumn colours on the right, was perfect. This was my second visit to North Preston, Nova Scotia, a town of about nine hundred residents, most of them the descendants of Black Loyalists. I was excited to reconnect with two young people who'd welcomed me a year earlier and taught me about their community. LaMeia Reddick and her sister Kardeisha Provo took me on a walk through their town in 2016. They told me about the racial profiling tactics employed by police in the area, such as RCMP officers setting up checkpoints on the main road into town to stop and question cars that enter and leave. They also spoke of negative stereotypes of the community in the media.

A story that had stuck with me was about the local parish church, St. Thomas United Baptist, that for a long time had doubled as a community centre. The church was still there but it was no longer an open community space. There was a government-run community centre across the street in a building that doubled as the RCMP facility, with a door connecting the two spaces. LaMeia said that kids still used it but that it wasn't always a welcoming spot. She and Kardeisha dreamed of having an alternative space for youth in the neighbourhood.

Two other young activist sisters, Amina and Aisha Abawajy, drove me back to North Preston that evening in 2017. I'd met these Black Muslim women, as well as LaMeia, Kardeisha, and nearly everyone else I knew in Halifax through El Jones, a professor, poet, author, and anti-prison activist who seemed to be connected to half the Black people in Halifax. Just as they were in Toronto, young women in Nova Scotia were leading many of the political and social struggles for Black life.

We arrived at LaMeia's family home around twilight. LaMeia and Kardeisha were there, along with several teenagers from the area. More kids were rolling in as we settled in the basement—by the time our hosts were ready to begin their programming, I counted seventeen Black teenagers. Kardeisha and LaMeia had done it: a year after we'd met, they'd succeeded in using the little space they had for community programming. I'd come on a good night, they told me—this was the most youth who'd ever attended at one time.

To accommodate us all, we split into two groups. We ate, talked about the meaning of friendship, and played a couple of games. I watched as our hosts dealt with a conflict in the room: at least two young people didn't want to be around each other. The conflict wasn't resolved that night, but LaMeia and Kardeisha got the kids to agree to share the space in peace.

Once the programming was over and the youths went home, I asked LaMeia and Kardeisha how they'd managed to put this all together. They had no access to outside funds or institutional support. They said they'd paid for the food themselves, and designed programming based on conversations with the youths. For example, in one session the group had watched a video of a teenage Tupac Shakur reflecting on childhood and masculinity, and then the youths had a discussion about it.

Thanks to the efforts of Kardeisha and LaMeia, I associate North Preston with Black kids laughing in a partly finished basement like the one I grew up in, eating chicken and talking shit and playing on their phones. But the mainstream media narrative of North Preston includes all the stereotypes associated with a concentrated Black community: gang violence, drugs, danger, and death.

Writing for *Atlantic Insight* magazine in 1981, Stephen Kimber described a visit to North Preston and the vibrancy he experienced there—the social life, the food, and the emphasis on faith. Kimber contrasted what he was seeing with the stigma he'd heard about the community: "Can this really be Preston? Isn't it true, after all, that truck drivers trying to do nothing more than drive their rigs through Preston are pelted with rocks and bottles by local hooligans? And isn't it true as well that Dartmouth taxi drivers refuse to take fares to Preston because they know they'll never get paid? Isn't it also a fact—perhaps the most frightening fact of all—that the RCMP won't go near the place, not even to answer a call for help?"

This image of North Preston as a place too dangerous for white people has persisted since the founding of the place in the late 1700s and the time of the Black Loyalists, who were given the rocky and less fertile lands of the area and restricted to the most menial jobs. In 1791, nearly twelve hundred of these Black immigrants left for Sierra Leone because they were disillusioned with their circumstances. Five years later, the British settled hundreds of Maroons from Jamaica on the same rocky soil of North Preston. The British brought in the Maroons to build fortifications for Citadel Hill, the military fort that British settlers constructed to keep American invaders at bay.

The Nova Scotia government's website says, "It's not an exaggeration to say Halifax, a city on the sea, owes its existence to the Citadel." The website doesn't mention the Maroons, many of whom left for Sierra Leone in 1799 due to the same racism and bleak economic prospects that had driven the earlier Black residents out.

Black people have been in Nova Scotia for well over two hundred years, but they were never meant to survive and thrive and feed themselves on that rocky soil. Our media and political operatives describe the Black immigrants running for the Canadian border today as a potential economic burden, as invaders who will bring crime and social upheaval. But it's a self-fulfilling prophecy—white settlers deny Black communities the necessities of life, then blame us for the social dysfunction that follows.

The 2015 census puts North Preston's child poverty rate at 40 per cent. In Fall River, a mostly white suburb only twenty-five minutes away, the child poverty rate is 4 per cent. How can Black people with more than two centuries of history in the area be doing so poorly relative to the white settlers around them? What about the great Canadian narrative of upward mobility, of sacrifice for the improved chances of the next generation? Generations of African Nova Scotians haven't seen this prosperity, even though it is all around them.

Kardeisha Provo, who is now in university, wrote a piece in 2019 titled "The North Preston I Know Isn't the One You've Heard About." In it she continues her years-long struggle to paint a different picture of her community. "The North Preston I know has provided me with the tools to conquer the world and claim everything I want out of it. North Preston taught me that limitations cease to exist. That when I want to walk 'around the world' all I have to do is take a step out my front door. The North Preston I know made my skin tough. That no words thrown at me will break me. Being a 'product of my environment' means I am resilient."

Provo's piece includes a photo of LaMeia and the smiling faces of several local Black youths in the community space that Kardeisha and LaMeia started themselves. I can only imagine how much more of this Black communion is happening out of sight across the country, and how Black women whose names we don't know are protecting, educating, and caring for the next generation of Black Canadians.

community policing
(november)

I could barely sit still in the balcony of the Toronto District School Board headquarters on November 22, 2017, awaiting a final vote to remove armed police officers from all TDSB schools—I knew for once that we would win. Knowing we will win is not the same as believing it. I fight because I believe. But on this night I knew. After a decade-long battle to protect young people in Toronto's high schools, I was confident of a victory.

For this final vote, every seat in the meeting room was taken. The gallery was filled with people who had been fighting the so-called School Resource Officer—or SRO—program even before the police and school boards had implemented it without public consultation or consent. Grassroots collectives representing people historically targeted by police had kept up the fight for almost a decade. And they were about to win.

———

One afternoon in the summer of 2017 I was buying groceries when I encountered a familiar face, a young Black man I hadn't seen in many years. We'd first met at a community centre in downtown Toronto in 2007, where I was a youth worker and he a teen who played basketball a couple nights a week in the gym. I'm protecting his identity in order to tell his story—I'll call him Gerald.

When we met in the grocery store, Gerald said he'd recently seen me on TV calling for the removal of police from schools. "It reminded me of some stuff that used to go down back at Settlement," he said, referring to the community centre where we'd met. "Did you know about what the cops there used to do?" I didn't, but I remembered a program called Cops and Kids, an initiative claiming to build relationships between police and local youth, and to talk about so-called community safety, that used to operate inside the same centre. Gerald agreed to meet me for coffee sometime so he could tell me more.

Gerald wasn't part of Cops and Kids—he went to the community centre to play basketball with other teens from the neighbourhood, most of whom were Black. The police program would begin as his basketball program was ending. He said the police used to insist he and his peers, who had just finished playing basketball and needed time to change their clothes, clear out immediately or face consequences.

"If we were not out of there in an orderly fashion, basically it's loitering," said Gerald. He told me police would threaten to ticket him and his friends. "They started asking every individual, 'What's your name? Where are you from?'" He remembers that sometimes there would be a lineup of boys waiting to leave the centre, but who were not allowed to leave unless they first identified themselves to police. "What the police would say is, 'We know that you're from a certain neighbour-hood, and as a result, if you don't forfeit your first and last name, you can't even leave from here.' So they tried to put people in a box, and some of those people were there for their first time, and they had no clue what [the police] were talking about."

Though I wasn't surprised to learn about this surveillance, it shook me to think I worked in the building and never saw it. I knew our manage-ment had trusted the police to be in the space. My supervisor, a white man named Ted, regularly bragged about the Cops and Kids program and appeared very friendly and deferential to its officers, who in their bulletproof vests and weapons belts never looked quite right among the kids. I had been aware of the type of police profiling Gerald described, just not in my workplace.

Gerald's story reminded me of a comment Ted once made at the gym before a basketball game between some of our older youths and a group of police officers from a local division. The game was yet another initia-tive to put youth and police in the same space. We even paid referees to call it. Just before tip-off, Ted turned to the players, who were almost all Black, and remarked very loudly in reference to the cops, "I know they look like normal guys right now, but they've got all their gear in the cars, so you boys better play fair!" You just couldn't let them enjoy this, I remember thinking. You see how excited they are to compete against the cops, and have to remind them of their place.

Cops and Kids has been in existence in Ontario since 1991 and is now a province-wide initiative that, according to its website, has engaged hundreds of thousands of children in the province. Gerald's story got me to thinking about community programs, policing, and surveillance: How many young people did police document under the guise of oper-ating a community program? What did they do with the information?

The Cops and Kids website features a group of predominantly Black students wearing T-shirts that say "POLICE & YOUTH." How much of the interaction between police and Black children includes the kind of surveillance and documentation Gerald and his peers experienced? How can officers, who engage with kids through everything from summer camps to cooking classes to sports programs, do so without substantial training and expertise working with children? Why did we allow them to bring their weapons into community spaces? And how many educators, community workers, and parents are eager for these interactions, despite the obvious risks to kids, especially Black kids? We often learn about police surveillance and mistreatment of our young people well after the fact, because kids don't feel safe talking about it, or because they don't realize it's happening to them.

On May 23, 2007, when I was working at the community centre, Jordan Manners was fatally shot in the chest inside C.W. Jefferys Collegiate Institute, in Toronto. He had just turned fifteen. Jordan's murder was the first time in the city's history that a student had been shot and killed inside a school. A couple of months later police arrested two seventeen-year-old boys and charged them with Jordan's murder. The two were later acquitted after the jury failed to agree on a verdict.

The public conversation in response to the shooting centred heavily on race—Jordan was Black, and C. W. Jefferys is located in northwest Toronto. The school is near Finch Avenue and Keele Street, but media immediately connected it to Jane and Finch, a neighbourhood that news stories use as shorthand for crime, street gangs, and blackness in the city.

Jordan's mother, Loreen Small, told the media that she waited for more than a day after her son's death before officials allowed her to see his body. At the hospital, on the evening Jordan died, police arrested his brother Calvin and held him for several hours for allegedly uttering threats. Police never made it clear who the young man may have threatened, and released him without any charges.

The *Toronto Star*'s Rosie DiManno, who reported this news, remarked, "It is hard to imagine any victimized family being treated with such a dearth of compassion in their moment of loss." After sympathizing with the family, DiManno reversed herself in the next paragraph when she observed that although Jordan had never been in trouble with the law, "others in the family were described to the *Star* as 'known to police.'" More than seven months after Jordan's death, Small's lawyer said that officials at the Toronto District School Board had never contacted her to express condolences. The initial disregard shown to Jordan's family after his death was a sign of things to come.

Shortly after Jordan died, the Toronto District School Board commissioned a report on school safety that initially focused on an area of schools called Northwest 2, which included C. W. Jefferys and others in the Jane–Finch area. In August 2007, the School Community Safety Advisory Panel, which was tasked with writing the report and included Julian Falconer (to represent Dafonte Miller) requested more time and a broader mandate to "investigate security concerns at other schools in the area."

Ultimately the panel investigated violence in schools across Toronto and found that "while it is clear that the NW2 family of schools seriously underreports incidents, it is also equally clear that violence in general, and gun incidents and sexual assaults in particular, is a City-wide phenomenon." Despite this finding, the initial focus on Jane and Finch created a public impression that Jordan's murder had something particular to do with his neighbourhood.

The panel's final report concluded that Jordan's death was the result both of "years of neglect of our marginalized communities" by the TDSB and of a new school funding formula that shortchanged schools in large urban centres. The report states that "in April 1998, early figures based on the new funding formula were released and the TDSB was advised that its funding would decrease from approximately $92 million to $63 million for textbooks and classroom supplies, including: books, learning materials, workbooks, resource materials, computer software, CD-ROMs, and internet expenses. As a result of the decreased funding, the TDSB announced that it would have to close 120 schools."

The report said schools, including C. W. Jefferys, simply didn't have the money and resources to support students who might be struggling in the classroom or at home. It blamed the provincial Conservative government of Mike Harris for years of underfunding and punitive measures against kids. "The impact was, in effect, to push youth out of the schools into a setting where essential supports had been removed," said the report. "Consultees, such as Dr. Akua Benjamin, refer to this resulting generation of youth as the 'walking wounded' for whom hope and pride have been replaced by alienation and radicalization."

The report also noted a culture of fear and hopelessness among many teachers and school officials who failed to report violence because they believed it would harm their careers. Jordan's homeroom teacher, Bruce Miles, told media that school administrators were in denial about the levels of violence and dysfunction within schools. "Survival is managing your career," said Miles. "And managing your career is keeping your school out of the newspapers."

It was under these circumstances that Toronto police approached local boards and recommended that armed, uniformed police officers be placed in certain schools. Police Chief Bill Blair pushed the idea without formally consulting the public or even the city's elected school board trustees. Neither the TDSB nor the Toronto Catholic District School Board held a single vote to implement the School Resource Officer program.

By the spring of 2008, police and board officials were talking about police in schools as a foregone conclusion, and they met privately to decide which schools would host officers. Despite the evidence that violence was a problem in schools all over the city, officials predictably decided not to station police in schools in predominantly white and affluent neighbourhoods. Instead, they selected many schools in predominantly racialized neighbourhoods in north Etobicoke, North York, and Scarborough. The school boards did not publicize the list of the schools chosen for the program, nor the methods by which they had been chosen.

Even some elected trustees were caught off guard by the board's decisions. "I'm appalled that the board would consider a police presence in our schools," said trustee Stephanie Payne, who represented the area that included C. W. Jefferys. "If we turn schools into a police state, kids will be scared to come to school." Like some other trustees, Payne initially asked the board not to place officers at any of the schools in her constituency. But months later, after a student was stabbed at Jefferys, Payne agreed the school should host a police officer. Parents opposed to the initiative and afraid for their kids had little input on police presence in schools.

During this time local community groups began organizing to resist the police-in-schools program. The Newly Organized Coalition Opposing Police in Schools—NO COPS—was founded in northwest Toronto in December 2008. One of its members, a high school student named Kabir Joshi-Vijayan, described the police-in-schools program as "another way to increase the harassment and targeting of marginalized people in the school." Like many of the program's critics, Joshi-Vijayan was worried the police presence would simply alienate Black and other racialized students and threaten their education. "If there's a kid that's troubled, that's maybe doing something bad in school, if you kick them out of school, that kid is right away in a situation where crime is the only alternative."

From the start, Chief Bill Blair tried to distance the police-in-schools program from Jordan Manners's death and the ensuing panic about student safety. He insisted he had not the presence of intention to militarize schools and that armed police were meant to build relationships with kids.

On October 2, 2009, Constable Syed Ali Moosvi, who was stationed at Northern Secondary School in central Toronto, arrested a sixteen-year-old Black student in the hallway. It was the first publicly reported arrest of a student in school by a school resource officer. According to several students who witnessed the incident, it escalated when the student referred to the cop as "bacon." So here was a Black student who had negative feelings about the police. An officer whose priority according to the police chief was relationship-building might have started a conversation, or simply said nothing at all.

Instead Moosvi demanded the student's ID, and when the kid refused, Moosvi told him to put his hands behind his back. At the time of this incident, Northern Secondary used a lanyard system to identify students. Each student had to wear identification around their neck to prove they attended the school. The student involved in the incident was wearing his lanyard when Constable Moosvi began questioning him.

As Moosvi arrested the student, other students demanded he stop, saying the student had done nothing wrong. Moosvi repeatedly ignored the student's insistence that he be told why he was being arrested. One young person filmed this part of the arrest on his cellphone and later uploaded it to YouTube.

Police charged the teen with assault with intent to resist arrest. Even though the student was wearing the school lanyard when Moosvi arrested him, and had no further responsibility to identify himself to anyone, the police continued to justify the charge on the basis that the youth had refused to identify himself. A police spokesperson acknowledged that the youth had been wearing his lanyard. "The student had an ID card, and flashed it at the officer, but not being able to read the name on it, the officer continued to speak with the student."

According to the spokesperson, Moosvi's apparent inability to identify the youth, "caused greater concern, making the officer think, 'What's this person hiding?'" She confirmed that the student "was being investigated as a trespasser at that time." Investigated as a trespasser in his own school. Northern's administrators decided to add to the criminal jeopardy the young man was already facing by suspending him, and he eventually left the school, while Moosvi remained stationed there.

Before Moosvi became an SRO, he was charged with assaulting a Black deaf man named Peter Owusu-Ansah in the Northern school parking lot in 2002. Owusu-Ansah, a twenty-five-year old carpenter from Ghana, said he and a group of friends—all of them Black and deaf or hearing-impaired—were carded by police after leaving a basketball game at a community centre. Owusu-Ansah told the court Moosvi assaulted him after asking him to identify himself. Moosvi claimed he and another officer had taken Owusu-Ansah to the parking lot located towards the rear of the school, at one o'clock in the morning, to have a safe place to talk away from traffic. Although the judge ultimately acquitted Moosvi and another officer of assault, he said Moosvi's explanation of the events "defied common sense."

A couple of weeks after the incident inside Northern, about a hundred students held a demonstration outside the school. One of the student organizers described the dynamic the program had introduced into schools, saying, "It creates incidents that weren't there before. If you look back at the incident that was put on YouTube, that's a situation that could have been resolved by detention or a trip to the principal's office if a teacher was dealing with it."

Around the same time, a student at a school in Scarborough said of his interactions with the police officer stationed there, "It's like they're not there to look out for you but are looking at you. It's all [B.S.] that they're trying to get to know me. They're here to do their job."

But the cops were hell-bent on "improving relationships," so the program continued—as did the stories of the disproportionate arrest of Black, Indigenous, disabled, and undocumented students. I can't tell you exactly how many other students were arrested or charged or suspended or expelled as a result of interactions with an officer stationed inside their schools—neither the police nor the schools documented any of this information. They didn't care to know.

In May 2017, the Toronto Police Services Board delayed a vote on the future of the SRO program, which in turn allowed the growing coalition of community groups and individuals against the program more time to organize. Ken Jeffers, the only Black member of the Police Services Board, had suggested a vote to temporarily suspend the program to explore the many concerns of students, teachers, and activists. Through a motion from Mayor John Tory, the board chose to delay Jeffers' proposal till the next meeting, which also gave the police and their allies more time to organize.

I arrived early to the police board meeting on June 15, 2017. The first thing I noticed was the twenty or so armed officers in the room. At other meetings I'd attended, police officers who wished to observe would sit in seats on the far side of the room, separated from the public side of the gallery by the board table. On this day the cops were all over the place. A number of them occupied seats on the public side of the gallery. I watched as several students entered the room and officers rose to move, as if they'd been saving seats for just these kids. I overheard one officer, as he offered up his spot, mention something to two students about having lunch after the meeting.

I looked at the agenda and saw the names of students from the Toronto Catholic District School Board scheduled to speak in support of the SRO program at the start of the meeting, while the dozens of speakers opposed to the program were slated lower down the list. Many students had the names of their schools next to their names on the list.

Within minutes, the entire public side of the gallery was filled with dozens of students from the Catholic school board, accompanied by their teachers. Teachers had pulled the students out of class, put them on buses, and brought them to the board meeting. Not only would the teachers have needed the board's permission to do this; the board would presumably have had to pay for substitute teachers to cover the classes taught by the teachers attending the meeting.

While the boardroom was packed with supporters of the police, critics of the SRO program were prevented from entering the meeting. Once all the students were inside, police officers stationed themselves outside the door, slowing the movement of other speakers into the room. Even some media had a tough time getting inside. Then, police officers carried bicycles up from the first floor and placed them in front of the closed meeting room doors.

There were at least two hundred people in the meeting room, and at first none of us realized we'd just been barricaded inside. If a fire had broken out, if any emergency had sprung up in that crowded space, a roomful of people who might naturally rush towards the door would unwittingly have been obstructed by the cops and their bikes on the other side, and by the throng of people in the lobby the cops were blocking from coming in. Ironically, the people police put most at risk were their own supporters, the mostly teenage students in attendance under the supervision of their teachers.

Despite our protests that police were keeping dozens of people out of the room, board chair Andy Pringle and the other board members—including Mayor John Tory, and councillors Shelley Carroll and Chin Lee—insisted the meeting proceed as scheduled. Jeffers, who had initiated the motion to vote on the SRO program, opened the meeting by announcing he was withdrawing his own motion for a temporary suspension. Something had changed in the intervening month, and Jeffers now seemed to be backing down.

Pringle invited the dozens of supportive students to give their three-minute speeches about how important and upright and life-saving the police in their schools were. A few of us spoke out of turn, interrupting to demand the removal of the barricade, and advocating to get the armed cops out of the room in favour of community members, many of whom had signed up to speak at the meeting.

Along with members of Black Lives Matter–Toronto and several others, I shouted my voice raw for ninety minutes, until the police finally removed their barricade and allowed everyone in the lobby to come inside. In the interim, the police had successfully convinced many of those who'd signed up to speak against the program to leave—I'm sure many concluded they would never get in. Meanwhile, supportive students sang the police's praises, and even a few of the police officers serving within the program gave speeches about its merits.

During a recess—there were several, thanks to our constant disruptions—I was approached by an officer and told that if I continued to interrupt the meeting, I would be arrested for mischief. I witnessed officers use similar intimidation tactics with BLM-TO members, standing within inches of them when they spoke out during the meeting. Even though many white attendees also disrupted the proceedings, they were not confronted by the police in the same way. Still, many of us were ready to be arrested and dragged from that room. Our opponents, however, were not prepared for the dozens of us who stayed, and who dominated the second half of the public meeting with the same arguments and evidence against the program we'd been repeating for years.

Melanie Willson of Educators for Peace and Justice, a grassroots group of teachers and parents, spoke to the folly of expecting students critical of the program to participate in such an intimidating process inside the police headquarters. "We acknowledge that there are hardworking SROs who have organized events, volunteered their time, connected with particular students and staff. But there is a reason that the students who don't feel safe around police are not here today. This is about well-documented systemic injustice and the lived experience of students in our care. This is about the impact of the mere presence of a police officer on the education of some of Toronto's most marginalized students."

Katie German of Education Not Incarceration highlighted the cruelty of lining up students who have no problems with police to drown out kids the police are more likely to surveil: "We've heard today about youth who participate in sports programs and music programs with SROs—I need you to care about the kids who do not go to those programs because there are SROs."

Andrea Vásquez Jiménez, one of the co-chairs of the Latinx, Afro-Latin-America, Abya Yala Education Network, questioned how board members could be so unaware of the consequences of policing on racialized students. Jiménez spoke of the criminalization of all students, but most especially students who were Black, Indigenous, and people of colour: "Our youth understand how they experience these negative impacts by police," she said.

BLM-TO's Syrus Marcus Ware spoke about the police brutality his daughter had witnessed at her school. "Her fear that she has around the police in our community comes based on her experience, and no SRO program, or pizza, or cops, or barbecue is gonna take away from what she witnessed at five years old." Ware noted that while money was found to fund that SRO program, teachers who were actually trained to provide programming to kids were often unable to access the resources they needed from their schools. Ware and BLM-TO presented a petition against the police program with the signatures of thousands of Torontonians.

Gita Madan, a scholar who wrote her master's thesis on the issue of police officers in Toronto schools, came with receipts. "Black, Indigenous, racialized and undocumented students are criminalized through school-based policing. There is a lot of research about it out there," Madan told the board members, "and it was actually your responsibility to do this research before you implemented this program." Madan's research highlights the disproportionate negative outcomes for racialized students in the United States when schools introduce police officers and other strict disciplinary measures. "In Delaware in 2010–2011, Black students were three and half times more likely to be arrested in school than White students. In 2007–2008 in Philadelphia, a Black student was three and a half times more likely, and a Latino student one and a half times more likely, to be taken into custody from school than a White student. Black students make up only 21% of the youth in Florida, but were the subject of 46% of all 2011 school-related referrals to law enforcement."

Madan further pointed out that the program appeared to violate a number of the schools' policies, including educators' duty to protect students and their personal information from police access without parental permission. Through her research, Madan had discovered an agreement between SROs and the Canada Border Service Agency to hold weekly meetings to share information, presumably about undocumented students—a direct contravention of Toronto's Access Without Fear policies, which are often referred to as Sanctuary City protections.

Sabrina "Butterfly" Gopaul, a longstanding organizer and resident of Jane and Finch who had fought against the SRO program from the start, spoke on behalf of Jane Finch Action Against Poverty. Butterfly talked about the untold cost of aggressively policing her community. "That money, given by the city of Toronto, province, and the feds, could have gone to mediation, restorative justice, youth workers, community workers, educators, sexual health workers, jobs for our young people."

I will never forget the words of Ren Niles, a Black woman and parent who refused to mince words. "Further desire to study this situation at the detriment of the community is both reckless, and an admission of failure to properly monitor a city program that involves the lives and safety of minors," said Niles. "That the minors in question are predominantly Black and youth of colour is further damning. Further study could also be interpreted as the infantilization of a community by paternalistic authority, in essence making a bold statement that the city of Toronto does not believe that a community of grown-ass adults are capable of deciding what is good for themselves, their children, or their community."

Members of Stand Up for Racial Justice Toronto (SURJ), Toronto Youth Cabinet, and No One Is Illegal–Toronto also spoke against cops in schools. After eight hours of resisting, of fighting for the opportunity to even speak, we watched as Mayor Tory and his board did what they usually do when faced with a demand from community to stand up to police authority—they stalled. The board ultimately voted to review the SRO program, and to keep it running during the review. As opponents of the program lambasted Jeffers for abandoning his efforts to suspend the program, he lashed out. Jeffers, who'd become more defensive as the meeting wore on, countered our criticisms by saying he'd risked his life for Black people by marching during the civil rights movement. "You ever had a gun pointed in your face?" he shouted.

That was the night the winds shifted. We endured threats, dirty tricks, a betrayal from a board member, and a literal police barricade, and by the end of the meeting we were still singing and chanting.

Many of the same people who brought the fight to the police board in June worked to influence the two major school boards. The Catholic board, which had helped to stack the June board meeting, was, unsurprisingly, cold to these efforts. But many of the TDSB's twenty-two trustees were finally willing to hear from advocates and to do their own homework. In August of 2017, the TDSB voted to conduct a review of the SRO program and suspend the program until the review was finished. Instead of simply surveying students and parents and siding with the majority, the board took an equity approach, focusing on the harm to students who faced systemic discrimination. Through its consultations, the board heard from thousands of students, parents, and teachers who said the program made them less safe and welcome. According to the review's final report, most students in the focus groups "noted that the presence of the SRO often made them feel intimidated, and frequently mentioned feeling that they were under continual surveillance and suspicion, leading many of them to stay away from school." That's how we arrived at the packed school board meeting in November 2017.

I listened as trustees rose in succession to say what we'd been saying for a decade: that police were targeting the same children they'd historically targeted for surveillance and documentation. That the permanent harm done to a minority of students should never be justified by claims of what was needed to make the majority "feel safe." That police were not the adults we wanted confronting our kids. Trustee Tiffany Ford rose to speak and prefaced her comments by honouring Jordan Manners, and acknowledging that his death had become a talking point to advance the SRO program for a decade. "I can't imagine how that has been for his family," Ford said. Although the police had denied Manners's death had sparked their introduction of the program, Ford clearly believed, as many of us did, that police used his death as the silent pretext to militarize our public schools.

Women trustees such as Ford, Marit Stiles, Ausma Malik, and Jennifer Story led the vote to cancel the program at the TDSB. And after they voted it down, those public officials came out into the lobby and danced with us in front of the news media. One of our friends had brought her daughter to witness the historic vote—she had tears in her eyes as we jumped and hugged and shouted. "I'm happy," she said through the tears, "but I'm still angry we had to fight so hard just to get here."

As I write this, the Toronto Catholic District School Board continues to host armed police officers in its schools, as do dozens of school boards in Ontario and across the country.

competing interests
(december)

I'm often uncomfortable attaching the label "activist" to myself but I try not to get hung up on it. This work to free ourselves, this "wake work" as professor Christina Sharpe calls it, exceeds any title I could give it. But so much of the public conversation surrounding our work focuses on what we call ourselves, and on what right we have to speak and act as we do. People who have time for these questions are dodging much more important ones: What is the purpose of activism? What are we all responsible for in the world, whether we call ourselves activists or not?

There are a million permutations of "who is an activist" in popular conversation. When I shut down the police board meeting in April 2017, too much of the public discussion focused on whether I had acted in those moments as a journalist or an activist. Commentators used this irrelevant question to sidestep the issue of carding, which was the substance of my protest. These arguments about titles put the propriety of the speaker above their message—if you are not the appropriate person to be speaking, and if you don't say it right, and at the right time and place, at the convenience of the people with the real power to change things, then they reserve the right to ignore you.

In December of 2017, I witnessed the public launch of the Federation of Black Canadians—the FBC—a lobby group founded in collaboration with and for the benefit of powerful political forces in Canada, particularly the federal Liberal Party. From its first appearance at the National Black Canadians Summit in Toronto, FBC declared itself a unified advocacy voice for Black people—yet almost no Black people in Canada had ever heard of it. This is not the first time political elites have tried to sell the Black community's tireless work back to us, to argue that all activism is equal, that all Black actors are pushing in the same direction, to offer us access to power in exchange for a less radical and urgent politics. Sorry, naw. Black people have to grapple with politics too, particularly the politics of class that allows a few of us to be comfortable and patient in the storm while many more of us are barely treading water.

In late 2017 I got an invitation to the inaugural National Black Canadians Summit, a three-day conference at the Toronto Reference Library hosted by the Michaëlle Jean Foundation. Jean, a former governor general and the only Black person to hold that position, is one of the most visible and celebrated Black people in recent Canadian history. The foundation asked me to attend the summit and take part in a panel discussion on media. I knew almost nothing about the foundation's work or the larger purpose of the summit. I only knew a lot of Black people from across the country whom I respect would be there, so I immediately accepted the invitation.

The first evening of the summit was a gala, and I sat near the back of the long library salon amongst many familiar faces, all of us curious to learn exactly what vision the organizers had for this seemingly historic gathering. The foundation's Peter Flegel was the first to address us. He said our coming together was inspired by Black youth, many of whom were artists whose work the foundation had promoted. He told us the youth had given his organization two mandates for the summit: first, to serve as "a national gathering where people would have an opportunity not only to share best practices and network but to take it a step further and begin working on a national strategic action plan." Flegel didn't identify any of these young artists, or explain why they believed his foundation was the right group to organize this forum.

The youths' second mandate, according to Flegel, was to address "the need for a national advocacy organization that could represent the interests and needs—that are diverse, of course—of Black Canadians across the country." Not once during the entire conference were any of these artists, who'd apparently inspired our collective presence, formally introduced. We never learned their names or what kind of "best practices" they meant to share with us.

Flegel went on about the need for advocacy, saying, "It just happened that we had the privilege of coming across a wonderful person, a judge who I'm sure many of you know, Justice Donald McLeod . . . who's spearheading a really interesting national project which I think resonates very much with the recommendations." So McLeod, a sitting Ontario Court judge was starting a Black political advocacy group? It seemed so bizarre. McLeod, a tall, bald Black man in a suit and thickly knotted black tie, was next at the mic.

"Good evening, everyone," he said. "So this starts about a year and a half ago, almost eighteen months. There's a shooting. The person that gets shot is a young girl, and she's pregnant. She dies and so does the baby. It resonates—I actually went to school with her aunt. It becomes something that's a never-ending story. So as a result there's a meeting, there's discussions, and then we find ourselves eighteen months later where we're standing today."

Although McLeod never mentioned her name, many of us knew that the "young girl" he referred to was Candice Rochelle Bobb, the thirty-five-year-old Mississauga woman who was killed in May 2016 during a drive-by shooting in Toronto's Rexdale neighbourhood as she sat in a parked vehicle. Bobb was five months pregnant at the time. Her baby boy, Kyrie, was delivered prematurely, and died three weeks later. I've since heard McLeod repeat this FBC origin story several times on television and in print interviews. Never once has he named Bobb or said anything about her, except that he was acquainted with one of her relatives. Nor has he explained how her death had informed the advocacy of FBC, or if FBC was supporting the family.

I wondered how you could be moved to start an organization based on such a story but say so little about the woman herself and even less about the work she inspired. The absence of that fuller context and connection seemed to dishonour Bobb's memory, and McLeod's easy manner of alluding to her and then moving on without further reference has stayed with me.

"The rallying cry of the federation is and continues to be 'nothing about us without us,'" McLeod intoned. He liked that line so much he said it three times. He didn't give any details of the Federation's advocacy. He didn't name or introduce a single member of the group or hint at its structure. Nor did he tell the hundreds of Black people in the room how we might get involved. But McLeod did challenge the idea that Black Canadians, in all our diversity, are not united. "Today I speak against the false narrative. Today I constitute a new season," the judge said. "Truth be told, we are more unified now than we have ever been."

I could feel the energy I had brought into the room flowing out of me. The next part of the gala was heavy on formal ceremony, on what I call colonial greetings: a bunch of Black people get together and we feel obliged to sit quietly while politicians and leaders of institutions speak at us about the significance of our blackness. The first to do so was Prime Minister Justin Trudeau in a videotaped message, who apologized that he couldn't be with us, speaking in his dramatic tenor: "When I met with the federation this summer, I got to hear directly about some of the issues facing Black communities across Canada. They included recommendations put forward by the UN to mark the Decade for People of African Descent. I look forward to continuing the conversation on that with all of you in the weeks and months ahead."

The United Nations International Decade for People of African Descent, a global push for economic and social change, was approaching the end of its third full year, and I'd not heard Trudeau mention it before, not even during his election campaign two years earlier. I was so struck by that detail that I almost missed the fact that, months before the public knew of any federation, the group had already met with the prime minister.

Next to speak was John Tory—the man who had waffled on carding and the police-in-schools program, and refused to cancel either. The man who, as a member of the police board, had stalled a proper investigation of the assault of Dafonte Miller. The man who on this evening boasted of organizing dozens of public meetings about anti-Black racism and overseeing the city's first ever anti-Black racism strategy and action plan. Tory didn't mention that for two years he had resisted Black Lives Matter's call to address anti-Black racism. Instead Tory took the credit: "I think the most important thing may well be that the city will have an anti-Black racism strategy and action plan for the first time, initiated by a mayor—and that is *me*—who has acknowledged, as I will again now, that anti-Black racism exists in the city of Toronto."

Around the time of Tory's speech, Sandy Hudson of BLM-TO tweeted, "I'm wondering why the fuck @JohnTory is being given a chance to campaign at the National Black Canadians Summit after his consistent track record of betrayal to Black communities."

Ahmed Hussen, the federal minister of immigration, refugees, and citizenship, spoke next, and disclosed that he not only knew about FBC but was some sort of member. "I met with the federation, and with Justice Donald McLeod, and I asked a very simple question. I said, do you want me to be an ally, or do you want me to roll my sleeves and actually join the federation and be part of the working group. And the enthusiastic response was, we're not gonna let you go off that easy, we want you to work with us."

If you're keeping score at home, a sitting Ontario Court judge started a group to lobby the federal government on Black Canadians' behalf without any broad public knowledge or input, and then made a sitting federal cabinet minister one of his partners. Hussen informed the gala that he'd helped to organize a lobby day on Parliament Hill and a face-to-face meeting with Trudeau that lasted over two hours. He didn't mention what they spoke about. A very interesting lobby group this was. By the time all the politicians had finished campaigning before us, the better part of an hour was gone, and even the polite people in the crowd were shifting in their seats.

The Black summit spent an untold fortune to fly Black people from all across the country to Toronto for three days. Most of those participants were given less time to speak, on smaller stages, than the mayor of

Toronto, the minister of citizenship, the federal leader of the New Democratic Party, and the leader of the provincial opposition party. The Black summit scheduled public officials to speak at the opening gala before Black elders and award recipients took the stage. Even the African drumming came after the politicians were finished speaking—we put off our very heartbeat to receive colonial greetings.

Rinaldo Walcott's words later on during the gala saved me. The renowned professor, author, and director of the University of Toronto's Women and Gender Studies Institute spoke about the enduring crisis for Black life in Canada, about the chasm between our "best in the world" backslapping and the actual conditions for Black people. "I have argued and I want to again clearly propose that any new policy actions must pass what I call the Black test," Rinaldo said. "By that I mean it should meet the test of ameliorating Black dispossession and making Black life possible. If the policy does not meet the Black test, then it is a failed policy from the first instance of its proposal."

Rinaldo's words captured my disappointment with the next two days of the summit, which sadly were not about dreaming and reimagining but about working within the existing restraints of systemic racism and calling it progress.

Among my many friends and comrades at the summit was El Jones, who for many years has done critical work with incarcerated people in Nova Scotia. Like Rinaldo, El had come to the summit to address specific government decisions and policies that harm Black people. She had recently told me about a young man in a Nova Scotia prison whom she feared would soon be deported. Abdoul Abdi, then twenty-three years old and a refugee from Somalia, had nearly finished serving a five-year prison sentence for multiple charges including aggravated assault. Upon his release in January, he would be at risk of deportation because of his criminal conviction and the fact he was not a Canadian citizen. Nova Scotia's child welfare system apprehended Abdoul and his sister Fatouma from their family when he was seven years old, only a few months after they had immigrated to Canada as refugees from Somalia. The Nova Scotia Department of Community Services became Abdoul's legal guardian and the only entity with the authority to apply for his citizenship.

Abdoul was shuffled through at least twenty group-home placements by the time he was twelve; as is so often the case in child welfare, he experienced abuse in some of these placements. But DCS never applied for Abdoul's citizenship, so when he was sentenced for a crime in his adult years, he became vulnerable to a deportation order. Minister Hussen was scheduled to speak again on the first full morning of the summit, and we planned to take the opportunity to ask him about Abdoul.

My spirit was sagging that morning after the gala, and I was late returning to the summit venue. El sent me updates on Hussen's speech as I raced over by subway. I stumbled into the salon just as Hussen began taking questions. When El and I got the mic, we explained Abdoul's situation. "There's a very simple solution to these cases," El said, "which is to recognize that Black kids, once they're taken into protection, need *protection from the state* most of all. They need protection from their high likelihood of incarceration and the resulting deportations." El said the government is responsible for the outcomes of government apprehension and family separation.

I repeated to Hussen four demands from Abdoul's supporters: a promise that non-citizen kids in care will always be granted citizenship; an acknowledgement of Canada's obligation to protect non-citizen children whom the government apprehends; recognition of Canada's international duty not to deport long-term residents who came to

Canada as children but didn't become citizens through government neglect; and an end to the deportation process of Abdoul and all former children in care who have been denied citizenship.

The room was now very quiet. Hussen told us he'd received information about Abdoul's case at the gala—we knew this because El had given a handout to Rinaldo, who had personally delivered it to Hussen. "I haven't had a chance to look at it," he told us. "I can't comment on a case where I don't know all the circumstances the way you do. What I can tell you is this: removals are not done without individuals having numerous, numerous avenues of appeal." I never know what to make of such comments. We demand justice and we get process. When Hussen repeated that he couldn't talk about Abdoul's case, I interrupted to remind him that Abdoul's was one of many such cases. "You're asking me to commit to an amnesty for all children in care," said the minister. "I can't do that because each case is unique, each case has its own circumstances, as you would know."

The minister and I had it out for a few moments more, as he refused to speak to our demands, reaffirming instead his faith in the immigration system. "I have intervened in cases, I have halted deportations hundreds of times since I became minister," Hussen said, as if to reassure us. "You have to give me the chance to look at the facts of the case, and then see whether there is an objective reason to halt or proceed with removal."

Our fight was with the system, not just with Hussen, the first Black person to inhabit his post. It's asking too much of any one person to decide who should be deported to places like Somalia, a country Canadian government officials refuse to visit and, because of dangerous conditions, warn citizens against travelling to. In many cases, deportation to certain places can be a death sentence. Our government recognized this after the earthquake in Haiti in 2010 with a pause on deportations there. But since the recognition was political, deportations were resumed while Haiti was still an extremely dangerous, unstable, and inhospitable place. No individual should be asked to consider sending human beings to places where they are likely to die. We were asking Hussen, as Rinaldo had encouraged us to do, to fundamentally change the system instead of trying in vain to operate within its immoral confines.

As the session ended, El and I were confronted by many other participants. A few were extremely supportive and asked how they could help advocate for Abdoul. But most people were upset with us. "I thought you were very rude to the minister," an older Black woman told me. "We don't often get our people in positions like his, and we need to be patient with them." No one who confronted me disagreed with our demands—they took issue only with my apparent lack of respect for Hussen.

It's one thing when white folks try to police our tone and endlessly advise us that we've chosen the wrong time or place or method to speak up. Hearing it from other Black people always hurts my heart. But it's part of the struggle I see before us, especially the younger generation of Black people fighting for radical change today. We have to be willing to challenge some of our elders and point out that, in spite of the progress they have made, we still can't afford to be polite and submissive in the face of power. In fact, now that people like Hussen who, even as they sell their personal Black success stories to us, are in a position to help kick out other Black people, we have to be extra vigilant about complicity with a state that keeps hurting us.

The Black summit did not seem to include Black people unless they had money, or a title, or a university degree, or a public profile. The Black summit didn't provide childcare, or sign-language interpretation, or a prayer room, or transit tokens. It didn't ask us about our pronouns. It definitely did not ask us about our politics.

The Black summit was sponsored and facilitated by the multinational consulting firm Deloitte, who provided a quote with their logo in the promo video: "Being inclusive isn't just the right thing to do, it's also the smart thing to do. Inclusive firms outperform the rest, and Canada needs more." One day we will stop asking multinational companies to be more inclusive of us and start taking our shit back.

The organizers of this summit just threw us into some workshops that we did not ask for or help to inform, with white facilitators from a professional consulting firm who claimed expertise in building consensus. They provided the shittiest of boxed lunches for Black people who woulda no doubt loved some fried plantain or chicken or rice and peas. Rice and *anything*, damn. But that was the Black summit.

The Black summit was organized by the Michaëlle Jean Foundation, which afterwards gave participants' contact information to the Federation of Black Canadians without asking our permission. An advocacy organization that had told us nothing about its mandate, structure, membership, or values now had the ability not only to contact us but to boast about its instant and unearned connection to influential Black people across Canada.

You can't just sit a bunch of Black people together and expect us to solve all our problems. This might sound basic, but too many of our people believe it. They preach of a presumably unique lack of unity among Black people. Black Canadian mythology will tell you that while Jewish, Chinese, and Indian people are united, we are not. If only we would stick together like they do, if only we could convene and resolve our differences without shouting or disagreeing with each other, we too could move forward.

When Donald McLeod declared at the gala that Black people are more united than ever, he was addressing the myth that there is something singularly deficient about Black people that prevents us from getting along. But in stating our unity as fact, McLeod also got it wrong. Black people are not united, although there is definitely an expectation that we ought to be, an expectation that experiencing hundreds of years of racism should naturally have brought us together. We are not united, and the idea that disagreement or infighting is our unique struggle as Black people is itself racist.

McLeod's misstatement of Black unity matters because it leads powerful and influential Black people like him to bypass the entrenched struggle for Black life that Rinaldo spoke of, to collapse all our differences as Black people. McLeod and his federation and the Michaëlle Jean Foundation got hundreds of Black people into a room and pretended solutions would naturally follow. Organizers bypassed the hard work of helping participants meet, get to know one another, learn about one another's work, and seek some consensus from diverse points of view. We could interpret this as a failed attempt at organizing, but that's too generous for Black folks with millions of dollars who are wooing us with their experience and knowledge. The federation, the foundation, and their political friends already had a political agenda, and were simply pushing us to get on board.

We knew almost nothing about the Federation of Black Canadians when the group introduced itself at the summit, and Justice McLeod gave us very little info during the event. Afterwards I did my homework and found out a few interesting facts. The federation was created in private and selected twelve individuals to form its steering committee, including McLeod as chairperson. Ebyan Farah was chosen as FBC's "stakeholder relations" representative—Farah is the wife of Minister

Hussen. Somehow this didn't come up during the summit, not even when Hussen described his own work with the group at the gala.

Obviously, the presence of a cabinet minister's wife in the formal leadership of a group that lobbies the government raises questions of conflict of interest. In February 2018, I published a report that included Farah's involvement with FBC—she resigned the following day. A statement on the FBC website read, "Recognizing the perception of conflict, Ebyan has not participated in any discussions with the government since 2016." A second FBC steering committee member also left her position immediately after my reporting.

McLeod's participation in lobbying the federal government while serving as a judge in Ontario also raised questions. It is against the rules of the Ontario judiciary for a judge to get involved with partisan interests, to use the prestige of their office for fundraising, or to engage in any activity that creates the appearance of conflict of interest. McLeod told media that he had met not only with Trudeau in recent months but with Trudeau's chief of staff and several cabinet ministers. A journalist who interviewed McLeod reported that the judge then "received a call from Ottawa indicating they would prefer the initiative to be national."

During its creation, FBC didn't reach out to any radical organizers or groups across the country. McLeod addressed his group's heavily institutional makeup in an interview. "Those that weren't on the list weren't shunned," he said. "It's just because I didn't know you or I didn't know you well enough to trust you. As a sitting judge, if I brought someone that I didn't know or trust could compromise my money. I had to make sure I understood who was going to be in that room."

Of course the government would rather work with FBC than with Black folks who will risk everything to challenge white supremacy.

FBC debuted at the end of a year of relentless Black activism that made our governments nervous, and eager for alternative ways to court our communities. FBC's real purpose is to create the veneer of a united Black community that is eager to work with the federal Liberal government. Unlike the troublesome Black radicals who keep challenging the government, FBC is a respectable group with connections and access. It's a group of Black professionals, particularly those in the public sector, who've "made it," and who want us to believe their personal successes are about to translate into gains for the whole community, as long as we behave ourselves and make nice with power.

How can the Black police officers, Crown attorneys, and corrections officials who founded FBC call for systemic change without angering their superiors and endangering their jobs? How can a Black judge whose job it is to sentence people to jail be an effective public advocate against racist laws, policing, and sentencing? That is not to say McLeod doesn't care, or that he is not a *real* advocate for Black people. But people like him are limited in what they can say about white supremacy by their participation in its institutions. There is a price to pay for being Black and wanting real change. Black people inside government institutions would have to risk their careers to call out white supremacy and anti-Black racism. I don't expect them to do that, and I'm deeply skeptical when any Black person or group offers us progress that doesn't require sacrifice, confrontation, and real demands.

I wrote several public blog posts and columns in early 2018 about my concerns with FBC. An up-and-coming Black lawyer in Toronto responded on Facebook: "I think that Donald, FBC and all players are well-intentioned. Even if this ends up being a Lib PR stunt it will result in 'Black issues' getting national attn, so why throw them under the bus?" I can only reply that I am not riding the same bus as McLeod and his FBC friends. We are not fighting for the same things, and that's fine as long as we can acknowledge it.

In November of 2018, Justice Donald McLeod faced a disciplinary hearing at the Ontario Judicial Council after a fellow judge named Faith Finnestad filed a complaint regarding his involvement with FBC. Although the council dismissed the complaint, it determined that McLeod's activities with FBC "was incompatible with judicial office," but was not serious enough to find him guilty of misconduct. The decision also made specific reference to public criticisms of FBC's works, saying, "There are real and reasonable disagreements within the Black community concerning both the goals that members of the community should pursue and the means they should employ to achieve those goals."

A passionate defender of FBC challenged me on social media, and argued that there was room for its advocacy as a complementary force to groups like BLM-TO. Think about Malcolm X and Martin Luther King, he told me. Well I've thought about it. Malcolm X told the truth about Africans enslaved on plantations in the United States. He told us to be wary of house negroes, the few people chosen to personally serve the oppressor and enjoy more comforts at the expense of the negroes in the field. If I understand Malcolm's teachings, oppressed Black people of his era couldn't wait for their more fortunate peers to save them or speak for them, and neither can we.

abdoul & fatouma

(january)

Happy new year, me no die oh!
Tell God tenki for long life!

We knew in December that Abdoul Abdi was at risk of deportation, and we brought the message to the highest level, to the immigration minister who'd boasted he'd stopped hundreds of other deportations. But Ahmed Hussen and his government didn't stop Abdoul's deportation. Instead, border officials carried on with their quest to expel a young man who has only known Canada as his home.

Canada invited Abdoul and his family to live here. Out of a presumed concern for his safety, a child welfare agency separated Abdoul and his sister, Fatouma, from their family. But we didn't care for them as we promised we would, and when Abdoul ended up in jail, our system deemed him disposable. Imagine all the money, time, and resources spent during the past two decades to bring Abdoul to Canada through the refugee system, to apprehend him into the child welfare system, and to put him through the prison system. We invested so much, only to decide that our failed experiment with a Black child's life was no longer worth the effort, that we should get rid of him. Meet the new year, same as the old year.

Abdoul was born in Saudi Arabia in 1993. He and his refugee family are of Somali heritage, and in the year of Abdoul's birth, Somalia was one of the most dangerous places in the world. Political instability, famine, and civil war caused hundreds of thousands of Somalis to make dangerous escapes across the Gulf of Aden to Yemen and to the neighbouring countries of Kenya, Ethiopia, Djibouti, and Uganda. With the endorsement of the United Nations, the United States had led a military operation into Somalia in 1992 on a mission to use "all necessary means" to create enough stability for humanitarian aid. Among the UN troops were 1,400 Canadian soldiers.

On March 16, 1993, several members of the Canadian Airborne Regiment apprehended a sixteen-year-old boy named Shidane Abukar Arone who had entered their military compound in the Somali town of Belet Uen. Under the direction of their superiors, who had given permission to shoot or assault civilians in such circumstances, the soldiers tied Arone up and blindfolded him. Over the next three hours, the Canadians tortured the boy: they punched him, kicked him with their boots, beat him with a baton, burned him with a lit cigarillo, and struck him with a metal bar. One soldier used a broom handle to sexually assault the boy. Although many other soldiers heard Arone screaming in pain, they didn't intervene. The teenager died close to midnight— soldiers said he repeated the same word several times before he lost consciousness: "Canada."

Several of the soldiers who participated in the torture posed for photos with Arone's bloodied body. Barry Armstrong, a military doctor, would later testify that senior military officials destroyed many of these pictures together with other evidence of the murder, but some photos survived and were ultimately published. Canadians were horrified by the images on TV and in newspapers.

In time the public learned of other acts of violence and murder committed by Canadian soldiers. Twelve days before the murder of Arone, Canadian soldiers shot two Somali civilians who were walking near a military compound. Both men were shot in the back; twenty-nine-year-old Abdi Hunde Bei Sabrie received a fatal shot to the back of his head. It was later reported that soldiers had intentionally left out food and water, presumably to bait Somali civilians to come near the camp. Again it was Dr. Armstrong who spoke up about the killing of Abdi. Without his acts of whistle-blowing, Canadians may never have learned all we did about our military's war crimes.

Before its deployment of troops to Somalia, the Canadian government had been investigating neo-Nazi organizations at CFB Petawawa, the base that was home to the Airborne Regiment that then engaged in the war crimes. In her book *Men, Militarism, and UN Peacekeeping*, Sandra Whitworth summarizes the chilling revelation that senior military officials had allowed members of the Airborne Regiment who were either "known members of racist skinhead organizations or who were under investigation for suspected skinhead and neo-nazi activity to be deployed to Somalia."

The Airborne Regiment's conduct was the subject of a federal investigation now known as the Somalia Inquiry. Nine soldiers were charged for their participation in Arone's murder. Kyle Brown was convicted of second-degree murder and torture, and Mark Boland pleaded guilty to negligent performance of duty. All others were acquitted, while Clayton

Matchee, who along with Brown was charged for murder, had his charges dropped after he tried to hang himself and sustained severe brain damage. The government ended the inquiry before investigators could fully understand the extent of the Armed Forces' misconduct, particularly the roles of senior government officials and military police. The inquiry's commissioners said that military officers lied to the inquiry and that they believed officials attempted to cover up the true nature of the abuses. Upon the release of the inquiry's report in 1997, Liberal Defence Minister Art Eggleton called it "a blanket condemnation of our military; an unfair and unjust one."

Today, a quarter century after Canada knowingly sent neo-Nazis to East Africa, a white supremacist group calling itself the Proud Boys boasts of chapters within the Canadian Armed Forces. The Southern Poverty Law Center notes that although the Proud Boys publicly claim they are not white supremacists, "their disavowals of bigotry are belied by their actions: rank-and-file Proud Boys and leaders regularly spout white nationalist memes and maintain affiliations with known extremists. They are known for anti-Muslim and misogynistic rhetoric. Proud Boys have appeared alongside other hate groups at extremist gatherings like the 'Unite the Right' rally in Charlottesville."

In the summer of 2017, CBC Television suggested that Canadians needed an introduction to this hate group, and invited Proud Boys co-founder Gavin McInnes on air. McInnes, who is also the co-founder of Vice Media and a self-described male chauvinist and Islamophobe, used the interview to deny the genocide of Mi'kmaq people in Nova Scotia by Edward Cornwallis, the so-called founder of Nova Scotia's capital city on that stolen territory. The interview was aired, complete with McInnes's lies. Canadians still don't understand the extent of the white supremacist organizing our government uncovered within the military twenty-five years ago. Now that it has resurfaced in plain view, we are giving it a hearing for novelty's sake.

Abdoul, his older sister, Fatouma, his mother, and two of his aunts were living in a refugee camp in Djibouti in 1997 when they made contact with Canadian Immigration officials. The family applied to be government-sponsored refugees at that time, but the process lasted three years, and Abdoul's and Fatouma's mother died while the family was waiting in Saudi Arabia. When the siblings came to Cape Breton in 2000 as permanent residents, their aunt Asha Ali had become their legal guardian.

The family soon moved to Halifax, and Asha enrolled the children in school. She says she still does not understand why Nova Scotia's Department of Community Services (DCS) investigated her and decided to apprehend both Fatouma and Abdoul only months after their arrival in Halifax. Asha was just learning English at the time and says DCS did not provide her with an interpreter to communicate in Somali. Abdoul was only seven and Fatouma nine when the government apprehended them. Asha fought unsuccessfully through the courts to get them back. Both children became permanent Crown wards, meaning the government was legally responsible for their care. As Fatouma would later observe, "The government was our parents."

Abdoul and Fatouma were separated during their first years in the system. It's hard to imagine how difficult it must have been for these children, who had recently lost their mother and been separated from their adult relatives, to then be without one another. Abdoul was moved through thirty-one different placements. The longest of those was a three-year stay with a foster family that Abdoul says was abusive to him. Although DCS was the only entity that could legally apply for

Abdoul's citizenship, it never did. In 2013, Abdoul was arrested on several charges and in 2014 pleaded guilty to aggravated assault, theft of a motor vehicle, dangerous driving, and assaulting a police officer with a vehicle. He was sentenced to five years in prison, minus the six months he'd already served while awaiting trial. Upon this decision, Abdoul's lawyer noted that his client's immigration papers were "messed up" and that Abdoul could therefore face deportation upon his release.

I met El Jones in 2016 while filming Charles Officer's documentary *The Skin We're In*. In collaboration with Charles and his producer, Jake Yanowski, I travelled to Halifax, Saskatoon, and my birthplace of Red Deer, Alberta, to tell stories about Black life in Canada. As part of the documentary, El helped to organize a gathering at Halifax's Kwacha House, a legendary Black community space where, fifty years earlier, the National Film Board had filmed a conversation with activist Burnley Allan "Rocky" Jones. Jones, together with his wife, Joan Jones, an activist, lawyer, and writer, founded Kwacha House as well as the Black United Front of Nova Scotia, a collective of residents seeking economic and political justice.

I barely had time to speak to El during our brief time in Halifax, but we stayed in touch and reconnected on several of my subsequent visits. It was El who first told me about Abdoul and introduced me to his lawyer Benjamin Perryman, who had agreed to take on Abdoul's deportation case. El also connected me with Abdoul's aunt Asha, who had moved to Toronto, and his sister Fatouma, who was still living in Halifax.

El, in turn, had met Abdoul through his cellmate Jordan Ward, a young man who happened to be the nephew of Ashley Smith, a teenager who died in 2007 while in custody at the Grand Valley Institution in

Kitchener, Ontario. El would later recount, "Because of the experience that that family had had with experiencing state injustice, I think [Jordan] was able to recognize the pain that Abdoul was going through." Jordan reached out to El, who for many years has been working directly with people incarcerated in Nova Scotia and across the country, and told her Abdoul needed help.

The first time I called Asha on the phone, I was with my friend Idil Abdillahi, a professor at Ryerson University's School of Social Work, an activist, and a clinician with deep experience in prisons and jails across Ontario. That night in early January 2018 when we contacted Asha, she spoke to both of us in English and to Idil in Somali—we both shared tears with Asha as she described Abdoul's story in detail. Although we knew the chances of success were slim, we began to make plans to stop his deportation using all our resources.

Between the two of them, El and Idil share extensive knowledge about immigration and incarceration. Idil and her family had also immigrated to Canada as Somali refugees. El had met other women and men in her work who faced deportation as a result of criminal convictions. I had several media platforms to sound the alarm. The three of us—El in Halifax, and Idil and me in Toronto—worked with Abdoul's family, who had long been fighting for him.

Happy New Year, me no die oh!

—

Abdoul was scheduled to be released from prison in Dorchester, New Brunswick, on January 4, 2018. Asha had been told that Abdoul would be sent to a halfway house in Toronto where he would live under strict supervision while he reacquainted himself with life out of prison.

Corrections staff, however, did not release Abdoul on January 4. Instead, they handed him over to officials with the Canada Border Services Agency, who took him into their custody and placed him in immigration detention at the Madawaska Regional Correctional Facility near Edmundston, New Brunswick. At first we didn't understand why CBSA chose this location, but we soon learned that Edmundston has an airport staffed by border agents. We had to move quickly. We didn't know when the government might strip Abdoul of his permanent residency and then attempt to deport him, perhaps flying him out of Canada from New Brunswick. We had also received word from Ben Perryman, Abdoul's lawyer, that Abdoul was in solitary confinement in his new place of incarceration.

Abdoul would later tell us that he was transported to Madawaska in a van during a severe snowstorm, and that border agents had to pull into another jail during the night before getting him to his destination the next morning. I don't know how often people are kept in immigration detention at Madawaska, or if the jail is used to receiving calls from advocates asking pointed questions about the status of new prisoners, but Idil called repeatedly to let staff know we were extremely worried about Abdoul's safety. We'd been preparing for Abdoul's possible apprehension by CBSA, and I was able to reach out to contacts I'd made at the National Black Canadians Summit to help spread the word. We did this work ourselves because the Federation of Black Canadians, our purported national advocacy group, would not speak publicly about Abdoul's dire situation.

The day after Abdoul arrived at Madawaska, he was able to call Asha. He told her that he was all right, but also afraid and confused. On January 6, Asha came on my radio show on Newstalk 1010 and spoke openly about the precarious future her nephew faced. Asha identified herself as a resident of the federal riding of York South–Weston, the area represented by Immigration Minister Hussen. It turns out Asha had met Hussen years earlier, before he was a member of Parliament, and had told him of Abdoul's case. Asha said Hussen had promised he would help Abdoul if he was elected. But the Liberal minister hadn't done anything for her since, and Asha said his office staff eventually told her, "Ahmed Hussen's not able to help you for this case—we're closing the file."

On January 9, Prime Minister Trudeau hosted a town hall meeting at a school gym in Lower Sackville, Nova Scotia. It was the latest stop in a tour he'd been conducting across the country to hear directly from Canadians. Fatouma and El organized a rally outside the event. Several of Abdoul's supporters demonstrated as hundreds lined up to see Trudeau. But Fatouma wasn't satisfied, and told her companions she wanted to go inside to see if she could ask Trudeau a question. So the group found seats in the gym.

Trudeau ran his town halls like a teacher calling on students in a classroom, and chose questions at random from the dozens of raised hands in the audience. By some small miracle, Trudeau chose one of Fatouma's supporters, who waited for the microphone and then walked it over to Fatouma. At home, I watched a livestream of the event as Fatouma stood face to face with the prime minister, the camera positioned behind Trudeau's shoulder as she asked, in a firm and even tone, "Why aren't you helping my brother?"

Flanked by El, Amina Abawajy—the young activist I had met in North Preston a few months before—and several other supporters, Fatouma explained to everyone in the room that Abdoul was currently in immigration detention. She then turned back to Trudeau. "My question to you is, if it was your son, would you do anything to stop this?"

Trudeau indicated immediately that he was familiar with Abdoul's story. "When we saw how the care system failed your brother . . . how the challenges he's facing have impacted upon him, and we saw the real challenges that we're facing in the system, it has opened our eyes to something that many of us knew was ongoing in many communities but we continue to need to address." This was the first formal acknowledgement by the government that Abdoul's specific circumstance was part of a systemic problem among non-citizens in Canada, and it was coming from the prime minister on a live broadcast. Trudeau continued, "I can assure you that our immigration minister, who himself came to this country as a sixteen-year-old Somali refugee, understands the challenges and the situation that your family is facing right now."

The next day, reporters began asking the Nova Scotia Department of Community Services, the agency that had failed to secure Abdoul's citizenship, for comment. While the department wouldn't comment on Abdoul's case for privacy reasons, it admitted that it had no policy to ensure it applied for citizenship on behalf of non-citizen children. Nova Scotia premier Stephen McNeil promised that the department would review all its cases to find out how many other children in Abdoul's situation might need support. The story was all over the news.

That night, January 10, Trudeau travelled to his next town hall, at McMaster University in Hamilton, and Idil and I watched the livestream of the event in her apartment. The very first question came from another supporter of Abdoul. The woman, who did not give her name, criticized Trudeau for not offering Fatouma firm reassurances the night before. She also pointed out that earlier in the event, Trudeau had praised Canada's peacekeeping efforts. "This is the same peacekeeping which led to the Somalia affair in which Canadian soldiers—supposedly in the country on a humanitarian mission—beat to death a teenage boy," she said.

She went on to mention Abdirahman Abdi, who had died at the hands of the Ottawa police the previous summer and whose death politicians had still not addressed in any meaningful way. She then returned to Abdoul: "He faces deportation and potentially death because of the failings of this nation's government and its institutions. So my question is: what rules and compassion exist within a system that at every level, from the police to the children's services to other institutions domestically to armed forces abroad, continues to perpetuate anti-Somali and anti-Black violence? Thank you."

They say luck happens when opportunity meets preparation. Every day as news spread, we urged Abdoul's supporters to contact the government and demand his release and the cancellation of his deportation. We also demanded that the government compile stats showing how many other children across Canada were at similar risk, and that it immediately grant all such children citizenship. These had always been our demands, and now they caught on.

On January 11, one week after Abdoul had been put in immigration detention in New Brunswick, CBSA officials transferred him to the Maplehurst Correctional Complex just north of Toronto. It was the clearest sign yet that our advocacy was working. Abdoul was no longer in solitary confinement, but he was not out of danger. We arranged for Asha to visit him, but when she arrived at the prison the staff told her he was no longer there. Abdoul had been in Maplehurst barely forty-eight hours before he was transferred again, to the Central East Correctional Centre in Lindsay, more than two hours' drive east of Toronto.

With this news our hearts sank—the jail in Lindsay is where so many men without citizenship in Canada have been kept on indefinite immigration holds while the government tries to deport them. We feared the worst but kept working, kept calling and urging others to do the same, kept sharing Abdoul's story with anyone who might listen and take action. Fatouma and Ben Perryman went on national radio and television to advocate for him.

Abdoul had an immigration hearing on January 15 to decide where he would remain while he continued to fight his deportation. Officials weren't even sure where they wanted to deport Abdoul, and at the hearing cited both his birthplace of Saudi Arabia and his family's homeland of Somalia as possible destinations. Abdoul had no status in either country, and did not know their languages or customs. As a stateless individual with criminal convictions, he had reason to fear for his life in both places.

I sat in a CBSA facility in downtown Toronto with Asha and her sister as a member of the Immigration and Refugee Board delivered his decision: he would release Abdoul to a halfway house in Toronto after all. After seeing so many others stay in immigration detention for weeks, months, or years, this was the unlikely outcome we'd been dreaming of. It wasn't the end of Abdoul's plight, but it meant he could see his family for the first time in years.

Minister Hussen requested a meeting with us only *after* Abdoul was released. We declined.

In March of 2018, a Jamaican immigrant named Kiwayne Jones announced that he was filing a $200-million class action lawsuit against the Ontario government on behalf of the province's non-citizen children who were apprehended by the child welfare system. Kiwayne, who is now in his thirties, had become a permanent resident of Canada with his family in 1999 but was taken by the Toronto Children's Aid Society a year later. Like Fatouma and Abdoul, Kiwayne has yet to be made a citizen. When announcing his lawsuit he said, "I felt I was Canadian, but, in reality, I wasn't."

In Federal Court, Ben Perryman continued to fight Abdoul's deportation on the grounds that attempts to deport him violated his Charter rights as well as international law. On July 13, 2018, the Federal Court, convinced by Ben's arguments, overturned Abdoul's deportation order. This was the second time the court had reversed a deportation order for Abdoul—after a similar ruling the previous October, the government had simply created a new order. Four days after the latest ruling, without warning, Public Safety Minister Ralph Goodale tweeted: "The Government of Canada respects the decision filed on July 13 by the Federal Court concerning Abdoul Abdi. The Government will not pursue deportation for Mr. Abdi."

To my knowledge, the government has never made such a public statement about a decision to abandon a deportation. It happened because we fought. Idil was on the phone day and night. El and her partner, Reed, an unseen and unsung brother in the struggle, drove Fatouma to appointments and organized people in Nova Scotia. Folks from Goodale's constituency in Regina, Saskatchewan stood in the snow to demonstrate on Abdoul's behalf when he was in CBSA custody. Supporters in Ottawa wrote letters to and called their members of Parliament. Black Lives Matter–Toronto took over Hussen's office and held a press conference demanding that Abdoul be released. People across Canada we didn't know stood up for a young man they'd never met.

Fatouma, who continues to live in Halifax with her two children, is also without citizenship as a result of the same government neglect her brother suffered, and she continues to struggle. It was Fatouma who led the public fight for Abdoul, and Asha who helped us understand their story. Abdoul lives in Toronto now. Since his release from CBSA custody, he's been working and starting a new chapter in his life. We still have no idea how many other young people in Canada are at risk of deportation because of government failures to apply for their citizenship.

In January 2018, when Abdoul was released from immigration detention, he did a feature interview on CBC's "The National." The reporter asked him what he wanted to say to Prime Minister Trudeau and the Liberal government. Abdoul replied, "Help me, and help kids never be in the situation I'm in right now. Because I guarantee you if I just get swept under the rug, that there will be another child in the same position as I am." He added that he wanted to be a good father to his daughter, whose life he'd missed out on while he was incarcerated. "I feel like what makes a person is their struggles in life."

postscript

All the stories I share in this book continue to evolve. Some court cases and other institutional battles I wrote about have moved forward since the original publication. Although no story can ever really be complete, the following are notable updates to some of the stories you've just read.

John Samuels has kept up his artistic pursuits, and in 2019 the collective he started won the Arts for Youth Award from the Toronto Arts Foundation. In his acceptance speech, Samuels spoke of the resilience of his artistic community: "They stood by us when we opened our first brick-and-mortar space. And they were right at the door when our locks were changed multiple times. They cheered triumphantly when we overcame police brutality." In November 2020, under the name Just John, Samuels released his debut solo EP *This Is Fate*.

———

In February of 2020, the Human Rights Tribunal of Ontario found that race played a factor in the treatment of "Symone," the six-year-old girl whom police had handcuffed inside her Mississauga classroom. In January of 2021, the tribunal awarded Symone $35,000 in damages for the police's conduct. HRTO adjudicator Brenda Bowlby noted Symone's "tender age" in experiencing anti-Black racism.

Bowlby wrote: "It is clear that, because of this incident, she became aware that as a Black person, she may be subject to different treatment than a white child. The full impact of this is unknown but it is now part of the applicant's lived experience and will affect her into the future."

Symone's mother, "Brenda," said she was happy this chapter of their lives is over. "I can now focus on what lies ahead, which is making my daughter whole. This decision gives my community hope where we often feel there's no recourse."

Charline Grant and nine others co-founded the group Parents of Black Children in 2019. PoBC works to "eliminate anti-Black racism and oppression for Black students within their schools and connected systems." PoBC advocates with Black students and their parents, and has created community-based tools for reporting anti-Black racism within Ontario schools.

In a 2020 article for *Chatelaine*, Charline explained that her fight to defend her son Ziphion from racism in York Region public schools led to a broader struggle. "As a family, we decided a long time ago not to accept racism. We will always fight against it, especially at the institutional level. As Ziphion begins university, our continued advocacy gives us a sense of closure and satisfaction. It hopefully also promotes healing, as we work to help motivate and inspire the next generation. The struggle continues."

———

On the first day of Daniel Montsion's 2019 trial for his attack on Abdirahman Abdi, dozens of armed Ottawa police offers flooded the lobby of the Ottawa courthouse to support their colleague. The courtroom itself was so small that some of the Abdi family's supporters were forced to wait outside.

In October of 2020, the court found Montsion not guilty on the charges of manslaughter, aggravated assault, and assault with a weapon. Lawrence Greenspon, the Abdi family lawyer, said, "They are truly devastated by the decision, and I have assured them that this is far from the end of our fight."

Farhia Ahmed of the Justice for Abdirahman Coalition spoke at a rally after the court decision: "Today we heard a verdict that has not only done irreparable harm to a family, to our community, and to the memory of a man undeserving of death at the hands of the state, but harm as well to what little semblance of trust remained between law enforcement and our city's most vulnerable."

In 2021, the family ended its $1.5 million civil suit against the Ottawa Police Services Board after both sides signed an agreement that Ottawa police would improve their responses to people experiencing a mental health crisis—details of that agreement are confidential.

Most of Toronto's official, in-person Pride festivities were cancelled in 2020 to prevent the spread of COVID-19, but Pride Toronto hosted virtual celebrations. Thousands did gather at Nathan Phillips Square for a teach-in and rally to defund Toronto police. Black Lives Matter Toronto and dozens of community organizations demanded an immediate 50 percent reduction of the Toronto Police Service budget.

Bev Bain, an organizer of the rally with the No Pride in Policing Coalition, welcomed the gathering by saying, "We are glad you are all here, prepared to raise your voices to demand that we defund and abolish policing here in Canada, and to celebrate a return of Pride to its political roots. No more corporatized Pride!"

Days later, two Toronto city councillors put forward a motion to defund the police by 10 percent. The city council, led by mayor John Tory, defeated this proposal and voted instead to equip police with 2,350 body cameras.

During the 2019 criminal trial of Michael and Christian Theriault, Durham police constable Barbara Zabdyr, who responded to the brothers' attack on Dafonte Miller, testified that she gave her handcuffs to Michael so he could handcuff Dafonte. Zabdyr said Theriault, the off-duty police officer, also searched Dafonte before handing him over to Durham officers. This was one of many revelations during the trial that demonstrated collaboration between the Durham police and the Theriault family.

Dafonte's testimony in the Oshawa courthouse lasted about thirteen hours and included over eight hours of cross-examination by Michael Lacy, the Theriaults' defence lawyer.

The courthouse was closed due to COVID-19 when Justice Joseph Di Luca delivered his decision in June of 2020, so the court produced a livestream of the judge reading his decision. Dozens gathered outside the courthouse and listened to the hours-long reading on speakers.

The brothers were both charged with aggravated assault and obstruction of justice. Di Luca found Christian Theriault not guilty of these charges, but found Michael Theriault guilty of a lesser charge of assault and ultimately sentenced him to nine months in jail. Both Theriault and the Crown are appealing his conviction.

Dafonte spoke after the decision:

I would like to show appreciation for the community supporting me, everybody who's been in my corner. It's meant a lot to me in these last few years, it's helped me go forward. We've come a long way, you know. 'Cause I remember the night when this happened to me, I ended up getting charged.

And now we're in a situation where an officer has been held accountable to some extent. There's a lot of people who are in my position who don't get the same backing that I got and don't get to have their day to really have any vindication for what they're going through. . . . I wanna thank everyone for the support, and I wanna bring awareness to all my brothers and sisters who are going through what I'm going through and don't have the resources that I had and don't have the support that I had.

As COVID-19 spread throughout Canada in the spring of 2020, CBC News in Montreal ran an article entitled "Quebec Relies on Hundreds of Asylum Seekers in Long-Term Care Battle against COVID-19." The story detailed the plight of a Haitian asylum seeker who had crossed into Québec in 2017. This woman, whose identity the CBC protected, had contracted COVID-19 while working as an orderly at a long-term care home.

The story noted that while Québec premier François Legault was praising front-line health workers as "guardian angels," the hundreds who were asylum seekers had no status in Canada or knowledge of how long they could stay in the country.

A group supporting Haitian asylum seekers released an open letter that included the following:

We appeal to your sensitivity and ask you to consider the fate of these essential workers who are claiming refugee status. In exceptional circumstances, these individuals offer us their skills, dedication and dignity to help us fight this pandemic, all while putting their own health and that of their families at risk. Many of them have nearly died, many have lost co-workers. We find it hard to believe that these *guardian angels* may be expelled from the country once the battle is won. This would run counter to our values as Quebecers and Canadians.

We ask that you implement a special immigration program to regularize their status on Canadian soil. Such a program would be a supreme gesture of gratitude to these people. Canada and Quebec have put in place similar special measures in the past that have proven beneficial for the country.

We are counting on your leadership to make a humanitarian gesture to these citizens who are fighting alongside us every day.

The movement to remove police officers from schools expanded to cities across Ontario and Canada. After sustained organizing in Hamilton, Ontario, by "HWDSB Kids Need Help," a group of mostly Somali and other Black students, the local school board voted to end its School Resource Officer program. Pressure from parents, students, educators, and local community members in Peel Region forced local police to cancel their SRO program.

Vancouver's school board cancelled its program in 2021, although it took an apologetic tone with police, voted to write them a letter of thanks for their service, and vowed to continue involving officers in other aspects of school life, including "school emergencies, lockdowns, critical incidents and VTRA (Violent Threat Risk Assessments)."

School boards and police in Calgary, Edmonton, Ottawa, Winnipeg,

Waterloo, Durham Region, and York Region are also reviewing their police-in-schools programs.

I continued my reporting on Justice Donald McLeod and the Federation of Black Canadians. In early 2020, the Ontario Judicial Council announced a second judicial hearing for McLeod. The OJC alleged that McLeod had committed perjury at his first hearing, had made an improper call to two Black advocates in order to silence them, and had attended funding meetings on FBC's behalf. The complaint cited my blog *Cole's Notes*, where I documented many of McLeod's questionable acts.

In June of 2021, the OJC concluded that McLeod had twice engaged in conduct that was "incompatible with judicial office." However, as it had done in McLeod's first hearing, the OJC decided his behaviour was not so serious that it would "diminish public confidence in Justice McLeod's ability to carry out the duties of his office or the administration of justice generally." The OJC dismissed the complaint and paid McLeod nearly $1.1 million for his legal fees, and spent $3.4 million on the hearing.

Fatouma and Abdoul Abdi announced a lawsuit against the province of Nova Scotia and the Nova Scotia Home for Colored Children in late 2020. The siblings' lawsuit describes the abuse they experienced in the child welfare system. In a piece by El Jones, Fatouma detailed publicly for the first time how social workers separated her and Abdoul from their aunts, punished the children for speaking Somali, and removed her hijab and refused to replace it. Fatouma also disclosed many other abuses she suffered while she was still a minor and in the province's custody, and said her guardians ignored her repeated attempts to report these abuses.

In her conversation with El, Fatouma reflected on the lawsuit she and Abdoul had filed. She said that although the courts could never reverse the harms she, her children, and Abdoul had experienced, "it's going to bring light to how they run the system and what they did to other kids, and I hope it forces them to change."

El wrote, "I am continuously humbled by Abdoul and Fatouma's courage, by how often they have opened themselves to the public gaze and criticism for other children they do not even know. I marvel at them, betrayed so often and still believing in hope and goodness. If we are left with any image of them, let us be left with that." In early 2022, Canadian senator Mobina Jaffer introduced a bill to ensure that non-citizens who went through child welfare services or foster care are able to become citizens, and to prevent such people from being deported.

Notes for Educators

Teaching books that address intersecting aspects of Black life and the struggle for freedom is an important and at times challenging task. This educator's guide highlights some of the key themes and questions in *The Skin We're In* with the goal of helping learners develop better questions, a deeper understanding of contemporary Black struggles, and a sense of responsibility towards their communities.

The style of the book is direct, citing statistics, writings, research, and interviews that illustrate the contours of Black experiences and resistance to anti-Blackness in the context of Canada. It is important to frame the discussion with this understanding in mind. The text is neither a how-to nor a personal recount of the author's life, so it offers many entry points and opportunities for discussion and collaborative learning. Readers should be encouraged to seek lifelong learning and participation in the struggle for freedom—as opposed to looking for a prescription or linear set of actions—within and beyond the scope of the text. Learning from the many examples of resistance and interventions in the book can offer a glimpse into the possibilities for our own work.

Space Agreement

In order to facilitate active reading and engaged discussion, and to create a productive and supportive learning environment, parameters should be given to learners. A space agreement can prepare learners for conflict, harm, and discomfort and should be developed in collaboration with the learners. Developing a short and clear set of practical guidelines helps learners find the courage to participate in uncomfortable and difficult conversations. Some examples of these guidelines frequently used by social justice educators can include:

- "No one knows everything, together we know a lot": An invitation to be co-learners with classmates and our teachers.
- "No one is disposable, everyone is accountable": An invitation to share and be responsible with our words and choices.
- "What's said here stays here, and what's learned here leaves here": An affirmation that respects the privacy of others and invites them to apply the lessons learned.

Most importantly, the agreement should outline how and when educators will intervene in instances of harm or conflict. Space agreements and competent facilitation can create a learning environment that supports cross-cultural dialogue without burdening Black learners in the spaces with the responsibility of teaching and affirming those around them or making Black people into object lessons.

Perhaps the most challenging and important practices for educators are modelling humble learning, self-reflection, and changed behaviour as key competencies for being co-learners in solidarity with Black lives.

When guiding learners through discussion, remember:

- Don't lie about, minimize, or misrepresent the impact or reality of racism and injustice. Introduce as much information as is appropriate for the age of the learner.
- Don't frame or present racism as a historical problem—situate it

as an issue with a past, present, and future. This can help learners feel a sense of responsibility, rather than guilt.

- Don't present anti-Black racism as the behaviour of a few "bad" people but as a system that we all participate in, which some benefit from at the expense of others.
- Do become familiar with and highlight examples of both anti-Black racism and resistance to it in the learners' local context.
- Do share about your learning journey and mistakes where possible to encourage accountability and change.

Tips for answering challenging questions

1. Acknowledge and reward curiosity and critical thinking. For example: "That's a great question, I am glad you're making that connection."
2. Provide an honest, fact-based answer. If you don't have one, offer to find out together. For example: "Yes, people in Africville were displaced from their homes due to racism," or "I am not sure I know enough about that; let's do some research and come back to discuss this."
3. Ask a question back. Take this as an opportunity to learn from and understand the perspective of a learner. For example: "Do you know anything about the descendants of Africville today?"
4. Explore an action. Take this opportunity to connect a historical injustice to a contemporary one, or a present injustice to a local context. For example: "We still see city planning and other policies that displace Black people from their communities. What does that look like here? Who is working to organize against it? How can we help?"

Notes for Learners

In *The Skin We're In*, Desmond Cole names over one hundred organizations, collectives, writers, activists, parents, youth organizers, and individuals engaged in everyday and organized struggle against anti-Black racism, as well as the names of dozens killed by state-sanctioned violence. This generous mapping represents a fraction of the resistance to anti-Blackness, which has been relentless since its onset. Additionally, the author cites resources, research, and bodies of knowledge that offer us an invitation to ongoing learning.

Like you, the people in the book didn't have a set of foolproof instructions. Instead, they took risks and disrupted, documented, and advocated. They learned from the resistance of those who came before them and from the knowledge and practices of Black people everywhere, acting from a love for themselves, their families, and their communities. Those who worked in solidarity with them affirmed Black lives through their support and organizing.

This archive of courage is a place where we can learn many lessons. These lessons allow us to look at practices of resistance that we can apply to our own circumstances, lessons we can work collaboratively to implement. They do not offer us a prescription; instead, they inspire us to ask ourselves *what have others done to resist that can inform our present moment?* rather than asking Black people and communities to give us a step-by-step guide for solidarity.

All learners have a responsibility to develop a lifelong political education and to increase capacity and skills to intervene in the injustices that shape all of our lives. It is important to approach this work with humility, which allows us to recognize when we have been ignorant to the realities of others and when we have participated in harming them—with or without intending to. We may feel guilt, but it is important not to allow that feeling to immobilize us. Instead, we should allow it to compel us to action and a sense of responsibility towards our communities and our world.

Learning about injustice is always difficult, especially when it intersects with our own lives and experiences. The text reminds us that we are not powerless and that, in fact, it has always been our collective work and relentless commitment that have changed the world in tiny and enormous ways. The discomfort that we feel when we learn about the lives of others, and by extension our complicity in the oppression they experience, is a part of learning. It is important not to allow that discomfort to be mistaken for harm. We are uncomfortable when our world views, our actions, our words, and our choices are being challenged. We are harmed when we are being devalued, insulted, assaulted, and dehumanized. We all deserve safety: comfort is often a luxury in the face of injustice.

Glossary of Terms

Ableism: Discrimination or prejudice against people with disabilities.

Anti-Black racism: Racism specifically targeting Black people.

Capitalism: An economy in which the production and exchange of goods and services is guided by profit-driven, private interests and the demands of a consumer marketplace, with little intervention from the state.

Carding: The police practice of stopping people who are not reasonably suspected of any crime and documenting their personal information before, during, or after the interaction.

Cisnormativity: The assumption that being cisgender is the "default" or norm for all people, thereby positioning other gender identities as exceptional or abnormal.

Decolonizing: Resisting and working to undo colonial structures by reasserting Indigenous values and voices.

Heteronormativity: The assumption that being heterosexual is the "default" or norm for all people, thereby positioning other sexualities as exceptional or abnormal.

Intersectionality: The understanding that different forms of oppression (such as racism, ableism, transphobia, homophobia, and classism) don't exist independently of each other but rather overlap, inform, and exacerbate each other, creating unique and distinct experiences of oppression. Intersectionality shows that a person's life is shaped by all their identities and social locations simultaneously and that people within the same group or community may experience systemic barriers and oppression differently based on their intersecting identities.

Patriarchy: A system of power in which men are privileged over women.

Oppression: A systematic exercise of power of one group over another.

"Race card": A term invoked to diminish claims of racism by suggesting those claims stem from an attempt to gain sympathy or advantage rather than actual acts of racism.

State violence: A state's use of its authority and resources to harm individuals, groups, or other nations.

Saneism: Discrimination or prejudice against individuals with mental health illnesses or challenges.

White supremacy: The political, economic, and cultural systems of power that encourage and maintain the predominance of white people over other races.

Mapping Resistance: Group Exercise

Many who engage with this book and other writings on Black life find themselves asking the question: *What should we do?* Because there is no prescription or "how-to" recipe to confront anti-Black racism, we must learn from past and contemporary struggles. Black people whose resistance is documented in the book, as well as those in solidarity with them, learned from the people who came before them, took risks, and disrupted injustice.

This exercise helps us draw from the interventions and triumphs in the text to explore possibilities for our own resistance. In small groups of up to six participants, choose a chapter in the text which outlines the struggle of an individual or group as they work to address the injustices they experience. Groups should be encouraged to tackle different chapters in order to contribute to a broader discussion.

Work to identify each of the following elements outlined in this chapter:

1. **Individuals or groups** immediately affected by the injustices of anti-Black racism and/or state-sanctioned violence, and the ways they are impacted.
2. **The cost of resistance:** What "price" did those who resisted pay? How were they punished, excluded, criminalized, silenced, and/or endangered because they dared to object to injustice?
3. **The broader community** that is also impacted by these injustices.
4. **Groups and individuals who support the resistance,** including those working in solidarity.
5. **The demands** stated by those who are impacted by the injustice. What were people asking for?

6. **Media and dominant narratives:** How did mainstream media in Canada tell stories of the resistance? What was the focus of their storytelling? How did they describe the Black people and communities impacted by the injustice?

7. **Responses (or lack thereof)** by individuals in positions of institutional power, such as the leadership of elected officials and public servants and their actions/inactions within policing institutions, school boards, etc.

8. **Strategies of resistance** used by the affected communities and by their supporters, including but not limited to: disruption, protest, social media campaigns, boycott, public education, advocacy, etc.

9. **Counter-resistance:** Those who actively worked against the goals and demands of the Black individuals and communities affected, and the stories they told.

10. **Historical context:** What existing struggles, practices, and legal contexts shape the conditions of resistance in the chapter? For example, the Safe Schools Act in the context of recent resistance to the School Resource Officer program.

11. **Triumphs and outcomes:** The wins, transformations, reforms, and restitution yielded from the courage of those who dared to resist. Please note promises made by individuals and institutions in positions of power to Black communities.

12. **Beyond the text—updates:** Since the publication of your edition of *The Skin We're In*, have there been developments or new events that relate to the chapter you're analyzing?

Groups should share and present their findings with the larger class, drawing parallels between different events and various forms of resistance.

Anti-Blackness at the Intersections

From the 2015 murder of Andrew Loku by the Toronto Police Service, to the attempted deportation of Beverly Braham in 2017 and the demands to remove uniformed, armed police from the Toronto Pride Parade, the text illustrates how anti-Black racism intersects with discrimination based on immigration status, sexual orientation, and gender identity, as well as ableism. The experiences of Black people at intersecting margins are illustrated at various points in the text.

Intersectionality is a term coined by Black writer, academic, and feminist Kimberlé Crenshaw. In a 2020 interview with *TIME* magazine, Crenshaw defined intersectionality as "a prism, for seeing the way in which various forms of inequality often operate together and exacerbate each other. We tend to talk about race inequality as separate from inequality based on gender, class, sexuality, or immigrant status. What's often missing is how some people are subject to all of these, and the experience is not just the sum of its parts."

Group activity

Using an intersectional lens, reflect on the book and work in four groups to answer the questions outlined below. Pass out four sheets of paper, each with a question at the top. Each group should identify and write down one or two examples as prompted by the question. The groups should exchange their notes and add more examples to the reflections outlined by their colleagues. Rotate questions until each group has had an opportunity to discuss each of the prompts. The goal of the exercise is to learn to build on existing knowledge while working collaboratively.

- How do ableism and saneism intersect with anti-Black racism to particularly harm Black people living with disability and mental illness? Illustrate with examples from the text.
- How have queer and trans Black people led movements and resistance? What price did they pay?
- How does anti-Black racism—exacerbated by patriarchy—shape the lives of Black women and trans people?
- In *women of exceptional merit*, the author describes the labour and resistance of Black women in the community as "protecting, educating, and caring for the next generation." How is this work documented in the text?

Beyond the text
What does intersectionality look like in your life and community?

We Keep Us Safe

While the police may claim that their role is to "serve and protect" our communities, it is evident that Black people and others impacted by injustice are neither granted safety nor support from law enforcement and other adjacent agencies (such as the Canada Border Services Agency). The author names dozens of Black people who were murdered and assaulted by these institutions and describes a blatant lack of accountability in the aftermath. Calls to defund, disband, and abolish the police have become more common in recent years, and many of us may be asking: What do we do now? What do we build instead? How do we keep ourselves safe?

Many abolitionist thinkers, writers, organizers, and educators have dared us to use our imagination and creativity to design interventions, supports, spaces, and by extension, a world where safety does not mean heavily funded and armed law enforcement agencies that often respond in the aftermath of crises. One such organizer is Mariame Kaba. She asks us to consider what the police say they do, and what the police actually do. With this in mind, her work invites us to reflect on the following questions:

- What does it mean to have safe communities? What actually ensures safety in our communities?
- What were the experiences of various Black people and communities in the text in relation to the police?
- What other kinds of support could have been offered first to various individuals harmed or killed by police?
- On page 21, the author states that "police enjoy a legal monopoly on violence." What are some examples that demonstrate this statement?
- Various points in the text illustrate the staggering amount of resources used to police, surveil, restrict, detail, and punish Black people. How might these resources be reallocated to support Black life?

Beyond the Text

What is the police budget in your local community (you can find this information by doing a web search of your city's name with the word "police board")? What services are underfunded in your community? How would you redistribute some or all of your local police budget to better serve your community?

Media, Stories & Black Life

From Symone, the pseudonym given to the six-year-old Black girl who was cuffed by police in her school in the Peel District School Board, to the work of Black Lives Matter Toronto, Canadian media has often told certain types of stories about Black life and the struggle for freedom. The media plays a huge role in shaping public conversations and maintaining Canada's narrative of innocence.

Cole cites many academics, organizers, and historians whose work address how Canada tells a passive and benevolent story about race, and Black people in particular, within Canada, often framing anti-Black racism and state-sanctioned violence as "American" problems and sending the message that ours is "an inclusive country" (page 109).

- What are some examples of this story?
- On page 152, Cole references "complementary Black origin stories." What are some examples of these?
- Give examples from the text of the ways that media organizations have excused anti-Black racism and/or given platforms to groups and individuals who devalue Black life and engage in anti-Blackness.
- Who tells stories about Black life in the media?
- How has social media been used as part of resistance by Black communities and those in solidarity with them? Draw on examples from the text as well as your own knowledge.

Beyond the text

Reflect on the stories of Black life and resistance you were familiar with prior to reading the book. What stories did you hear? Where did you hear them? How do you feel about them now?

Family & Kinship Ties

In Chapter 13, we learn that when Abdoul Abdi was a child, his mother died and his aunt Asha Ali became he and his sister's guardian. When he was at risk of deportation after years of abuse and abandonment by the state, his sister Fatouma Abdi was a vocal and courageous advocate for his safety. Black families push back against educational institutions that harm their children, immigration systems that separate them from their loved ones, policing institutions that kill and maim our families, and the everyday injustices of anti-Black racism.

- What are some examples of this resistance from the text?
- What are some examples from your community?

Education & Freedom

On page 24, the author writes that "Canadian education systems suspend, expel, devalue, and discourage Black kids with efficiency and intention." Citing statistics and research, as well as organizers inside and outside the school setting, we learn of the ways that the education system engages in anti-Blackness and intersects with other institutions to the detriment of Black life. Policies and practices such as zero tolerance policies, the Safe Schools Act, and the School Resource Officer program, among many others, disproportionately impact Black learners.

- How does policing intersect with education? How does it

impact Black, Indigenous, racialized, and disabled learners as well as their communities?

- In the book, how did individuals and organizations resist anti-Black racism within the context of education? Provide three examples.

Beyond the text

What other "wins" have there been for those organizing against School Resource Office Programs across the country? What work to address anti-Black racism is ongoing within your local context?

Beyond Borders: Black Liberation as a Global Struggle

Across the globe, anti-Black racism shapes the material conditions and experiences of Black life. Connections between the histories and contemporary realities of Black people transcend borders. These parallels are evident across the text and in the solidarity in Black organizing across and beyond Canada.

- How does Canadian foreign intervention such as military and "peacekeeping" missions and international aid work contribute to destabilizing and displacing Black communities and people?
- What are the connections between Somali experiences of anti-Black racism and Canada's history in Somalia?
- How does Canada work to restrict and regulate the movement and presence of Black people within its borders? Give historical and contemporary examples.

About the Author

RANIA EL MUGAMMAR is a Sudanese artist, liberation educator, abolitionist, anti-oppression consultant, multidisciplinary performer, speaker, and published writer. Her work explores reproductive justice, transformative justice and abolition, art as liberation, and digital justice. She has worked extensively with contemporary arts institutions, STEM-based enterprises, media organizations, educational institutions, and community/grassroots groups. She lives in Toronto.

notes

NEGRO FROLICKS (JANUARY)

5   The photographer's previous tweet read Vonny Lorde (@LASTNAMELORDE), Twitter, January 1, 2017, https://twitter.com/LASTNAMELORDE/status /815659398206988288.

7   In order to control the "freed" Black loyalists, Shelburne officials created a bylaw "forbidding Negro Dances and Negro Frolicks in this town" Stephen Kimber, *Loyalists and Layabouts: The Rapid Rise and Faster Fall of Shelburne, Nova Scotia, 1783–1792* (Toronto: Anchor, 2002), p. 202.

8   White power works . . . to create what feminist scholar and author bell hooks describes as "dominator culture" bell hooks, *Teaching Community: A Pedagogy of Hope* (New York and London: Routledge, 2003).

8   White power works in concert with . . . cisnormativity (the dominance of people who feel that their gender identity matches their body/sex Jessica Cadwallader, "Diseased States: The Role of Pathology in the (Re)Production of the Body Politic," *Somatechnics: Queering the Technologisation of Bodies*, ed. Nikki Sullivan and Samantha Murray (Milton Park, UK: Routledge, 2009).

9   As U.S.-based writer Yawo Brown puts it: "White America has been playing a centuries-long game of 'stop hitting yourself'" Yawo Brown, "The Subtle

Linguistics of Polite White Society," Medium, August 14, 2015, https://medium.com
/@YawoBrown/the-subtle-linguistics-of-polite-white-supremacy-3f83c907ffff.

12   **According to the modern-day government of Manitoba** Manitoba, Education
and Training, Grade 6 Social Studies, "Numbered Treaties: Key," https://www
.edu.gov.mb.ca/k12/cur/socstud/foundation_gr6/blms/6-1-4f.pdf.

16   **When I was nineteen and a student at Queen's University in Kingston, Ontario,
two white police officers stopped me** For more on this and similar incidents, see
my "The Skin I'm In: I've Been Interrogated by Police More than 50 Times—
All Because I'm Black," *Toronto Life*, April 21, 2015, https://torontolife.com
/city/life/skin-im-ive-interrogated-police-50-times-im-black/.

ZERO TOLERANCE (FEBRUARY)

20   **Colley said two officers arrived at the school** Cynthia Mulligan, "Mom
Outraged After Six-Year-Old Daughter Handcuffed by Police in School,"
CityNews, February 2, 2017, http://toronto.citynews.ca/2017/02/02/exclusive
-mom-outraged-six-year-old-daughter-handcuffed-police-school/.

23   **The force would conduct an internal review** https://www.cbc.ca/news/canada
/toronto/human-rights-tribunal-peel-police-girl-handcuffed-1.5483456.

23   **In his book *The Civil War in 50 Objects*, Harold Holzer reflects** Harold Holzer
and the New-York Historical Society, *The Civil War in 50 Objects* (New York:
Viking, 2013), https://erenow.com/ww/the-civil-war-in-50-objects/2.php.

25   **For that same school year, the TDSB suspended about 3 per cent of white
students** Toronto District School Board, "Caring and Safe Schools," Fact
Sheet, Issue 3 (June 2013), http://www.tdsb.on.ca/Portals/research/docs/reports
/CaringSafeSchoolsCensus201112.pdf.

26   **However, a 2003 report by the Ontario Human Rights Commission noted**
Ontario Human Rights Commission, "The Ontario Safe Schools Act: School
Discipline and Discrimination" (Toronto: Ontario Human Rights Commission,
2003), http://www.ohrc.on.ca/en/book/export/html/2471.

26   **And yet that same year, Black students across all age groups were still suspended**
Toronto District School Board, "Caring and Safe Schools."

26   **In 2014 the TDSB struck its Task Force on the Success of Students of Somali
Descent.** Toronto District School Board, "Task Force on the Success of Students
of Somali Descent: Report and Recommendations" (2014).

27   **The report's introduction states** Black Learners Advisory Committee, "BLAC
Report on Education: Redressing Inequity—Empowering Black Learners"
(Halifax: 1994), p. 13.

27   In 2016 the Halifax Regional School Board reported Halifax Regional School
      Board, "Report on Student Suspension Data" (2016), https://www.hrsb.ca/sites
      /default/files/hrsb/2016-05-20.pdf.

28   The York study includes findings from the 1990s that "by the end of 1992 . . ."
      C. E. James and T. Turner, *Towards Race Equity in Education: The Schooling of
      Black Students in the Greater Toronto Area* (Toronto: York University, 2017), p. 14.

28   The same study summarizes findings from "The Roots of Youth Violence"
      James and Turner, *Towards Race Equity in Education*, p. 9.

28   The words of one participant in the York study give us some insight
      James and Turner, *Towards Race Equity in Education*, p. 56.

30   Lawyer Paula Rusak said, "The optics are not great . . ." Wendy Gillis, "Peel
      Cops Had 'No Alternative' But to Handcuff 6-Year-Old Black Girl at School,
      Police Lawyer Argues in Human Rights Case," Mississauga.com, May 29, 2019,
      https://www.mississauga.com/news-story/9398501-peel-cops-had-no-alternative
      -but-to-handcuff-6-year-old-black-girl-at-school-police-lawyer-argues-in
      -human-rights-case/.

31   Two weeks later, the *Toronto Star* reported that Nancy Elgie was under
      investigation Kristin Rushowy and Noor Javed, "York Board Probing Trustee
      over Alleged Racial Slur," *Toronto Star*, December 8, 2016, https://www.thestar
      .com/yourtoronto/education/2016/12/08/york-board-probing-trustee-over
      -alleged-racial-slur.html.

31   The writer of a letter to Elgie's local newspaper explained Piri Pandy,
      "Nancy Elgie a Dedicated Public Servant," *Georgina Advocate*, February 6, 2017,
      https://www.yorkregion.com/opinion-story/7101739-letter-to-the-editor-nancy
      -elgie-a-dedicated-public-servant/.

33   When the *Toronto Star* asked Elgie why she had used such a hateful word
      Rushowy and Javed, "York Board Probing Trustee over Alleged Racial Slur."

33   In early February, the *Toronto Star* undermined its own reporting of Elgie's racist
      remark Stewart Elgie and Allyson Harrison, "Facts to Consider When Judging
      Nancy Elgie," *Toronto Star*, February 7, 2017, https://www.thestar.com/opinion
      /commentary/2017/02/07/facts-to-consider-when-judging-nancy-elgie.html.

34   "Anyone who knows my mother will tell you she doesn't have a racist bone in her
      body . . ." Laura DaSilva, "York Region Trustee at Centre of Racism Controversy
      on Indefinite Medical Leave," CBC News, February 7, 2017, https://www.cbc.ca
      /news/canada/toronto/york-region-trustee-nancy-elgie-medical-leave-1.3971342.

34   Vicky Mochama . . . clapped back via Twitter Vicky Mochama (@vmochama),
      Twitter, January 20, 2017, https://twitter.com/vmochama/status/822589458948194306.

35 "I propose a voluntary sanction that I be prohibited from participating in all board meetings" Desmond Cole (@desmondcole), Twitter, January 24 2017, https://twitter.com/desmondcole/status/824056811162583040.

37 American journalist and author Ta-Nehisi Coates has said "racism is not merely a simplistic hatred . . ." Ta-Nehisi Coates, "Fear of a Black President," *The Atlantic*, September 2012, https://theatlantic.com/magazine/archive/2012/09 /fear-of-a-black-president/309064/.

JUSTICE FOR ABDIRAHMAN (MARCH)

40 The pastor asked the staffer, "Is that man with it?" Aedan Helmer, "A Full Picture of Abdirahman Abdi's Final Moments Has Finally Been Painted," *Ottawa Citizen*, updated May 2, 2019, https://ottawacitizen.com/news /local-news/a-full-picture-of-abdirahman-abdis-final-moments-has-finally -been-painted.

42 This officer "immediately jumped into the altercation . . ." Kristy Nease and Matthew Kupfer, "Witness Describes Fatal Confrontation between Abdirahman Abdi and Police," CBC News, July 26, 2016, https://www.cbc.ca/news/canada /ottawa/witness-confrontation-abdirahman-abdi-1.3695047.

42 He told a CBC reporter, "I heard the screaming . . ." Trevor Pritchard, "SIU Investigating After Ottawa Man Taken to Hospital Critically Injured Following Arrest," CBC News, July 24, 2016, https://www.cbc.ca/news/canada/ottawa /siu-investigate-hilda-street-arrest-hospital-1.3693073.

43 According to testimony from paramedic Yannick Roussel Aedan Helmer, "Paramedics Responded to 'Pepper Spray' Incident at Hilda St. on Morning of Abdi Arrest," *Ottawa Citizen*, updated March 12, 2019, https://ottawacitizen .com/news/local-news/paramedics-responded-to-pepper-spray-incident-at -hilda-st-on-morning-of-abdi-arrest.

43 "We don't know the cause of death right now" Laura Osman, "Abdirahman Abdi's Injuries Called in as Pepper Spray Incident," CBC News, March 12, 2019, https://www.cbc.ca/news/canada/ottawa/paramedic-abdi-montsion -trial-1.5051911.

43 "I was surprised, relieved and happy . . ." Helmer, "Paramedics Responded to 'Pepper Spray' Incident."

44 Nimao Ali, a spokesperson for the family, addressed the media Paul Jay (@PaulJayCBC), Twitter, July 25, 2016, https://twitter.com/PaulJayCBC /status/757725734349799424.

44 The report noted that Montsion "usually apprehends gang members . . ." Paul Cote Jay, "2 Officers Under Investigation in Death of Ottawa Man Identified,"

CBC News, July 26, 2016, https://www.cbc.ca/news/canada/ottawa/police
-officer-in-abdi-death-identified-1.3695996.

44 But in court the judge called Montsion's testimony "difficult to both understand
    and accept" Gary Dimmock, "Officer in Abdi Arrest Once Panicked During
    Violent Takedown of Another Somali-Canadian Man," *Ottawa Citizen*, updated
    September 10, 2016, https://ottawacitizen.com/news/local-news/police-officer
    -in-abdi-arrest-once-panicked-during-violent-takedown-of-another-somali
    -canadian-man.

44 Two days after police attacked Abdirahman, CBC Ottawa tweeted CBC News
    Ottawa (@CBCOttawa), Twitter, July 26, 2016, https://twitter.com/CBCOttawa
    /status/757965654448279552.

45 Months later, in an interview with the CBC, Watson was asked again about his
    silence CBC News, December 28, 2016, https://www.cbc.ca/news/canada/ottawa
    /jim-watson-2016-year-end-interview-police-1.3914339.

45 Writer and communications professional Jared Walker described the silence Jared
    A. Walker, "Welcome to Canada: Abdirahman Abdi and the Selective Silence
    of Canadian Leadership," Medium, July 26, 2016, https://medium.com/unfadable
    /abdirahman-abdi-the-selective-silence-of-canadian-leadership-7f5309b2175b.

47 "The call came in, there was violence involved . . ." Kristy Nease, "Ottawa Police
    Union President Calls Racism Speculation in Fatal Arrest 'Inappropriate,'"
    CBC News, July 26, 2016, https://www.cbc.ca/news/canada/ottawa/matt-skof
    -abdirahman-abdi-amran-ali-1.3695349.

47 Tracey Clark, the president of the Bridgehead coffee shop chain, confirmed
    "Abdirahman Abdi Worried Bridgehead Customers on Previous Occasions
    before Fatal Arrest, Owner Says," CBC News, August 5, 2016, https://www.cbc
    .ca/news/canada/ottawa/bridgehead-owner-speaks-abdirahman-abdi-1.3708589.

48 In response to questions about the officers' knowledge Nease, "Ottawa Police
    Union President Calls Racism Speculation in Fatal Arrest 'Inappropriate.'"

49 Skof rejected claims that Abdirahman had been treated harshly because of
    his race Laura Stone, "Witnesses Recount Abdirahman Abdi's 'Gruesome'
    Encounter with Ottawa Police Before His Death," *The Globe and Mail*, July 29,
    2016, https://www.theglobeandmail.com/news/national/funeral-held-for-somali
    -canadian-man-who-died-after-altercation-with-police/article31199886/.

49 "That's unfortunate that we're seeing the bleeding of that very difficult rhetoric . . ."
    Nease, "Ottawa Police Union President Calls Racism Speculation in Fatal Arrest
    'Inappropriate.'"

50 The CBC conducted a study of SIU investigations of Ottawa police officers
    Amanda Pfeffer, "SIU Data Reveals Criminal Charges Against Ottawa Police

Didn't Stick from 2011–2015," CBC News, October 27, 2016, https://www.cbc.ca/news/canada/ottawa/siu-track-record-ottawa-police-1.3822575.

50 **In a 2008 case that predated the CBC's investigation, Sergeant Steven Desjourdy arrested twenty-seven-year-old Stacy Bonds** Robyn Maynard documents Bonds's story and others in chapter 4 of her *Policing Black Lives: State Violence in Canada from Slavery to the Present* (Halifax and Winnipeg: Fernwood, 2017). See also Angela Ritchie, *Invisible No More: Police Violence against Black Women and Women of Color* (Boston: Beacon Press, 2017).

51 **In 2014, the *Ottawa Citizen* reported that only four days before Desjourdy cut Stacy Bonds's clothes** Gary Dimmock, "Desjourdy Had Previous Run-In for How He Treated Female Prisoner," *Ottawa Citizen*, updated May 20, 2014, https://ottawacitizen.com/news/local-news/desjourdy-had-previous-run-in-for-how-he-treated-female-prisoner.

51 **According to the CBC, "Three deaths involving Ottawa police in 2007, 2009 and 2013 . . ."** Kristy Nease, "70% of SIU Probes into Ottawa Police Never Publicized," CBC News, November 9, 2017, https://www.cbc.ca/news/canada/ottawa/siu-ottawa-police-investigations-news-releases-1.4389221.

52 **Marriner asked, "If we're not even aware that sexual assault allegations are being investigated . . ."** Catharine Tunney, "SIU Doesn't Publicize all Investigations into Ottawa Police," CBC News, April 18, 2017, https://www.cbc.ca/news/canada/ottawa/siu-sexual-assault-allegations-ottawa-police-1.4066639.

52 **Between 2001 and 2016, investigators cleared an average of 97 per cent of the officers it investigated** Calculated from SIU Annual Reports from 2001–2002 through 2015–2016, available at https://www.siu.on.ca/en/annual_report_2017.php.

52 **From its creation in 1990 until 2017, the SIU defined serious injuries** Ontario, Ministry of the Attorney General, "Implementation of the Recommendations— The Review (Recommendations 1 to 8)," October 29, 2015, https://www.attorneygeneral.jus.gov.on.ca/english/about/pubs/adams/recommendations1to8.php.

53 **At the coroner's inquest into Loku's death, Doyle described his own act of killing Loku** Paola Loriggio, "Toronto Police Officer Who Fatally Shot Andrew Loku Says He's 'Devastated,'" *The Globe and Mail*, June 14, 2017, https://www.theglobeandmail.com/news/toronto/toronto-police-officer-who-fatally-shot-andrew-loku-says-hes-devastated/article35307281/.

53 **Cerqua said at the inquest into Eligon's death** The Canadian Press, "Toronto Officer Who Shot Michael Eligon Feared for His Life," December 2, 2013, https://www.cbc.ca/news/canada/toronto/toronto-officer-who-shot-michael-eligon-feared-for-his-life-1.2448192.

54 **Badenoch said Abdirahman did not resist the two police officers who struck him** Judy Trinh, "The Unreleased Video: Woman Who Watched Fatal Arrest of Abdirahman Abdi Speaks Out," CBC News, March 8, 2017, https://www.cbc.ca/news/canada/ottawa/abdirahman-abdi-unreleased-video-siu-charges-1.4014423.

54 **Skof had seemed prepared . . . when he'd argued, "The SIU has a mandate to investigate . . ."** Pfeffer, "SIU Data Reveals Criminal Charges Against Ottawa Police Didn't Stick from 2011–2015."

55 **He said, "This has nothing to do with the relations we have with the community"** Amanda Pfeffer, "Ottawa Police Don Wristbands in Support of Officer Charged with Manslaughter," CBC News, March 29, 2017, https://www.cbc.ca/news/canada/ottawa/ottawa-police-daniel-montsion-wristband-abdi-1.4044425.

55 **Three days later, CBC reported that more wristbands had been ordered** Pfeffer, "Ottawa Police Don Wristbands in Support of Officer Charged with Manslaughter."

56 **Madut's cousin would later explain that he'd recently been served with an eviction notice** Erin Brohman, "From Terror to Tragedy: Witness Describes Events Leading Up to Police Shooting," CBC News, February 27, 2019, https://www.cbc.ca/news/canada/manitoba/police-shooting-witness-risbey-1.5035063.

57 **"Unfortunately sometimes people, for whatever reason, they leave no other choice"** Beth Macdonell, "Winnipeg's South Sudanese Community Demands Answers into Why Man Was Fatally Shot by Police," CTV News, February 25, 2019, https://winnipeg.ctvnews.ca/winnipeg-s-south-sudanese-community-demands-answers-into-why-man-was-fatally-shot-by-police-1.4311797.

57 **Sandy Deng, a South Sudanese community member, questioned the police's use of deadly force** Glen Dawkins, "South Sudanese Community Demands Answers After Police-Involved Shooting," *Winnipeg Sun*, February 25, 2019, https://winnipegsun.com/news/news-news/south-sudanese-community-demands-answers-after-police-involved-shooting.

57 **A CBC News investigation that analyzed 461 fatal civilian encounters with police** Katie Nicholson and Jacques Marcoux, "Most Canadians Killed in Police Encounters Since 2000 Had Mental Health or Substance Abuse Issues," CBC News, April 4, 2018, https://www.cbc.ca/news/investigates/most-canadians-killed-in-police-encounters-since-2000-had-mental-health-or-substance-abuse-issues-1.4602916.

58 **The CBC also found that, of the 461 deaths, "criminal charges were laid against 18 police officers . . ."** Kristin Annable and Vera-Lynn Kubinec, "Criminal Consequences for Police Officers Are Rare When a Civilian Dies," CBC

News, April 6, 2018, https://www.cbc.ca/news/canada/manitoba/deadly-force -police-criminal-charges-1.4607134.

58 **In a 2017 report on police use of force in Ontario, Independent Police Review Director Gerry McNeilly stated** Office of the Independent Police Review Director (Ontario), *Police Interactions with People in Crisis and Use of Force: OIPRD Systemic Review Interim Report* (Toronto: 2017), pp. 4–5, https://www .oiprd.on.ca/wp-content/uploads/Police-Interactions-with-People-in-Crisis -and-Use-of-Force-Systemic-Review-Report-March-2017-Small.pdf.

58 **Durand described Abdirahman as a "teddy bear" and told the *Globe and Mail*** Stone, "Witnesses Recount Abdirahman Abdi's 'Gruesome' Encounter with Ottawa Police Before His Death."

59 **"I told the police he's a crazy man," she told local media** Evelyn Harford and Aedan Helmer, "Updated: SIU Investigates After Man Dies Following Confrontation with Police," *Ottawa Citizen*, updated July 25, 2016, https: //ottawacitizen.com/news/local-news/man-in-hospital-siu-called-after -pepper-spray-incident-in-hintonburg.

59 **In the days following Abdirahman's death, a collective of agencies . . . released a statement** "LASI and OCASI Statement on the Death of Abdirahman Abdi," Ottawa, July 28, 2016, http://ocasi.org/lasi-and-ocasi-statement-death-abdirahman -abdi.

60 **"This is not a beating that caused the death of Mr. Abdi"** "Abdirahman Abdi's Death not Due to Beating, Lawyer Claims," CBC News, October 26, 2017, https://www.cbc.ca/news/canada/ottawa/daniel-montsion-abdirahman-abdi -not-a-beating-1.4373493.

DIRECT ACTION (APRIL)

63 **"Public associations between blackness and crime can be traced back to . . ."** Robyn Maynard, *Policing Black Lives: State Violence in Canada from Slavery to the Present* (Halifax and Winnipeg: Fernwood, 2017), p. 85.

64 **Hayter Reed . . . described his vision in a letter to a superior** Haytor Reed to Edgar Dewdney, July 20, 1885, Library and Archives Canada, RG10, vol. 37 10, file 19,550-3.

66 **In 2012 the *Toronto Star* published "Known to Police"** Jim Rankin and Patty Winsa, "As Criticism Piles Up, So Do the Police Cards," *Toronto Star*, September 27, 2013, https://www.thestar.com/news/gta/knowntopolice2013/2013/09/27/as _criticism_piles_up_so_do_the_police_cards.html.

66 **According to the *Star*'s investigation, "from 2008 to 2012, the number of young black males . . ."** Rankin and Winsa, "As Criticism Piles Up, So Do the Police Cards."

67 **Farah could no longer work at the airport** Colin Perkel, "Judge Slams Government for Nixing Woman's Airport Security Clearance," CBC News, August 16, 2016, https://www.cbc.ca/news/politics/airport-security-clearance -ayaan-farah-1.3723432.

67 **In 2014 ... the *Star* documented that the total number of carding stops** Jim Rankin and Patty Winsa, "Carding Drops but Proportion of Blacks Stopped by Toronto Police Rises," *Toronto Star*, July 26, 2014, https://www.thestar.com /news/insight/2014/07/26/carding_drops_but_proportion_of_blacks_stopped _by_toronto_police_rises.html.

67 **The *Star*'s 2002 series "Race and Crime" had revealed** Jim Rankin, Jennifer Quinn, Michelle Shephard, Scott Simmie, and John Duncanson, "Singled Out," *Toronto Star*, October 19, 2002, https://www.thestar.com/news/gta/knownto police/2002/10/19/singled-out.html.

68 **His successor, Mark Saunders, defended carding and promised to "keep the community safe ..."** Neil Armstrong, "Toronto Has Its First Black Police Chief," *Pride News Magazine*, April 22, 2015, http://pridenews.ca/2015/04/22/toronto -has-its-first-black-police-chief/.

69 **"When we as a service started to train the officers on what street gangs were about ..."** Mark Saunders, interview by Dwight Drummond, CBC TV, May 28, 2015, https://www.cbc.ca/player/play/2668312453.

76 **Though he had been ... "about *carding* all the time"** Shree Paradkar, "It Was Wrong to Rein in Desmond Cole," *Toronto Star*, May 12, 2017, https://www.thestar.com /news/gta/2017/05/12/it-was-wrong-to-rein-in-desmond-cole-paradkar.html.

76 **The *Star*'s public editor, Kathy English, wrote a piece** Kathy English, "Journalists Shouldn't Become the News: Public Editor," *Toronto Star*, May 4, 2017, https: //www.thestar.com/opinion/public_editor/2017/05/04/journalists-shouldnt -become-the-news-public-editor.html.

77 **The same public editor ... wrote that "Porter is right in her understanding ..."** Kathy English, "Catherine Porter, Ezra Levant and Journalism Standards," *Toronto Star*, July 17, 2015, https://www.thestar.com/opinion/2015/07/17/catherine -porter-ezra-levant-and-journalism-standards.html.

77 **Another important response to the Star's ... came from Michele Landsberg** Michele Landsberg, "Former *Toronto Star* Columnist Michele Landsberg Calls Out Paper's Bosses for Desmond Cole 'Blunder,'" *NOW Magazine*, May 15, 2017, https://nowtoronto.com/news/michele-landsberg-toronto-star-s-desmond -cole-controversy/.

HONOURED GROUP (JUNE)

83   **CBC News ran an opinion piece by a Black gay man** Orville Lloyd Douglas, "I'm Black and Gay. Black Lives Matter Toronto Doesn't Speak for Me," CBC News, June 12, 2017, https://www.cbc.ca/news/opinion/blm-pride-toronto-1.4153736.

91   **Forrest Picher documented some of the testimonies of men arrested in those raids** Forrest Picher, "Coming Clean about Operation Soap: The 1981 Toronto Bathhouse Raids," Active History, June 23, 2015, http://activehistory.ca/2015/06/coming-clean-about-operation-soap-the-1981-toronto-bathhouse-raids/.

93   **Chanelle Gallant, one of the Toronto Women's Bathhouse Committee organizers, wrote in 2001** Chanelle Gallant and Loralee Gillis, "Pussies Bite Back: The Story of the Women's Bathhouse Raids," *torquere: Journal of the Canadian Lesbian and Gay Studies Association* 3 (2001): 158, https://torquere.journals.yorku.ca/index.php/torquere/article/download/36620/33268/0.

93   **In 1999, Pride organizers estimated their attendance had doubled . . . and credited "greater corporate involvement . . ."** "Toronto Comes Out for Gay Pride," CBC News, June 28, 1999, https://www.cbc.ca/news/canada/toronto-comes-out-for-gay-pride-1.193072.

94   **"This gathering was spearheaded by Jamea Zuberi . . ."** Beverly Bain, "Fire, Passion, and Politics: The Creation of Blockorama as Black Queer Diasporic Space in the Toronto Pride Festivities," in *We Still Demand! Redefining Resistance in Sex and Gender Struggles*, eds. Patrizia Gentile, Gary Kinsman, and L. Pauline Rankin (Vancouver and Toronto: UBC Press, 2017), pp. 81–82.

95   **That first year, Zuberi recalls the space "overflowing . . ."** Ryan Adamson, "Complicating Queer Space in Toronto: How the Development of Toronto's LGBTQQ2I Spaces Fits within Homonormative and Homonationalist Scripts" (master's thesis, York University, Toronto, 2017), p. 90, https://yorkspace.library.yorku.ca/xmlui/bitstream/handle/10315/34706/MESMP02750.pdf?sequence=2&isAllowed=y.

95   **Of the immediate impact of putting Blockorama in a smaller venue, Ware said** natalie samson, "Yet Another Pride Scandal: The Marginalization of 'Blackness Yes!'" This.org, July 2, 2010, https://this.org/2010/07/02/pride-toronto-blocko-blackness-yes/.

96   **According to Bain, "The paradox of re-entering a space . . ."** Bain, "Fire, Passion, and Politics," p. 95.

96   **Pride said its staff and volunteers "all openly welcome the opportunity . . ."** Pride Toronto, "Pride Toronto Announces Black Lives Matter–Toronto as 2016 Honoured Group," press release, February 10, 2016, http://www.pridetoronto.com

/wp/wp-content/uploads/2016-02-10_2016-Pride-Toronto-Honoured-Group
-Black-Lives-Matter-Toronto-Media-Release.pdf.

96   **According to a 2015 study on human rights and trans people in Ontario** Greta R.
Bauer and Ayden I. Scheim, "Transgender People in Ontario, Canada: Statistics
from the Trans PULSE Project to Inform Human Rights Policy" (London, ON:
Trans PULSE Project Team and University of Western Ontario, 2015), p. 4,
http://transpulseproject.ca/wp-content/uploads/2015/06/Trans-PULSE
-Statistics-Relevant-for-Human-Rights-Policy-June-2015.pdf.

97   **Khan would later ask, "What does it mean . . ."** LGBT Canada in the Media,
"Janaya Khan: Blackness Yes Been Erased by Gay Pride Toronto—Black
Lives Matter," YouTube video, posted July 22, 2016, https://www.youtube.com
/watch?v=iCZ1QZNvBB0.

97   **"The idea that we could be black and queer, black and trans, is unfathomable
to too many people . . ."** Desmond Cole, "Pride Has Divorced Blackness
from Queerness," *Toronto Star*, July 7, 2016, thestar.com/opinion/commentary
/2016/07/07/pride-has-divorced-blackness-from-queerness-cole.html.

97   **"In Pride, there is often a delegation of police who are there . . ."** Arshy Mann,
"Black Lives Matter to Be Honoured Group at Toronto Pride," *Daily Xtra*,
February 16, 2016.

98   **But Stormé fought back, recounting years later, "The cop hit me, and I hit him
back"** Julia Diana Robertson, "Remembering Stormé: The Woman of Color
Who Incited the Stonewall Revolution," HuffPost, June 4, 2017, https://www
.huffpost.com/entry/remembering-storm%C3%A9-the-woman-who-incited
-the-stonewall_b_5933c061e4b062a6ac0ad09e.

98   **The *Toronto Star* had reported on this vehicle at previous Pride parades,
describing it as** Eric Andrew-Gee, "Gotta have pride," *Toronto Star*, July 1, 2013,
https://www.pressreader.com/canada/toronto-star/20130701/281487863931974.

99   **As a former federal prisoner said** Chester Abbotsbury, "Pride Toronto Has a
Prison Problem," *NOW Magazine*, July 20, 2016, https://nowtoronto.com/news
/pride-toronto-has-a-prison-problem/.

99   **"We are fighting for our people . . . We fought for you . . ."** Michael Toledano,
"BLMTO: Black Pride," YouTube video, posted July 10, 2016, https://www
.youtube.com/watch?v=w9UhcQ3tcyI.

101   **Chantelois told media, "Their requests were completely reasonable . . ."**
Oliver Sachgau, "Executive Director of Pride Toronto Resigns Amid 'Serious
Allegations,'" *Toronto Star*, August 10, 2016, https://www.thestar.com/news
/gta/2016/08/10/executive-director-of-pride-toronto-resigns.html.

DESMOND COLE

101   **Chantelois offered this explanation of his decision to sign** Jeremy Grimaldi, "York Regional Police Caught in Toronto Pride Parade Can," *Aurora Banner*, July 4, 2016, https://www.yorkregion.com/news-story/6751695-york-regional -police-caught-in-toronto-pride-parade-ban/.

102   **"That's one of the most successful things that have come out of this . . ."** LGBT Canada in the Media, "Janaya Khan: Blackness Yes Been Erased by Gay Pride Toronto—Black Lives Matter."

103   **"Lacking familiarity of 'the other' . . ."** Martin Regg Cohn, "Pride's Principles Should Matter to Black Lives Matter," *Toronto Star*, July 12, 2016, https://www .thestar.com/news/queenspark/2016/07/12/prides-principles-should-matter-to -black-lives-matter-cohn.html.

103   **Media obtained an email it attributed to Pride staff** Adam Miller, "Pride Toronto Executive Director Resigns After Allegations of Racism, Sexual Harassment," Global News, August 10, 2016, https://globalnews.ca/news/2875763/pride-toronto -executive-director-resigns-after-allegations-of-racism-sexual-harassment/.

104   **"All of the things that they apologized for are deeply appreciated but we still need action plans"** "Pride Toronto Apologizes for 'Deepening the Divisions' in LGBT Community," CBC News, September 20, 2016, https://www.cbc.ca /news/canada/toronto/pride-toronto-apoloply-black-lives-matter-1.3770107.

104   **The group said the operation targeted men** "Project Marie," Queers Crash the Beat, http://queerscrashthebeat.com/project-marie/.

104   **"Queer and trans people of colour actually started this . . ."** Shanifa Nasser, "Black Lives Matter NYC 'Inspired' by Toronto Chapter's Call for Removal of Uniformed Police," CBC News, June 25, 2017, https://www.cbc.ca/news/canada /toronto/black-lives-matter-toronto-pride-2017-1.4177554.

105   **The demonstrators had something to say to Toronto's visiting police, too** "No Justice, No Pride in NYC," press release, Facebook, June 25, 2017.

THE UNSETTLING (JULY)

108   **"Problem was," King writes, "Live Indians didn't die out . . ."** Thomas King, *The Inconvenient Indian: A Curious Account of Native People in North America* (Toronto: Doubleday Canada, 2012), p. 67.

108   **"Canadians who do recognize historical injustice seem to understand it in this way . . ."** Chelsea Vowel, *Indigenous Writes: A Guide to First Nations, Métis and Inuit Issues in Canada* (Winnipeg: Highwater Press, 2016), p. 120.

109   **It was Vowel who set the tone for the sesquicentennial year, tweeting on January 1** Chelsea Vowel (@apihtawikosisan), Twitter, January 1, 2017, https: //twitter.com/apihtawikosisan/status/815612534128525313.

256

110   **As researcher and writer Febna Caven wrote of Spence** Febna Caven "Being Idle
      No More: The Women Behind the Movement," *Cultural Survival Quarterly
      Magazine*, March 2013, https://www.culturalsurvival.org/publications/cultural
      -survival-quarterly/being-idle-no-more-women-behind-movement.

111   **Idle No More organizers said its "Unsettling 150" day of action** "Unsettling 150:
      A Call to Action," IdleNoMore, May 5, 2017, http://www.idlenomore.ca
      /unsettling_150_a_call_to_action.

112   **In the words of Elizabeth Cooke of the Bawaating Water Protectors** Joanne Laucius
      and Paula McCooey, "PM, Wife Visit Ceremonial Teepee on Parliament Hill,"
      Ottawa Citizen, June 30, 2017, http://ottawacitizen.com/news/local-news/teepee
      -erected-on-parliament-hill-was-for-ceremony-not-protest-says-grassroots-group.

113   **But he did commend them for "being these strong voices, for being courageous"**
      John Paul Tasker, "Justin Trudeau Visits 'Reoccupation' Teepee on Parliament
      Hill," CBC News, June 30, 2017, http://www.cbc.ca/news/politics/trudeau-visits
      -reoccupation-teepee-1.4185758.

113   **In a poll of a thousand Canadians, 70 per cent thought it was too expensive**
      Monique Scotti, "Most Canadians Feel $500M for Canada 150 Is Too Much,"
      Global News, June 26, 2017, https://globalnews.ca/news/3538958/canada-150
      -budget-too-much/.

114   **"The Trudeau government's first budget doubled the program's size," wrote the
      *Globe and Mail*** Chris Hannay, "Ottawa Spending Half a Billion Dollars for
      Canada's 150th Anniversary," *Globe and Mail*, January 4, 2017, https://www.the
      globeandmail.com/news/national/canada-150/ottawa-spending-half-a-billion
      -dollars-for-canadas-150th-anniversary/article33508942/.

114   **"Just about a month ago," he said, "I was at a vigil for Missing and Murdered
      Indigenous Women . . ."** Hilary Beaumont, "Canadian Police Spied on
      Indigenous Protesters on Parliament Hill," Vice News, November 10, 2017,
      https://news.vice.com/en_ca/article/a3jjxa/canadian-police-spied-on-indigenous
      -protesters-on-parliament-hill.

115   **After the ruling, Freddy reflected on his decision to stay at the camp** Leslie
      Knibbs, "All Charges Against Freddy Stoneypoint Dismissed," *Anishinabek News*,
      June 13, 2018, http://anishinabeknews.ca/2018/06/13/all-charges-against-freddy
      -stoneypoint-dismissed/.

115   **In its 2004 report *Stolen Sisters*, Amnesty International cited many causes . . .
      including** Amnesty International, *Stolen Sisters: A Human Rights Response to
      Discrimination and Violence Against Indigenous Women in Canada* (2004), p. 2,
      https://www.mmiwg-ffada.ca/publication/consolidated-literature-review
      -violence-against-women-and-girls/.

116 **A passage from that report . . . summarizes some of its findings** Human Rights Watch, *Those Who Take Us Away: Abusive Policing and Failures in Protection of Indigenous Women and Girls in Northern British Columbia, Canada* (2013), https://www.hrw.org/report/2013/02/13/those-who-take-us-away/abusive-policing-and-failures-protection-indigenous-women.

117 **As she opened the press conference, Wabano-Iahtail addressed the media directly** These and the following direct quotes from the press conference are taken from "News Conference—Families Discuss MMIWG Inquiry," CPAC, June 29, 2017, http://www.cpac.ca/en/programs/headline-politics/episodes/51361495.

120 **In Edmonton, for example, police carded Indigenous women at ten times the rate of white women** Andrea Huncar, "Indigenous Women Nearly 10 Times More Likely to Be Street Checked by Edmonton Police, New Data Shows," CBC News, June 27, 2017, http://www.cbc.ca/news/canada/edmonton/street-checks-edmonton-police-aboriginal-black-carding-1.4178843.

120 **At a community meeting in Edmonton, a woman shared her experience of vulnerability** Meeting transcript, July 15, 2017.

121 **In mid-2017, dozens of Indigenous chiefs, elders, and grassroots groups signed a letter** "Open Letter to Chief Commissioner Marion Buller on the National Inquiry on Missing and Murdered Indigenous Women and Girls," May 16, 2017, http://nbmediacoop.org/2017/05/16/open-letter-to-chief-commissioner-marion-buller-on-the-national-inquiry-on-missing-and-murdered-indigenous-women-and-girls/.

121 **When the Liberals countered with a six-month extension, the commissioners said** Connie Walker (@connie_walker), Twitter, June 5, 2018, https://twitter.com/connie_walker/status/1004010093116092416.

122 **"There were a lot of people who did not want this inquiry to happen . . ."** Jessica Deer, "Lack of Police Co-operation 'Slowed' Work for MMIWG Inquiry, Says Chief Commissioner," CBC News, March 22, 2019, https://www.cbc.ca/news/indigenous/mmiwg-inquiry-slowed-police-says-commissioner-1.5066313.

122 **"Settler colonialist structures enabled this genocide . . ."** National Inquiry into Missing and Murdered Indigenous Women and Girls, *Reclaiming Power and Place: Executive Summary of the Final Report* (Vancouver: 2019), p. 3, https://www.mmiwg-ffada.ca/wp-content/uploads/2019/06/Executive_Summary.pdf.

123 **"A decolonizing approach aims to resist and undo the forces of colonialism . . ."** National Inquiry into Missing and Murdered Indigenous Women and Girls, *Executive Summary*, p. 56.

HERE FOR DAFONTE (AUGUST)

127 "Christian Theriault caught up to Dafonte first and grabbed him . . ."
"Schedule A to the Complaint of Dafonte Miller, OIPRD TPS Complaint
E-file # E-20170815160311I6254, OIPRD DRPS Complaint E-file #
E-2017081516000962I5," August 15, 2017, pp. 8–9, http://www.falconers.ca
/wp-content/uploads/2017/08/REDACTED.Miller.Schedule-A-to-the
-Complaint.FINAL_.Aug-15-2017.pdf.

128 "DRPS Officers Jennifer Bowler and Barbara Zabdyr were the first DRPS
officers to arrive . . ." "Schedule A to the Complaint of Dafonte Miller," p. 11.

129 Dafonte's complaint says Constable Theriault and his brother both gave
statements "Schedule A to the Complaint of Dafonte Miller," p. 11.

130 "When police are on the job, their licence to kill is only valid if . . ."
"Schedule A to the Complaint of Dafonte Miller," p. 12.

132 In his decision, SIU director Tony Loparco said Special Investigations Unit,
"SIU Lays Additional Charges in Case Where Man in Whitby Sustained
Serious Injuries," press release, July 21, 2017, https://www.siu.on.ca/en/news
_template.php?nrid=3123.

132 Dafonte's mother, Leisa Lewis, took the lead on speaking to the media "Mother
Speaks Out about Son's Recovery," CBC News, July 18, 2017, http://www.cbc.ca
/news/canada/toronto/mother-speaks-out-about-son-s-recovery-1.4210625.

132 When Lewis was asked if she believed race played a factor in her son's
treatment, she replied Peter Goffin, "Alleged Victim's Family Speaks Out After
Toronto Cop Charged with Assault," *Toronto Star*, July 18, 2017, https://www
.thestar.com/news/gta/2017/07/11/toronto-cop-charged-after-man-assaulted-in
-whitby.html.

133 Briggs won a 2015 Human Rights Tribunal decision https://www.durhamregion.com
/news-story/6206701-rights-tribunal-orders-durham-regional-police-to-pay-
10-000-to-joseph-briggs-who-was-racially-targeted.

133 In the video, Briggs accuses Theriault of racially profiling the people in the car
CityNews, "Bother of Toronto Police Officer Also Charged with Assaulting
19-Year-Old," YouTube video, posted July 21, 2017, https://www
.youtube.com/watch?v=5vduHZbs_Nk.

133 According to the SIU, "all Ontario police services are under a legal obligation . . ."
Special Investigations Unit, "Frequently Asked Questions," https://www.siu.on.ca
/en/faq.php.

134 "Under the legislation, it is the responsibility of the police service . . ." "Who
Was Responsible for Contacting SIU in the Dafonte Miller Case?" CityNews,

July 28, 2017, http://toronto.citynews.ca/2017/07/28/who-was-responsible-for
-contacting-siu-in-the-dafonte-miller-case/.

134 **"There will be no exceptions," said Martin at a subsequent meeting** Jeff Mitchell,
"Durham Police Chief Implements New Policy on Contacting SIU After Review
of Dafonte Miller Case," DurhamRegion.com, September 11, 2017, https://www
.durhamregion.com/news-story/7548991-durham-police-chief-implements-new
-policy-on-contacting-siu-after-review-of-dafonte-miller-case/.

134 **Martin disclosed a critical fact about his officers' actions that night in December
2016** "Durham Police Chief Paul Martin Says Toronto Police Should've Called
SIU in Dafonte Miller Case," Durham Radio News, July 28, 2017, http://www
.durhamradionews.com/archives/104031.

134 **One week later, Toronto Police Chief Mark Saunders contradicted Pugash**
Mark Saunders, interview by George Lagogianes, CP24, July 25, 2017, https:
//www.cp24.com/video?clipId=1174866.

135 **Saunders went on to offer a bewildering explanation** Codi Wilson, "'There
Was No Cover-Up,' Police Chief Says about Dafonte Miller Case," CP24,
July 26, 2017.

135 **The SIU goes further in explaining exactly what it expects in cases of off-duty
police officers** Special Investigations Unit, "Frequently Asked Questions."

136 **The document alleges that the elder Theriault "repeatedly contacted DRPS
investigators . . ."** "Schedule A to the Complaint of Dafonte Miller," p. 13.

136 **When the board members were seated . . . Andy Pringle addressed the audience
by saying** Transcribed from video of the Toronto Police Services Board meeting
July 27, 2017, https://www.youtube.com/watch?v=FP_GARyD178.

139 **In September of 2017, the Anti-Racist Network of Durham . . . issued the
following demands** Anti-Racism Network of Durham Region, "Two Cities,
Two Police Chiefs, Zero Accountability," press release, September 26, 2017,
https://www.newswire.ca/news-releases/two-cities-two-police-chiefs-zero
-accountability-648033483.html.

UNCONTROLLED MOVEMENT (SEPTEMBER)

144 **"I was shocked, I was traumatized, I was injured . . ."** "Toronto Woman Alleges
Officer Sexually Assaulted Her at Police Headquarters," CityNews, October 4,
2017, https://toronto.citynews.ca/video/2017/10/04/toronto-woman-alleges
-officer-sexually-assaulted-her-at-police-headquarters/.

147 **The twenty-two-page report confirms that Pardy did indeed grab D!ONNE**
SIU Director's Report, 17-TSA-278, p. 20.

150 **One year later, Trudeau's government increased targets for deportation** Kathleen

Harris, "Canada Border Services Agency Moves to 'Substantially' Increase
Deportations," CBC News, October 30, 2018, https://www.cbc.ca/news/politics
/cbsa-deportations-border-removals-1.4873169.

150　The report's summary states that "over the past several years, Canada has . . ."
Hanna Gros and Yolanda Song, *"No Life for a Child": A Roadmap to End
Immigration Detention of Children and Family Separation* (University of
Toronto Faculty of Law: 2016), p. 5, http://ihrp.law.utoronto.ca/utfl_file
/count/PUBLICATIONS/Report-NoLifeForAChild.pdf.

150　As reported by the *National Post* in the summer of 2019 Maura Forrest, "CBSA Has
Increased Deportations, Though Removals of Irregular Asylum Seekers Remain
Low," *National Post*, July 7, 2019, https://nationalpost.com/news/politics/cbsa-has
-increased-deportations-though-removals-of-irregular-asylum-seekers-remain-low.

150　Since 2000, at least sixteen people have died while in immigration detention
in Canada Petra Molnar and Stephanie J. Silverman, "Migrants Are Dying
in Canadian Detention Centres. The Government Needs to Act," *Maclean's*,
November 15, 2017, https://www.macleans.ca/opinion/migrants-are-dying-in
-canadian-detention-centres-the-government-needs-to-act/.

151　From *The Canadian Encyclopedia*: "The earliest written evidence of . . ." Natasha L.
Henry, "Black Enslavement in Canada," *The Canadian Encyclopedia*, updated April 26,
2019, http://www.thecanadianencyclopedia.ca/en/article/black-enslavement/.

153　"Founded in 1783, Birchtown was named in honour of . . ." Nova Scotia,
"Birchtown, Nova Scotia," https://ansa.novascotia.ca/birchtown.

154　A caveat in the agreement stated that "any women found unsuitable for work . . ."
Ping-Chun Hsiung and Katherine Nichol, "Policies On and Experiences of
Foreign Domestic Workers in Canada," *Sociology Compass* 4, no. 9 (2010): 767,
http://www.utsc.utoronto.ca/~pchsiung/docs/ForeignDomesticWorkers2010.pdf.

155　"Beverley said that during a CBSA appointment . . ." "Jamaican Woman
Facing Deportation Loses Bid to Stay in Canada," CityNews, September 20,
2017, https://toronto.citynews.ca/2017/09/20/jamaican-woman-facing-deportation
-loses-bid-stay-canada.

156　"I acknowledge that there would be a period of transition . . ." Desmond Cole
(@desmondcole), Twitter, September 20, 2017, quoting from the Canada Border
Services Agency appeal decision, https://twitter.com/DesmondCole/status
/910588369939439617.

WOMEN OF EXCEPTIONAL MERIT (OCTOBER)

157　Overall in 2017, 8,286 Haitians applied for asylum in Canada Phillip Connor and
Jens Manuel Krogstad, "Asylum Claims in Canada Reached Highest Level in

Decades in 2017," Pew Research Center, April 16, 2018, https://www.pewresearch. org/fact-tank/2018/04/16/asylum-claims-in-canada-reached-highest-level-in -decades-in-2017/.

159 **The Canadian government can't tell us exactly . . . but the government's esti-mates** Giuseppe Valiante, "U.S. Vietnam War Draft Dodgers Left Their Mark on Canada," *Maclean's*, April 16, 2015, https://www.macleans.ca/news/canada /u-s-vietnam-war-draft-dodgers-left-their-mark-on-canada/.

159 **The Canadian Vietnam Veterans Association estimates . . . some historians put the number closer to** Chris Corday, "Lost to History: The Canadians Who Fought in Vietnam," CBC News, November 10, 2015, https://www.cbc.ca /news/canada/british-columbia/lost-to-history-the-canadians-who-fought-in -vietnam-1.3304440.

160 **In the words of Bee Quammie** Bee Quammie, "The Black Women Who Helped Build Canada," Medium, January 18, 2016, https://medium.com/the-establishment /the-black-women-who-helped-build-canada-ed8eo8e2dfde.

160 **The late Dr. Agnes Calliste, a professor of sociology and anthropology, observed** Agnes Calliste, "Women of 'Exceptional Merit': Immigration of Caribbean Nurses to Canada," *Canadian Journal of Women and the Law* 6, no. 1 (1993): 88.

161 **Take, for instance, Toronto-born Bernice Redmon** Joan Lesmond, "Celebrating Black Nurses This February and Beyond," *Registered Nurse Journal* 18, no. 1 (Jan./Feb. 2006): 5, http://rnao.ca/sites/rnao-ca/files/Jan-Feb_2006.pdf.

161 **Lesmond names other trailblazing Black women** Joan Lesmond, "Celebrating Black Nurses This February and Beyond."

162 **Their 2011 study showed that, on average, for every dollar a white man earned** Sheila Block and Grace-Edward Galabuzi, "Canada's Colour Coded Labour Market: The Gap for Racialized Workers" (Ottawa: Canadian Centre for Policy Alternatives, 2011), p. 11, http://www.wellesleyinstitute.com/wp-content /uploads/2011/03/Colour_Coded_Labour_MarketFINAL.pdf.

162 **A 2019 study . . . found that "recent immigrants . . ."** Mental Health Commission of Canada, "Immigrant, Refugee, Ethnocultural and Racialized Populations and the Social Determinants of Health: A Review of 2016 Census Data" (Ottawa, 2019), p. 14, https://www.mentalhealthcommission.ca/sites/default/files/2019-03 /irer_report_mar_2019_eng.pdf.

163 **"They're criminals," he said. "If they're willing to jump the border . . ."** Jason Markusoff, "In Emerson, Man., Asylum-Seekers Find Love and Fear," *Maclean's*, February 7, 2017, https://www.macleans.ca/news/canada/fear-and-love-of -asylum-seekers-in-a-manitoba-town/.

164 **Mamadou later said that as he lay in the forest he thought to himself** Jonathan

Montpetit, "Mamadou's Nightmare: One Man's Brush with Death Crossing the U.S.-Quebec Border," CBC News, March 13, 2017, https://www.cbc.ca/news /canada/montreal/safe-third-country-agreement-mamadou-quebec-border -trump-1.4023285.

164   **The accompanying tweet read: "Here's Canadian Mounties greeting refugees . . ."** Canadian Press (@CdnPress), Twitter, February 17, 2017, https://twitter.com /CdnPress/status/832691566636576768.

164   **In November we learned that of the 6,304 citizens of Haiti who had sought asylum** Stephanie Levitz, "Canada Rejecting 90% of Asylum Claims Filed by Haitians," CTV News, November 22, 2017, https://montreal.ctvnews.ca/canada -rejecting-90-of-asylum-claims-filed-by-haitians-1.3689859.

165   **The coup, as Diverlus observes, "would lead to thousands of deaths . . ."** Pascale Diverlus, "Canada Has an Obligation to Help Haitians Fleeing Trump," *Toronto Star*, December 6, 2017, https://www.thestar.com/opinion/contributors /2017/12/05/canada-has-an-obligation-to-help-haitians-fleeing-trump.html.

165   **Haitian senator Moïse Jean-Charles said in 2013** Kim Ives, "Uruguay Will Withdraw from MINUSTAH, President Says," The Canada-Haiti Information Project, October 29, 2013, https://canada-haiti.ca/content/uruguay-will -withdraw-minustah-president-says.

166   **"Having work permits of short duration . . ."** Canada, Standing Committee on Citizenship and Immigration, "Apply Without Fear: Special Immigration Measures for Nationals of Haiti and Zimbabwe," May 2016, https://www .ourcommons.ca/DocumentViewer/en/42-1/CIMM/report-4/page-36.

167   **One of the envoys . . . described the effort by saying** Sylvia Thomson, "MPs Prepare to Head South to Dissuade Asylum Seekers in U.S. from Heading North Once Protected Status Expires," CBC News, November 8, 2017, https: //www.cbc.ca/news/politics/canada-migration-haiti-united-states-trump-1.4392219.

167   **Early in the twentieth century . . . "Immigration officials sent two agents to Oklahoma . . ."** Eli Yarhi, "Order-in-Council P.C. 1911-1324—the Proposed Ban on Black Immigration to Canada," *The Canadian Encyclopedia*, September 30, 2016, http://www.thecanadianencyclopedia.ca/en/article/order-in-council-pc -1911-1324-the-proposed-ban-on-black-immigration-to-canada/.

168   **Prime Minister Justin Trudeau apologized in May of 2016** "Justin Trudeau Apologizes in House for 1914 *Komagata Maru* Incident," CBC News, May 18, 2016, http://www.cbc.ca/news/politics/komagata-maru-live-apology-1.3587827.

168   **The *Globe and Mail* reported in 2018 on the progress of negotiations** Michelle Zilio, "Canada in 'Exploratory' Talks with U.S. over Border Agreement on Asylum Seekers," *Globe and Mail*, May 1, 2018, https://www.theglobeandmail

.com/politics/article-canada-in-exploratory-talks-with-us-over-border
-agreement-on/.

170   Writing for *Atlantic Insight* magazine in 1981, Stephen Kimber described
a visit to North Preston Stephen Kimber, "Must Preston Die?" *Atlantic Insight*,
December 1981.

172   Kardeisha Provo, who is now in university, wrote a piece in 2019 Kardeisha
Provo, "The North Preston I Know Isn't the One You've Heard About," CBC
Radio, July 13, 2019, https://www.cbc.ca/radio/noworneveral/the-resilience
-of-north-preston-nova-scotia-1.4932179/the-north-preston-i-know-isn-t-the
-one-you-ve-heard-about-1.4936766.

COMMUNITY POLICING (NOVEMBER)

174   I'm protecting his identity in order to tell his story—I'll call him Gerald All
quotes are from my recorded interview with Gerald in Toronto on June 1, 2018.

177   After sympathizing with the family, DiManno reversed herself in the next paragraph Rosie DiManno, "'Don't Die Jordan,' Best Friend Pleaded," *Toronto Star*,
May 25, 2007, https://www.pressreader.com/canada/toronto-star/20070525/textview.

177   More than seven months after Jordan's death, Small's lawyer said Caroline
Alphonso and Omar El Akkad, "Fears of Career Suicide Stopped Educators
from Reporting Violence," *Globe and Mail*, January 11, 2008, https://www.the
globeandmail.com/news/national/fears-of-career-suicide-stopped-educators
-from-reporting-violence/article666394/.

177   In August 2007, the School Community Safety Advisory Panel . . . requested
"School Safety Panel Releases C. W. Jefferys Report," CBC News, August 29,
2007, http://www.cbc.ca/news/canada/toronto/school-safety-panel-releases
-c-w-jefferys-report-1.689651.

177   Ultimately the panel . . . found that "while it is clear . . ." School Community
Safety Advisory Panel, *The Road to Health: A Final Report on School Safety—
Executive Summary* (Toronto: 2008), p. 3, http://www.falconerschoolsafetyreport
.com/pdf/executive_summary.pdf.

178   The panel's final report concluded that Jordan's death was the result both of
"years of neglect . . ." School Community Safety Advisory Panel, *The Road
to Health—Executive Summary*, p. 5.

178   The report states that "in April 1998 . . ." School Community Safety Advisory
Panel, *The Road to Health—Volume 1*, pp. 19–20, https://www.falconerschool
safetyreport.com/pdf/finalReport_volume1.pdf.

178   "The impact was, in effect, to push youth out of the schools . . ." School
Community Safety Advisory Panel, *The Road to Health—Executive Summary*, p. 5.

178 **"Survival is managing your career," said Miles** Iain Marlow, "'Busted' School System Failed Jordan Manners, Teacher Says," *Toronto Star*, June 2, 2007, https://www.thestar.com/news/2007/06/02/busted_school_system_failed _jordan_manners_teacher_says.html.

178 **Police Chief Bill Blair pushed the idea without formally consulting the public** Toronto Police, Toronto District School Board, Toronto Catholic District School Board, "School Resource Officer Program: 2011 Follow-Up Evaluation," p. 2. http://www.torontopolice.on.ca/publications/files/reports/2008,2009-sro _program_follow-up_evaluation.pdf.

179 **"If we turn schools into a police state, kids will be scared to come to school"** Louise Brown, "$5.5M to Be Spent on Improving Safety," *Toronto Star*, May 22, 2008, https://www.thestar.com/life/parent/2008/05/22/55m_to_be_spent_on _improving_safety.html.

179 **One of its members . . . described the police-in-schools program** Hilary Barlow, "Do Cops Belong in Schools?" *The Varsity*, March 23, 2009, https://thevarsity .ca/2009/03/23/do-cops-belong-in-schools/.

181 **"The student had an ID card, and flashed it at the officer . . ."** Kristin Rushowy and Louise Brown, "Arrested Student Suspended from Northern Secondary," *Toronto Star*, October 7, 2009, https://www.thestar.com/life/parent/2009/10/07 /arrested_student_suspended_from_northern_secondary.html.

181 **According to the spokesperson, Moosvi's apparent inability to identify the youth** Timothy Appleby, "Toronto Student Charged with Assaulting Cop at School," *Globe and Mail*, October 7, 2009, https://www.theglobeandmail.com /news/toronto/toronto-student-charged-with-assaulting-cop-at-school /article4288137/.

181 **She confirmed that the student "was being investigated as a trespasser . . ."** Rushowy and Brown, "Arrested Student Suspended from Northern Secondary."

181 **Although the judge ultimately acquitted Moosvi . . . he said Mossvi's explanation of the events "defied common sense"** Gay Abbate, "Two Constables Found Not Guilty of Assaulting Deaf Man in 2002," *Globe and Mail*, October 14, 2004, https://www.theglobeandmail.com/news/national/two-constables-found-not -guilty-of-assaulting-deaf-man-in-2002/article1005205/.

182 **One of the student organizers described the dynamic the program had introduced** Victoria Wells, "Police Presence Draws Fire at Northern Secondary," The Toronto Observer, October 22, 2009, https://torontoobserver.ca/2009 /10/22/police-presence-draws-fire-at-northern-secondary/.

182 **Around the same time, a student at a school in Scarborough said** Sandie Benitah, "Police School Program: Hit-and-Miss with Teens," CTV News,

October 24, 2009, https://toronto.ctvnews.ca/police-school-program-hit-and
-miss-with-teens-1.446653.

185 **"We acknowledge that there are hardworking SROs . . ."** Toronto Police Service,
"Toronto Police Services Board Meeting—LiveStream—Thursday, June 15, 2017,
1pm," YouTube video, https://www.youtube.com/watch?v=J6lVDtmlATk.

188 **According to the review's final report, most students in the focus groups "noted
that the presence of the SRO . . ."** School Resource Officer Program Review,
Toronto District School Board, November 15, 2017.

COMPETING INTERESTS (DECEMBER)

193 **He told us the youth had given his organization two mandates for the summit**
National Black Canadians Summit, Toronto Reference Library, December 4,
2017, https://www.torontopubliclibrary.ca/programs-and-classes/featured
/national-black-canadians-summit.jsp.

196 **Around the time of Tory's speech, Sandy Hudson of BLM-TO tweeted**
Sandy Hudson (@sandela), Twitter, December 4, 2017, https://twitter.com
/sandela/status/937850012410691584.

203 **A journalist who interviewed McLeod reported that the judge** "Federation of
Black Canadians Launched at National Summit," ByBlacks.com, December 14,
2017, https://byblacks.com/news/item/1767-federation-of-black-canadians
-launched-at-national-summit.

203 **McLeod addressed his group's heavily institutional makeup in an interview**
"Federation of Black Canadians Launched at National Summit," ByBlacks.com.

204 **An up-and-coming Black lawyer in Toronto responded on Facebook** Chritien
Levien, Facebook, February 25, 2017.

205 **The decision also made specific reference to public criticisms of FBC's works**
Ontario Judicial Council, *In the Matter of a Complaint Respecting The Honourable
Justice Donald McLeod*, December 20, 2018, p. 35, http://www.ontariocourts.ca
/ocj/files/ojc/decisions/2018-mcleod-EN.docx.

ABDOUL & FATOUMA (JANUARY)

209 **In her book *Men, Militarism, and UN Peacekeeping*, Sandra Whitworth summarizes** Sandra Whitworth, *Men, Militarism, and UN Peacekeeping: A Gendered
Analysis* (Boulder, CO, and London: Lynne Renner Publishers, 2004), p. 101.

210 **Upon the release of the inquiry's report in 1997, Liberal Defence Minister Art
Eggleton called it** "Somalia Debacle a High-Level Cover-up," CBC TV, July
1997, https://www.cbc.ca/archives/entry/somalia-debacle-a-high-level-cover-up.

210 **The Southern Poverty Law Center notes that although the Proud Boys publicly**

claim Southern Poverty Law Center, "Proud Boys," https://www.splcenter.org
/fighting-hate/extremist-files/group/proud-boys.

211 **As Fatouma would later observe, "The government was our parents"**
"'The Government Was Our Parents': Abdoul Abdi's Sister Says Somali Refugee
Failed by Canadian Foster System," CBC Radio, January 15, 2018, https://www.cbc
.ca/radio/thecurrent/the-current-for-january-15-2018-1.4487410/the-government
-was-our-parents-abdoul-abdi-s-sister-says-somali-refugee-failed-by-canadian
-foster-system-1.4487428.

212 **Upon this decision, Abdoul's lawyer noted that his client's immigration papers
were "messed up"** Steve Bruce, "Young Man Headed to Prison for 'Vicious'
Handgun Attack," *The Chronicle Herald*, July 7, 2014.

213 **El would later recount, "Because of the experience that that family had . . ."**
"How Abdoul Abdi's Defenders Helped Keep Him from Being Deported,"
CBC Radio, July 21, 2018, https://www.cbc.ca/radio/day6/episode-399-russia
-keeps-meddling-sacha-baron-cohen-keeps-punking-impeach-o-meter-che
-s-brother-and-more-1.4753119/how-abdoul-abdi-s-defenders-helped-keep
-him-from-being-deported-1.4753129.

215 **But the Liberal minister hadn't done anything for her since, and Asha said**
Desmond Cole, "'I Need My Son Back': A Refugee Family's Fight to Stop a
Senseless Deportation," Cole's Notes, January 8, 2018, https://thatsatruestory
.wordpress.com/2018/01/08/i-need-my-son-back-a-refugee-familys-fight
-to-stop-a-senseless-deportation/.

216 **Trudeau continued, "I can assure you that our immigration minister . . ."**
"Trudeau Asked Why Are You Deporting My Brother?" CBC News,
video, January 9, 2018, https://www.cbc.ca/news/canada/nova-scotia/abdoul
-abdi-somalia-refugee-immigration-deportation-1.4479509.

216 **The very first question came from another supporter of Abdoul's** CBC Politics,
"Prime Minister Justin Trudeau Is Taking Questions . . ." Facebook, January 10,
2018, https://www.facebook.com/CBCPolitics/videos/1930280503667442/.

219 **When announcing his lawsuit he said, "I felt I was Canadian, but, in reality,
I wasn't"** Jacques Gallant, "Lawsuit Accuses Ontario Government of Leaving
Foreign-Born Crown Wards in the Lurch," *Toronto Star*, March 9, 2018,
https://www.thestar.com/news/gta/2018/03/09/lawsuit-accuses-ontario
-government-of-leaving-foreign-born-crown-wards-in-the-lurch.html.

219 **Four days after the latest ruling . . . Ralph Goodale tweeted** Ralph Goodale,
Twitter, July 17, 2018, https://twitter.com/RalphGoodale/status/1019371039128674304.

acknowledgements

This book is the unexpected outcome of "The Skin We're In," a 2015 feature in *Toronto Life* magazine. I'm grateful to Emily Landau for editing that piece and supporting me during its production. This is my first book, and my editor, Martha Kanya-Forstner, guided me with patience, curiosity, and skill—I treasure our partnership and Martha's extensive contribution to these pages. My thanks to the entire Doubleday Canada team, especially Ward Hawkes for his editorial support, Scott Sellers for his marketing expertise, and Terri Nimmo for designing the cover. I have tremendous gratitude for Rania El Mugammar, who created the brilliant study guide for the paperback edition.

Thanks to my literary agency Westwood Creative Artists, especially Jackie Kaiser, who supported me throughout the writing process, and to Jake Babad, who helped me sign the deal. In 2016, filmmaker Charles Officer, with his excellent producer Jake Yanowski, took me to three provinces, connected me with Black people, and helped inform and inspire the book. One fateful evening in 2017, Dionne Brand gave me feedback that led to the present-day, month-by-month structure of this work. Thanks Dionne for that, and for every gift you've given to Black people.

Before I knew what this book would be, family and friends helped me speak it into existence. My loved ones cared for me, fed me, and helped me work through ideas. Thank you El Jones, Idil Abdillahi, Reed Jones, Hentrose Nelson, Shama Rangwala, Abdi Osman, Darja Davydova, Matthew J Godfrey, Courtney Skye, Huda Hassan, Azeezah Kanji, Terrence Hamilton, Estefania Alfonso Falcon, Rinaldo Walcott, and Melissa Filomena D'Souza. The research and scholarship of Black people, Indigenous people, and other people of colour made this book possible. Thank you Wine Club. Mom, I love you very much.

Thank you to all the Black and Indigenous people whose stories I share here, and to your families. Love to all the storytellers, artists, and messengers in our communities. My staple meal during my writing was a bowl of oatmeal with berries and flaxseed. I'm grateful to the land that produces this food and keeps us alive.

© Kate Yang-Nikodym

DESMOND COLE is an award-winning journalist and activist. His writing has appeared in the *Toronto Star*, *Toronto Life*, *The Walrus*, *NOW Magazine*, *Ethnic Aisle*, *Torontoist*, *BuzzFeed*, and the *Ottawa Citizen*.